Selling Yourself and Your Ideas

A Text/Workbook for Building Presentation Skills

Third Edition Revised Printing

R. Michael Bokeno
Crystal Rae Coel Coleman
Tina A. Coffelt
Stephen A. Cox
Cami Pierce Duffy
David M. Gesler
Mickey D. Miller
Patty S. Parish
Frances L. M. Smith
Lou Davidson Tillson

Murray State University
Department of Organizational Communication

Kendall Hunt
publishing company

www.kendallhunt.com
Send all inquiries to:
4050 Westmark Drive
Dubuque, IA 52004-1840

Contents

■ CHAPTER 8 Delivery: It's Not Only What You Say but How You Say It   165

Acknowledgments

The Department of Organizational Communication would like to acknowledge the following for their tireless effort in the edit of this edition:

John W. Dale
Greg Wurth
Jenilee Williams
Patty S. Parish

Selling Yourself and Your Ideas

A Text/Workbook for Building Presentation Skills

1 The Importance of Communication Skills

R. Michael Bokeno

CHAPTER OBJECTIVES

At the end of this chapter, you will be able to:

- Possess a greater understanding of the importance of effective communication skills in profession, personal, and public contexts.

- Identify specific contributions of classical theorists to the study of effective communication.

- Identify the contribution of classical theorists with respect to the relationship of rhetoric and ethics.

- Understand the contribution of Aristotle, in particular, to the art of effective presentational skill.

- Understand definitions of rhetoric by both Aristotle and theorist Donald Bryant as the foundation for contemporary presentational skill.

Communicating and Breathing Are Not the Same

We are fairly certain that you enter this course with a number of reservations. One of them – the one we hear most – goes something like this: "I already know how to communicate, I've been doing it all my life. Why do I need to take this course?"

We could accept that challenge from you, if not for the assumptions hiding in it. First, the challenge assumes that doing something for a long time means that you do it well. I've been doing many things for many years, and still don't do them well, like gardening, yard work, and building and fixing things.

Second, the challenge assumes that since you've done something like *communicate* all your life, it's normal, effective and easy, like breathing. So let's talk about your breathing for a minute. True, as long as you are not doing anything out of the ordinary physiological pattern of your life, and assuming no health issues, breathing is normal and easy. But what about those times when you have to do it in a specific way for a specific purpose in a specific context? If you have ever lifted weights for any reason, you had to learn to exhale on exertion and inhale on release. Similarly, if you run to keep in good cardiovascular condition, didn't you have to learn to adjust your breathing to speed, stride, and distance as you went along? Doesn't your breathing get faster when excited or when arguing with someone? Or consider a more common experience: if breathing is normal and easy, why do we always find it a little bit *uncomfortable* when the doctor puts the stethoscope on our back and chest and says "Ok, big deep breath for me . . . ok, another one . . . and another one . . . another . . . and one more . . . ." (My breathing gets irregular just writing that. You try it: focus on your breathing for a minute – not as easy, is it?)

Our point here is that while communicating may seem normal and easy, it's only that way if you don't think about it. And isn't your communication something you want to think about? Communication

Image © digitalife, 2009. Used under license from Shutterstock, Inc.

has been a specific practice, as well as a discipline that is taught and learned, for over two thousand years. Indeed, there is a *necessity* for *effective* expression.

The Necessity of Effective Expression

There are three broad categories of reasons why "effective expression" is a necessity: your **professional** life, your **personal** life, and your **public** life.

Your Professional Life

I cannot pick up a popular business or management magazine, e-newsletter or blog, or trade publication anymore without seeing an article devoted to the importance of effective expression in some way, shape, or form. In fact, there is virtually no occupation anymore that can escape the necessity of good oral communication skills. We typically think of accountants, for example, as working only with numbers and calculations; yet, at some point the accountant has to make sense of those numbers to his or her clients, and the numbers have to make sense to the clients as well. This depends on the communication ability of the accountant. Scientists and technologists also are typically understood as working with their own computations and experiments with little need for enhanced communication skills. Yet, the way a scientist is successful is to persuade other scientists that his or her experiments are viable and worthwhile. Persuasion is a communication skill.

More commonly, you are likely planning to enter an occupation in which interacting with others is an everyday affair, and in which you can foresee *managing* other people. Thinking about your communication is certainly important in these contexts.

Indeed, study after study in the past two decades has revealed the tremendous importance that business organizations place on communication skills in a variety of contexts. Let's start with the hiring process. Peterson (1997) asked 253 personnel interviewers to rate the importance of the communication skills of job applicants. Her findings were as follows:

- 68% of respondents strongly agree, and 29% of respondents agree that *oral and nonverbal communication skill significantly impact hiring decisions*.

- 68% of respondents strongly agree, and 23% of respondents agree that *higher level positions require more effective communication skills*.

- 5% of respondents strongly agree, and 54% of respondents agree that *job applicants display adequate communication skills*.

- 50% of respondents strongly agree, and 41% of respondents agree that *increased communication skills are needed for jobs in the 21st century*.

More telling is what Peterson (1997) revealed as *communication inadequacies* reported during the study. There are 20 of them, but I will show you only the top ten in ranked order:

Eye contact

Topic relevance

Response organization

Listening skills

Response clarity

Grammar

Feedback response

Vocabulary adequacy

Content accuracy

Self-confidence

Similarly, Windsor, Curtis, and Stephens (1997) found oral (speaking) communication, written communication, and listening ability to be the top three factors most helpful for graduating college students seeking employment.

Let's assume you communicate well enough to get hired. Can you do it well enough for sustained effective job performance, and/or to be promoted to a position of managing others? Guess what the top three factors are there? For successful job performance, in order[*]:

- Interpersonal communication skills
- Oral (speaking) communication skills
- Written communication skills

For managers, communication skills are the top six on the list of desired traits in the Ideal Management Profile[*]:

- Ability to listen effectively and counsel
- . . . work well with others one-on-one
- . . . work well in groups

Image © Dean Mitchell, 2009. Used under license from Shutterstock, Inc.

■ . . . gather accurate information from others to make decisions

■ . . . write effective business reports

■ . . . give effective feedback (appraisal)

And finally, the courses recommended for aspiring management personnel, in ranked order, are[*]:

1. Written communication

2. Interpersonal Communication

3. Management

4. Public Speaking

5. Ethics

So, indeed, have you really thought about your communication lately? If you still think communication, like breathing, is normal and easy, try imagining yourself in an interview situation or managing other people.

Your Personal Life

While most students do, or will eventually recognize the importance of effective expression in their professional life or chosen occupation, few realize fully that effective expression – communication ability – aids tremendously in enhancing personal growth. To view a course in presentational skill only as a "requirement" or as something that stands between you and graduation is to prevent yourself from seeing *beyond* the class, *beyond* the difficult speech assignments, and *beyond* the semester, to the ways in which speaking ability actually benefits you personally.

Importantly, the confidence provided by the focused cultivation of effective presentation skills tends to become part of your general communication "attitude" or mental model; it tends to foster increased levels of self-esteem and therefore helps you feel better and more comfortable about yourself in day-to-day communication situations. Thus, presentational skill can be much more beneficial to you than simply the acquisition of some specific skills for your profession. The development of such skills inspires a confidence that is useful in most other aspects of life.

Your Public Life

We might call this your "socio-political" life, in that this dimension involves all non-professional interactions with others – your spouse or significant other, friends, family, community and neighborhood folks, and anyone with whom you could carry on a public conversation.

Our families, for example, are a major force in shaping not only who we are, but the kinds of interactions we have with others. Developing romantic relationships and friendships are the most important sources of satisfaction in your lives right now; these relationships help us to cultivate great sources of understanding and trusting other people, which in turn helps us to shape our communication skills in particular ways.

Beyond families, friends, and lovers, however, as members of a democratic society, we have an obligation to contribute – or at minimum understand – the free and open exchange of ideas that makes democracy work. Rhetorical theorist and public speaking teacher Wayne Minnick (1983) writes that:

> A society organized on democratic principles . . . needs to promote the general welfare. This welfare requires that ideas and information be communicated rapidly to vast portions of the population. . . . The rapid spread of ideas and information is necessary to create informed, enlightened and productive citizens. . . . Underlying this process is the assumption that if ideas and information are widely communicated in a society, its people will be able to influence

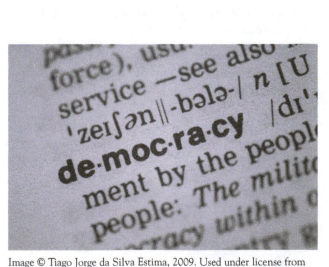

Image © Tiago Jorge da Silva Estima, 2009. Used under license from Shutterstock, Inc.

---

[*]From Curtis, Windsor Stephens (1997).

the legislatures, the courts, and other agencies to make decisions that are reasonable and beneficial for everyone.

We all enjoy our democracy, but outside of voting, how many of us are prepared to participate in it? Certainly we are all well aware of how technology has made the spread of information not just rapid, but instantaneous. Even so, our obligation to democratic communication requires effective communication in order for our voice to be heard. While the punctuated symbolism in chat, texting, and IM might be both efficient and fun, would we contact the police that way? Talk to our parents that way regularly? Compose an editorial that way, speak to a civic group that way? Say anything of any importance that way?

A Short History of Communication: The Relevance of the Ancients

What we call "communication" today, even specifically as organizational communication, interpersonal communication, intercultural communication, group or team communication, etc., derives from the tradition of **rhetoric.** The study of rhetoric, as well as the effective practice of the craft, began in the Golden Age of Greece's democracy. In fact, this classical understanding of communication grounds just about everything we know about it today. In what follows, although I believe the history to be important, I will stay close to that history with the most contemporary relevance – that is, how the history shapes and informs what we should know and do today with regard to effective expression.

Classical Rhetoric

In many ways, classical rhetoric is a focus on presentation skills – the ability to sell yourself and your ideas. As rhetoric became important in ancient Greek democracy, so too did the importance of being able to communicate one's ideas effectively to argue in court, to praise and honor people, and to participate publicly in legislative affairs. This is much like you would do today if you had to make your own case in court without a lawyer, make a case for a new idea, project or campaign to your manager, say a few words after dinner to honor your guest or new client, entertain a small audience of new clients, or speak on behalf of your community or organization on some local government issue.

The ability to express yourself effectively became so important that classical philosophers and theorists began to study it in a systematic way; communication became a *discipline* so it could be taught and learned. Part of the role of the new democracy in Greece was to return parcels of land that had been confiscated by the previous government to their rightful owners. But the rightful owners had to make a case for their land claim. Would you want your land taken away from you just because you couldn't make a convincing argument – deliver an effective presentation – that it belonged to you? So, rhetorical skill or effective expression became a necessity for everyone in ancient Greece.

Rhetoric became a systematic study in ancient Greece due to the writings of the Sophists, Plato, and Aristotle. Each had their own view of rhetoric, and, more importantly, each had their own view of how the practice of rhetoric related to ethics as well.

Classical rhetoric scholar James Murphy reports on an interesting dilemma that arises from the absence of a certain or probable truth, as well as the ability to prove both sides of a question.

Apparently, Corax and Tisias got into a legal dispute about fees and public speaking lessons. Murphy reports that the case went something like this:

Corax: You must pay me if you win the case because that would prove the worth of my lessons. If you lose the case, the court will force you to pay. So in either case you pay.

Tisias: I will pay nothing because if I lose the case it would prove your instruction was worthless. If I win, however, the court will absolve me from paying. In either case I will not pay.

The **Sophists** were contemporaries of Plato, and much of what we know of the Sophists comes to us from Plato's writings. In those writings, known as "dialogues," Plato has Socrates arguing with many of them: Corax, Tisias, Gorgias, Parmenides, Protagoras, and others.

The Sophists had a particular understanding of rhetoric. And, given the need in Greek society for instruction in rhetorical skill, they taught it to people for a fee. For the most part, they believed that rhetoric was the art of persuasion by any means, sometimes involving trickery and manipulation. For them, rhetoric was an art of proving opposites, and they delighted in being able to argue both sides of any issue with equal conviction; for this, they were often accused of "making the worse seem the better cause." Moreover, an emphasis on the ability to prove both sides of an issue implies that there is a certain amount of truth to both sides of an issue. Ethically speaking, this makes "truth" relative to what one can make others believe. In fact, the Sophists would do well in today's post-millennium culture, where image is everything and something like "truth" seems impossible to find anywhere; you can find 124,692 versions of the truth on any issue in 0.0213 seconds on the web. The Sophist conversation in Box 1 illustrates this very well.

Plato was frustrated by the Sophists. Traveling the Greek countryside teaching people to "flatter and mislead" others was for Plato not the way to educate the citizenry of an increasingly powerful nation. For Plato, rhetoric was a secondary skill as establishing the Truth of an issue was of primary importance. Truth was established through a philosophical method of questioning, called **dialectic**. Dialectic resembles group discussion or interviewing more than public speaking. After the Truth was established in this manner, then rhetoric was necessary to persuade others to see the Truth. For Plato, Truth was an absolute; and because all people couldn't participate in the almost divine form of philosophy he had in mind, he believed that rhetoric would ultimately be necessary to persuade others to see it. Ethically speaking, where the Sophists had a relativist conception of truth, Plato had an absolutist conception of Truth: things were true or false, right or wrong and could be determined absolutely. Anyone who thought differently was not seeing the Truth correctly. Plato would not do well in contemporary postmodern culture.

Fortunately, it is between the extremes of Plato and the Sophists that we find the basis for almost all modern communication theory and practice, in the form of Aristotle. Aristotle defined rhetoric as:

The art of discovering in any given case the available means of persuasion.

Now, while that seems a little bit like what the Sophists would say, the "available means" for Aristotle had limits. For Aristotle, persuasion was accomplished by three main forms of proof:

- **Ethical Proof (Ethos)** – the credibility of the speaker due to good character.
- **Logical Proof (Logos)** – the proof the speaker employs through evidence or reasoning.
- **Emotional Proof (Pathos)** – the ability to influence others by inspiring the passions or emotions.

Importantly, for Aristotle, these three forms of proof worked together. A speaker would not be effective using only one alone. Additionally, we can see the practical value of Aristotle's view. Unlike Plato's absolutism of truth and secondary emphasis on rhetoric,

Aristotle saw the outcome of rhetoric as a matter of probability; using the three forms of proof, a speaker could establish, and an audience could see, what is probably true or reasonably true.

As I mentioned, much of what we teach and practice today in terms of effective expression is based on Aristotle's definition of rhetoric above. In 1958 contemporary communication theorist Donald Bryant offered a definition of rhetoric that seems remarkably similar to Aristotle's:

The art of adjusting ideas to people and people to ideas.

Intriguingly, if we look back at the communication skills necessary to be employed, promoted, and expected of aspiring management and leadership personnel, doesn't Bryant's definition sort of cover it all?

◼ Chapter Review

Ultimately then, the current relevance of the rhetorical tradition is kind of self-explanatory. Your life – personal, professional and public – depends on your ability to discover in any given case the available means of persuasion, or to adjust ideas to people and people to ideas. The extent to which you can do that is the extent that you will be successful in these areas of life.

The ability to sell yourself and your ideas is not easy or normal. The reason for this is that you are always doing it in a specific way with a specific purpose and in a specific context. That is, you are thinking about it!

Professionally, the necessity of effective expression is revealed when you interview for a position, to maintain competence in your job, and to obtain a managerial position. Personally, the cultivation of effective communication skills is something that will help you throughout your life in a number of ways. Primarily, it helps give you the confidence you need to handle any communication situation. Publicly, or socio – politically, effective expression is necessary to develop relationships in a way that is satisfying to you and others, as well as to actively participate in democratic processes.

Thus, the necessity of effective communication skills is much the same as it was for the classical theorists who began the systematic study of communication, called rhetoric. From the Sophists, we understand the importance of at least understanding both sides of an issue in order to understand the argument as whole. From Plato, we understand that even though there may be an obvious or objective truth to an issue, it is often necessary to persuade others to see it. From Aristotle, we get most of the theory that informs public speaking today. "The art of discovering in any given case the available means of persuasion" tells us the task ahead of us in any presentation situation; the forms of proof ethos, logos, and pathos – provide us the guidelines for how that task is to be accomplished. Indeed, Donald Bryant's definition of rhetoric as "the art of adjusting ideas to people and people to ideas" sums up effective managerial and professional performance.

Throughout this course, you will learn concepts and practices that will refine your presentation skills in substantial ways. Our hope is that you use the information in this introductory chapter as tacit knowledge that will inform your practice.

◼ Epilogue

◼ COM 161 Is a Doorway

This chapter gave you an introduction to Public Speaking—how to sell yourself and your ideas in a pubic context. But public speaking is just the doorway into studying communication and building key communication skills while in college. Contemporary business and society have changed in ways only visionaries could have imagined. We don't live or work the same as we did even 10 years ago. Changes in the workplace, technology, and globalization have placed more value on human communication skills than ever before. Indeed, if you have ever seen the show *Mad Men*—about executive life and work in the 1960s—you can easily see fundamental differences in the way we work and communicate in organizations today.

Although Aristotle and other scholars mentioned earlier outlined the foundation for effective self-presentation, you will need to build many other communication skills to have a successful career. Effective communication at work is now about . . .

- listening to customers,
- sharing information,
- asking smart questions,
- guiding discussion,
- collaborating with coworkers,
- facilitating creativity,
- resolving conflict,
- building strategic relationships,
- facilitating teamwork,
- developing employees,
- promoting products and services,
- managing change, and
- leading others so everyone succeeds!

These communication processes go beyond COM 161's singular focus on presenting well to an audience. The Organizational Communication Department can help you gain all of the communication skills that you will need for career success.

We tend to think of good management as accounting, finance, marketing, sales, strategic planning, calculated decisions, and visionary leadership. But none of these is effective without strategic and mindful communication. Because the communication discipline has always studied how message strategies create unity in thought and action, companies are now focusing on how "better" communication contributes to "better" organizational success—in both profit and nonprofit sectors. Remember, any group of people organized around the achievement of common goals is an organization. But how did they become organized? By luck, accident, magic, DNA . . . NO! Only effective communication produces organization. Can you think of an organization that could "get organized" and function well without effective communication? Thus, the *Organizational Communication* discipline provides a substantial body of knowledge that can make organizations work better for all of us.

Unfortunately, too many organizations and managers fail to practice ethical and effective communication. All you have to do is look at the news—public corporate mistakes, unethical con-

The Major/Minor in Organizational Communication

Organizational Communication major (39 hrs)

Required Courses..30 hrs
COM 201 Communication Foundations and Theory
COM 331 Interpersonal Communication
COM 340 Intercultural Communication
COM 353 Team Communication and Leadership
COM 361 Career Presentations
   or
COM 461 Persuasive Communication
COM 380 Organizational Communication
COM 384 Communication Skills for Professionals
COM 390 Communication Research
COM 580 Advanced Organizational Communication
COM 595 Senior Seminar in Organizational Communication

Required Electives ....9 hrs
Choose from the following:
COM 215 Introduction to Sports Communication
COM 260 Communication Ethics
COM 315 Coaching as Communication
COM 345 Diversity, Communication, and the Workplace
COM 361 Career Presentations
COM 367 Communication and Critical Thought
COM 401 Contemporary Issues in Communication
COM 422 Communication and Technology
COM 439 Conflict and Communication
COM 461 Persuasive Communication
COM 488 Cooperative Education/Internship
COM 489 Cooperative Education/Internship
COM 510 Internship
COM 530 Seminar in Interpersonal Communication
COM 553 Advanced Team Communication and Leadership
COM 577 Organizational Learning and Dialogue
– *A maximum of 3 hours may be chosen with advisor approval from courses not on the elective list.*

duct, a bottom-line mentality that ignores communities and the environment, employee mistreatment, hazardous products that harm consumers, questionable policies and practices concerning gender/age/race issues, and the list goes on. That's not even taking into account poor superior–subordinate relations, managerial arrogance, narrow-minded leadership decisions, unclear channels of communication, frequent misinformation, or disregard for the employees' need to voice their objections and ideas. But there is a solution—YOU! Your communication competencies will be the key to addressing these issues, and many others, throughout your career.

Moreover, your "soft" communication skills matter because they make your "hard" skills shine. Sure, you may have great math, biology, music, nursing, or computer skills, but "while your hard skills may get you in the door, your people skills will open every other door that is to come" (http://www.mindtools.com/pages/article/newCDV_34.htm). But such soft skills are very much underdeveloped—to the organizations' own detriment—as managers have learned that graduates of "hard skill" training do not come automatically equipped with soft skill accompaniment. Because employers now seek job candidates with exceptionally effective communication skills, every company will expect you to have developed these while in college! Good news, *we teach that!*

Organizational Communication Minor (24 hrs)

COM 201, 331, 380, 384, 390, 595 and six hours of restricted electives from the following: COM 215, 260, 340, 345, 353, 361, 367, 386, 422, 439, 461, 580. (*Three hours may be other courses if approved by minor advisor.*)

Our COM courses prepare you not only for effective organizational membership but also for humane management and leadership. Starting with **COM 161** and your ability for effective self-presentation, to **COM 201** where you see the diverse communication practices that influence all organizational and social environments, to **COM 353** where you are exposed to teamwork and leadership

and the communicative collaboration that these require, you begin to gain the foundation for what makes work *work better.*

COM 380 exposes you to the variety of organization and management structures and the way human communication operates within each of them to maximize their effectiveness. **COM 367** and **COM 390** immerse you in the kind of critical thinking and data analysis skills that is so often lacking in organizational problem solving and decision making. **COM 331** exposes you to the advanced interpersonal dynamics relevant to workplace communication; **COM 439** teaches you the negotiation and conflict management skills crucial to nearly every interaction in organizational contexts. **COM 361** and **COM 461** provide you with the persuasive and presentational polish that is crucial for every proposal you will make in the work environment. **COM 340** and **COM 345** directly examine the necessity of intercultural awareness and the diversity issues that complicate communicating/organizing in globalized work contexts. **COM 384** builds your managerial communication skills ranging from conducting job interviews and providing performance feedback and conducting interviews to managing meetings and training employees. **COM 422** takes a close and informed look at how communication technologies affect both personal and organizational interactions. And **COM 580** and **COM 595** conclude the degree by integrating these diverse organizational communication competencies and applying them to your career goals and personal aspirations.

We even have a set of courses that constitute a minor in Sports Communication!

Sports Communication Minor (21 hrs)

COM 215, 315, 386, 439 and nine hours of restricted electives from the following: COM 353, 401, 510; HIS 330; JMC 384; MGT 370; MKT 285; PSY 222; SOC 436.

▌ *Preparing for Your Career*

So, as businesses plead time and time again for the "soft" communication skills their applicants, employees, and managers seem to lack, our curriculum will prepare you to fill this void and advance in your career as a result. Indeed, making the most of what "Org Com" offers will bring the best out of you—to achieve those professional goals you may have in mind now and will realize in days ahead. YOU can be the value-added employee who brings more to the workplace and makes all the difference in the lives of others, so "fast track" management is within sight shortly after organizational entry, then leadership positions where you combine your analytical and strategic communication skills to make you, your coworkers, and your organization thrive.

WE are the key to YOUR future professional life and career success. Anyone on 3rd floor Wilson Hall can help you realize your aspirations in this way, with a degree in Organizational Communication. *What's holding you back?*

Think about this as you decide your major, or trudge through others.

References

1. Minnick, W. (1983). *Public Speaking*. Boston: Houghton Mifflin.

2. Murphy, J. (1972). *A synoptic history of classical rhetoric*. New York: Random House.

3. Peterson, M. (1997). Personnel interviewers' perceptions of the importance and adequacy of applicants' communication skills. *Communication Education*, 46 (4), 287-291.

4. Windsor, J., Curtis, D. and Stephens, R. (1997). National preferences in business and communication education: A survey update. *Journal of the Association of Communication Administrators* (3), 170-179.

2 Developing and Presenting the Message

Mickey D. Miller

CHAPTER OBJECTIVES

At the end of this chapter, you will be able to: identify the following components of an effective presentation:

- The Five Canons of Rhetoric
- Topic Selection and Development
- Supportive Information and Sources
- The General Purpose (P.I.E.)
- Outcome Statements
- Thesis
- The Introduction, Body and Conclusion (I.B.C.)
- Outlines
- Presentation Aids
- Audience Analysis
- Four Methods of Presentation Delivery
- Ethos, Logos, and Pathos
- Five Areas of Evaluation
- The Five P's of Great Presentations

Introduction

Chapter 1 introduced you to concepts of rhetoric, discussed rhetorical history in the development of civilization, and impressed the importance of communication in many aspects of your life and career. Consider this chapter as a general guide to "jumpstart" you toward presentation success. There will be many concepts discussed, most of which will be covered in greater detail within subsequent chapters. Here, to start, we will examine the key components of conceptualizing, developing, and delivering a successful presentation.

Why Develop Speaking Skills

You may be asking, "What are the chances I will give a presentation in my lifetime", or "How often will I be asked to speak?" The reality is that as organizations are reducing their number of employees and eliminating layers of leadership, employees at all levels are being required to assume more responsibilities, which include developing and delivering presentations. Today's employees will have greater opportunity than their predecessors to represent or serve their organization by presenting information in a public venue. It may be as a "mentor," training new employees on how to perform their duties, instructing on safety procedures, or deliv-

Image © Oshchepkov Dmitry, 2009. Used under license from Shutterstock, Inc.

ering information on company benefits. Outside of work, opportunities may include delivering a sermon or testimony at your place of worship or delivering an appeal for a local charity. Therefore, developing the skills to research, develop, and deliver content in an effective manner will serve you well in your occupation and vocation. The idea of the citizen delivering presentations is nothing new. The following suggests historical proof for the need of effective delivery skills and how early rhetoricians addressed them.

ROSE-D: The Five Canons of Rhetoric

About 2500 years ago, the ancient Greeks freed themselves from a series of invading conquerors to establish the first viable, participatory democracy. Citizens governed themselves by presenting and defending their ideas, grievances, or innocence before their fellow citizens gathered in a community courtyard. Citizens soon realized they needed to be trained on how to deliver effective presentations or they would lose!

Aristotle and other ancient thinkers began developing and teaching the fundamentals of oral presentation skills that they called "The Five Canons of Rhetoric." Equivalent modern terms create a handy mnemonic device to help you remember each canon: ROSE-D stands for Research, Organization, Style, Extemporaneous, and Delivery.

Research is the gathering of effective supporting materials. The Greeks called it *Invention*.

Organization is structuring the material in a logical pattern, which the Greeks termed *Arrangement*.

Style is a presentation's distinctive character, what makes it memorable. It involves writing and language style. The Greeks also called it *Style*.

Extemporaneous presentations combine both preparation and spontaneity. A *delivery* (key *word) outline* triggers planned and rehearsed thoughts, yet specific words are chosen "in the moment." Conversely, the Greeks advocated reciting a presentation from *Memory*.

Delivery technique is the way a speaker uses the voice and body during a presentation to create a desired effect. The Greeks also called this *Delivery*.

These ancient "canons" remain the foundation of effective presentation skills.

Choosing a Topic

Public speaking professors often hear the comment from their students, "I don't know what to talk about." Topic selection is indeed an important facet in effective presentations and should be your initial consideration along with determining your purpose. Ideally, the successful presenter should select their topic and determine their purpose congruently. This can seem an imposing task, but not to worry! If you follow a couple of guidelines, topic selection will not be difficult.

To be effective speech, topics should have two attributes. They should be *relevant* and *researchable*. Let's look at these two qualities individually.

Topics Should Be Relevant

Often in high school and college-level speech courses, students pick topics based singularly on their own interests or experiences. This may work well for the speaker, but may be irrelevant for the audience to hear. Whether giving a presentation within or without the classroom you should consider speaking on a topic that is relevant to the occasion and the audience. In other words, your presentation should be "audience-centered" and not "speaker-centered." By definition, Webster's Dictionary (2007) states that relevance implies "a close relationship with, and an importance to, the matter under consideration." Based on this definition of relevance, audience-centered presentations should include elements that address *appropriateness* (does the topic fit the occasion?), the audience's *interest* (does the topic have general appeal to the masses?), the audience's *knowledge* or *experience* on the subject (will the topic miss its mark because it is far outside the audience's knowledge, or too elementary for their knowledge?), and a suitable level of *importance* (something that benefits the audience; for example, a "how to" speech on the making of the perfect peanut butter and jelly sandwich may not be beneficial to the audience).

Topic relevance is dictated by:

- Appropriateness

- Audience Interest

- Audience Knowledge

- Topic Importance

In the world of work the topic may have a predetermined relevance due to the presenter's role, the presenter's qualifications, and the occasion. For example, if you were a human resource director, you might review your company's hiring policy with future employees. In this situation your topic is predetermined by your job responsibilities, your qualifications, and a specific audience. Table 2.1 illustrates other situations where your topic may be pre-selected as a function of your role or the situation.

TABLE 2.1 Examples of Pre-Selected Topics as a Function of Role or Situation

Audience	Topic	Presenter's Role
Civic Organization	Fundraising Activity	Chairperson
Church Members	Implementing a Clothing Drive	Pastor/Minister
Employees	Fire Extinguisher Training	Safety Manager
Company Managers	Sexual Harassment Policy	Human Resource

In each of the examples in the table, the topic is predetermined by the audience or the situation. In these instances, your role as a presenter is to determine what you want to do with the topic (your purpose) and develop the content accordingly.

However, there will be opportunities in and out of the classroom where you will choose the topic you want to present and what your purpose will be. In these situations, it is very important to understand the attributes of your audience. We will discuss audience analysis later in this chapter and later in the textbook, but for now, you should be aware of who comprises your audience and choose your topic so that your presentation has relevance.

Topics Should Be Researchable

Is the topic substantive enough that it has undergone previous and credible research? If the answer is "yes," then it is likely that your topic has a broad appeal. Often students become frustrated due to not being able to find supportive material on a topic. If you have a topic in mind, check with your library or an electronic search engine and determine how much quality data exists on your subject. If little is found, consider modifying your subject or changing it altogether.

Finding appropriate external supportive information for your topic is essential for establishing your credibility and reinforcing your claim. You may select presentation topics in which opinions (yours or a quoted source) will be of value. The use of opinion within the presentation can be an effective and credible tool for substantiating your point; however, the overuse of opinion can be a detriment to your effectiveness. Unless you have documented expertise in a subject (for example, you are a medical doctor and the subject is internal medicine), it is good to have access to credible information to support your ideas. Opinion alone is not always supportive material!

What then is supportive material and how do you find it? With respect to presentations, *supports* are information that effectively validate your claim. Supports come in many forms. Supports can be statistical information, facts, explanations, analogies, definitions, narratives (stories), and yes, even opinions or experiential information when supported with other data. The effective use of supportive material will elevate your credibility and strengthen your claim. Always examine your supports to be certain that your supportive material is appropriate for your topic and your purpose.

Sources are where you get your supportive material. Forms of reliable sources are numerous. Sources of supportive information can be your university library or local municipal library (book, periodicals), the Internet (websites, databases), or qualified individuals (subject matter experts) who are acknowledged as experts in their field. The caveat with any source is to ensure that the data is accurate and current. For example, with the accelerating turnover and updating of information, the use of data as recently as the 1970s and 80s should be used with caution as some of the information may be superseded. Using outdated material will quickly lessen your credibility and weaken your claim.

In a following chapter you will learn in more detail about research and the proper use of supports. In the meantime, be certain that when you select a topic that it not only has relevance to your audience, but is also a topic that can be researched.

> **Supports:** Information that supports your idea or claim
> **Sources:** Where you get your supportive material

Topic Selection: A Process

Now that the attributes of appropriate topics have been defined, the next step is to discuss some processes that you may use to generate ideas for topics. We earlier stated that in some circumstances your topic may be predetermined. In other situations you may be given free course to select a topic of your choosing.

There are multiple ways to select and narrow a topic for presentation. Let's consider a couple of ideas to help you in the public speaking classroom (and outside of the classroom).

Internet Search Engines

One of the quickest ways to generate a large list of topic ideas for presentation is to use an Internet search engine. For example, if you were looking for topics for an information presentation, you would type "information speech topics" in the search field to locate a number of websites that list information speech topics alphabetically. Some sites have hundreds of topic ideas, while one site surveyed had over 5000 topics! You can use these lists to help spark a topic idea that you and your audience will be interested in.

Library

Your library is ALWAYS a good place to research presentation topics. Most libraries have someone who serves as a reference librarian. This person will direct you to those resources that will help you. It may be books, journals, periodicals, DVDs, the Internet, or other forms of reference. Consider the library your best friend in researching and developing your presentation.

Brainstorming

Another method is to brainstorm ideas. The process is simple: Get a sheet of paper and a pen or pencil. Give yourself a time limit of two to three minutes while using a stopwatch to help you keep time. To maintain focus on your goal, write at the top of the page "Proposed Speech Topics." Now, start your stopwatch and begin by writing down the first topic idea that comes to mind. Write down

be more effective and generate more topic ideas if you can get the aid of a couple of your friends or classmates.

Narrowing Your Topic

As you look at your list you may find that your topics are relevant but may be too broad for presentation purposes. Examine the following list:

- Baseball
- Music
- War
- Food

You can see how these topics may be unmanageable when determining what you will discuss in your presentation. You should think about your topic and narrow it to be more specific. Notice how each of the above subjects are narrowed:

Narrowing a subject may feel uncomfortable at first for the fear of leaving out important information about your topic. However, developing skills in narrowing your topic will make your research more effective and aid in the organization of your content.

Baseball	Music	War	Food	Broad
Major League	Rock and Roll	United States	Ethnic	
National League	1960s	Civil War	Sushi	
Central Division	Psychedelic			
Chicago Cubs				Narrow

your idea without forming an opinion about the quality of the idea (don't judge, just write). Now, write down a second idea. It may be a new topic or one that was generated by the first idea. Again, write down a third idea . . . you get the point. Start writing ideas as if you were "popcorn" and ideas begin to "pop" out of your head, slowly at first, then more quickly. Remember the purpose is to generate a quantity of ideas. Keep thinking and writing until your time is up.

At the end of the session you should have a good number of ideas to work from. This process will

Purposes of Presentations

After selecting your topic but before getting too deep in the planning and development of your presentation, you should first understand "why" you are giving your presentation. What is it you want to accomplish? What do you want to do with your topic? Stated in another way, what is your overall purpose? Much like being able to narrow your topic, having a clear sense of the "why" of your presentation will validate your topic choice, focus your research, and aid in the organization of your material.

There are two levels of speech (presentation) purposes. The higher purpose is referred to as the **general purpose**. After determining your general purpose, you will refine your process by developing a more specific purpose called an **outcome statement**.

The General Purpose

According to Beebe and Beebe (2000), the general purpose is the "over-arching goal of the presentation." Virtually any presentation will fall within one of three general purposes; to *persuade*, to *inform* or to *entertain*. This is not to say that your presentation will solely focus on one of these three purposes at the exclusion of the other two. In reality, any effective presentation will have an emphasis on one general purpose and will manifest attributes of one or both of the others.

The idea of a *persuasive presentation* implies that your purpose is to deliver information for altering or strengthening an audience's beliefs, attitudes, or behaviors (Woodward and Denton, 2000). Examples of persuasive presentations include: encouraging a driver's education class to wear seatbelts when riding in an automobile, encouraging the donation of blood at the local American Red Cross, or advocating for a political candidate.

An *informative presentation* has a more simplistic design in that its main purpose is to disseminate information. Even though you may want to influence your audience positively regarding your credibility or the accuracy of your data, your main focus will be only to inform. Examples of informative presentations include: university lectures, state-of-the-business presentations at stockholder meetings, changes in health benefits at work, or the appropriate method of exiting a building during a fire drill.

A *presentation to entertain* focuses on the "building of goodwill" component. Presentations that have an emphasis to entertain include: after dinner speeches, acknowledging an individual who is retiring from an organization, a "send-off" for someone moving to another city, roasts, or toasts to name just a few examples. The main purpose is to create a positive and light-hearted examination of an issue or topic or to present something/someone in a favorable manner. Humor or the effective use of anecdotes is often utilized in presentations to entertain.

Remembering the Three General Purposes is as easy as **P.I.E.!**

- Persuade
- Inform
- Entertain

When you have determined your topic (or it is determined for you), you will decide what your general purpose will be.

As you can see from the three brief definitions above, speeches to persuade, inform and entertain very well may share attributes of each purpose. Let's consider the 60-30-10 rule. If you are developing and delivering a persuasive presentation on the importance of wearing a seat belt when riding in an automobile, you would want to deliver meaningful information with a persuasive emphasis, while engaging and energizing the audience. Your purpose is to persuade (60%) while delivering supportive information (30%) in a way that engages your audience (10%).

Whereas, in a presentation to inform, such as a safety information meeting, your main purpose is to deliver important safety information (60%) that convinces your audience of the importance of the data (30%) in a way that engages them (10%).

The same may be said about presentations to entertain. An after-dinner presentation would be designed to entertain (60%) with information on a specific topic (30%) that influences the audience (10%). The following figure graphically models this concept:

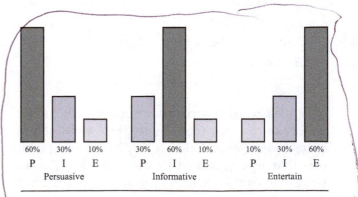

FIGURE 2.1 Different configurations of presentations.

The percentages are arbitrary, yet the principle is concrete. It is most probable that your presentation will be a representation of all three components, while the main general purpose of your presentation will have a focused theme of, "to persuade, to inform or to entertain".

The Outcome Statement

As mentioned earlier, after determining your general purpose, you will refine your process by developing a more specific purpose called an *outcome statement*. An outcome statement is a defining statement that reflects your general purpose, identifies your topic, and dictates an observable, measurable action you want your audience to achieve. You will notice that an outcome statement has a greater degree of specificity than the general purpose and that the language is more precise. Outcome statements should be worded to indicate what the audience will achieve as opposed to what the speaker will achieve. Notice the distinction of the two phrases:

Speaker-centered: "I will talk about the benefits of wearing a seatbelt."

Audience-centered: At the conclusion of my presentation, the audience will be able to list the three elements of effective seatbelt use."

Notice in the first example how the emphasis is on what the speaker will perform and not on what the audience will glean from the presentation. Whereas, in the second example, it is easy to determine what the audience will be expected to know or do. Be sure in writing your outcome statement that you use precise action words such as "list, define, write, etc . . . ." Writing clearly stated outcomes will help you develop the main points of your presentation in a way that is relevant to your topic, to your purpose, and to the audience.

Thesis

In your presentation development, the crafting of the *thesis* will signal that your presentation is about to take form. The *thesis* is sometimes referred to as a "thesis statement" or "central idea" and in one sentence makes known the main points of your presentation. The thesis should include your outcome statement. To illustrate, the following is a properly written thesis:

Smart automobile operators know the importance of wearing their seatbelt, inspecting it for wear, and properly donning it each time they use their vehicle.

Notice how the thesis statement comprehensively states what the presentation will include; seatbelt importance and the three components of seatbelt use.

The general purpose, the outcome statement, and the thesis when effectively combined will provide a strong foundation for further development of your presentation. Look at the three components discussed so far (general purpose, outcome statement, and thesis). Notice that when they are in concert with one another, a comprehensive view of the presentation appears and will keep the presenter on a successful track:

General Purpose: To Persuade

Outcome Statement: "At the conclusion of the presentation, the audience will be able to list the three elements of effective seatbelt use."

Thesis: "Smart automobile operators know the importance of wearing their seatbelt, inspecting it for wear, and properly donning it each time they use their vehicle."

Let's now look at how to build upon this stable foundation by examining the three building blocks of an effective presentation.

The Introduction, Body, and Conclusion

Think back to a presentation that made a strong and positive impression on you. What were its qualities that made you sit up and take notice? It may have been the speaker's polished presentation style, the creative use of visual aids, or the topic itself. It is a given that if the presentation appeared coherent and the information flowed in a logical order, the presenter had a clear method of organizing the information.

As we continue the discussion of preparing and developing the successful presentation, knowing the main components of your "speech" will help you in managing your material, so that your delivery will appear to flow in a smooth and logical order. An effective presentation almost always will have three main components into which the information is divided. The components are: the *introduction*, the *body*, and the *conclusion*. Plato is credited with personifying these elements by referring to them as parts of a living creature, appropriately proportioned, much like our own bodies. Think of your presentation as having parts that are appropriately proportioned with respect to one another. Let's examine these components individually.

The Introduction

The introduction of the presentation is where the presenter gets to make the good "first impression." It is also the section where the presenter "*tells them what he/she is going to tell them.*" Although the introduction is much shorter in length than the body of the presentation, the introduction is where you "set the table" for presentation success. This is accomplished by the successful completion of four items: The attention grab, topic identification, establishing credibility and presenting your thesis (Table 2.2).

TABLE 2.2 Four Elements of an Effective Introduction
Grabbing the Audience's Attention
Identifying Your Topic
Establishing Speaker Credibility
Presenting the Thesis

Grabbing the Audience's Attention

The attention grab is designed to accomplish what the term suggests; to grab the audience's attention, to metaphorically have the audience say, "tell me more." The amount of time a speaker has to capture the audience's attention is indeed brief. Therefore, it is important that the beginning of the presentation contain an effective attention-grabbing device. There are a number of methods to do this. The *dramatic statement* can be effective as such a device. A *quotation* from someone renowned or of historical significance is also effective. These devices are easy to use and effective when they have relevance to your topic and purpose. The presenter should remember when using someone else's quote, ALWAYS give attribution to the person that originated the content.

The well-crafted *question* is another excellent thought-provoker and attention-grabbing device. Questions also are easy to manipulate and can be used as information gathering tools. Questions can come in two forms, *response* and *rhetorical*. Response questions are posed for the purpose of gathering

information and in the case of a presentation, introducing a topic or a concept. An example of a response question is:

By a show of hands, how many of you ate a healthy breakfast this morning?

As evidenced by the directness of the question, the presenter has an expectation of audience response. This can be an effective method of building common ground between the speaker and the audience; however, caution is in order when using the response question. Should the presenter require a vigorous response from the audience and no response is given, this could diminish speaker credibility at the onset of the presentation.

The rhetorical question is another effective attention grab when used properly. A rhetorical question differs from a response question in that the sole purpose of the rhetorical question is to generate thought within the minds of the audience and not to solicit information. An example of a well-crafted rhetorical question might be:

Why is it that most Americans fail to eat a healthy breakfast in the morning?

By the wording, one can see that the answers are numerous and the question does not readily lend itself to audience response. However, if the presenter poses this question to stimulate thought, the audience can consider the question internally and prepare themselves for the direction the presenter will take them.

The last attention grab we will discuss is the narrative or "story telling." This form of attention grab is usually reserved for the more seasoned presenter. Although effective, the narrative can be difficult to use, especially when brevity is critical. However, if you can professionally deliver the relevant, concise, and engaging story, your audience will be eager to consider your thesis.

Identifying Your Topic

The second element of the introduction is the identification of your topic. It is imperative that the topic is fully revealed in the introduction of your speech. The presenter may hint at their topic in the attention grab, but the professional speaker should never "mask" their topic for novelty or effect. Always use explicit language in your introduction such as, "Today I want to talk to you about . . ." or "Seatbelts save lives." Deferring your topic identification until later in your presentation will only create confusion for your audience and may frustrate them.

Establishing Speaker Credibility

Think about the times you have listened to a speech or presentation. Did you ever question the speaker's honesty or their expertise on the subject? If you did, you were questioning the **"credibility"** of the speaker. Likewise, you as a presenter need to ensure when you stand before an audience that you establish yourself as ethical and knowledgeable on your subject. By definition, credibility is that which is believable or reliable (Webster, 2007). You must tell the audience early in the process why you are a legitimate speaker.

As a student, you may not have established a huge body of work nor had many experiences with respect to your topic, but you can let the audience know what specific knowledge or experiences you have had. For example, if your topic is the importance of wearing seatbelts, you should inform your audience of a personal experience in which seatbelts prevented yourself or someone you know from serious injury or death. It can be effective to explain how much research you have committed to the topic. Look at the following statements that establish or increase your credibility:

> Personal Experience: "Seatbelts save lives. I am a benefactor from having worn my seatbelt in a head-on collision."

> Personal Knowledge: "Seatbelts save lives. I have researched the seatbelt issue for four years and the numbers are staggering!"

As you can see, both statements have the effect of establishing prior experience or knowledge. Emphasizing this information in the introduction of your speech will quickly let the audience know you are capable of presenting accurate content.

Your credibility (ethos) determines if people trust you enough to listen to your ideas. When making a presentation, there are three phases of credibility that must be managed:

1. **Initial Credibility:** This is the credibility you initially bring to the presentation. Do you have a prior reputation, credentials, experiences, training, etc., that boost (or diminish) your trustworthiness? Are you known to have a good character and goodwill towards the audience? Always establish or remind the audience why you are credible enough to address this topic and why they should trust you enough to begin listening.

2. **Derived Credibility:** This is the credibility you build or create while making the presentation. This credibility builds (or diminishes) based on the quality of cited sources, language, facts, examples, logic, organization, delivery style, vocal variety, multimedia, etc., that you use throughout your presentation.

3. **Terminal Credibility:** This is the credibility you have at the end of the presentation. The quality of your conclusion, how you respond to audience questions, and even your facial expressions and body posture as you return to your seat will leave a final, lasting impression on the audience. Hopefully, your credibility level increased throughout the presentation and the audience now thinks more highly of you and your ideas than before you spoke.

There are other methods of establishing or increasing your credibility and these concepts will be discussed in a later chapter. But the value of letting your audience know that you are a reliable and plausible speaker is a must if you are to deliver an effective presentation.

Presenting the Thesis

Lastly, revealing your **thesis** completes the "table setting" section of the presentation. In formal terms a thesis is "a proposition maintained or defended" (Webster, 2007). In the presentation, a thesis is a one-sentence statement that explains what your presentation is about. You will be stating your proposition in the thesis. In the thesis you should be able to state your topic (implicitly or explicitly) and state your main points. Look at the thesis that was previously mentioned:

> *Smart automobile operators know the importance of wearing their seatbelt, inspecting it for wear, and properly donning it each time they use their vehicle.*

In this sentence the audience is treated to the topic of the presentation (seatbelts) and the three main points (importance, inspection, and donning).

A well-crafted thesis can be considered a map. It tells the audience what their destination is and the stops they will make along the way.

As stated earlier, the introduction has brevity, yet its importance cannot be overstated. A creative and appropriately-structured introduction will comfortably guide the audience into the next section of your presentation, the body.

The Body

It can be said that within the body of your presentation is the reason you are giving your presentation. In the body is the information that supports your general purpose, applies your outcome statement, and details your thesis. This is the section where you "*tell the audience*" the information you have prepared. You should devote considerable thought to the content and organization of the material in the body.

The content of your presentation is the relevant information you gathered during your research, including your supports and the citation of your sources. There should be an apparent structure for your content that manifests an evident flow. As suggested in the thesis portion of the introduction, a well-crafted presentation should contain about three **main points**. Certainly this is not a fixed number as some presentations will require more information. But, to help maintain audience engagement and retention, three main points is a good benchmark. Let's examine the previous thesis to illustrate the three main points:

Smart automobile operators know the importance of wearing their seatbelt, inspecting it for wear, and properly donning it each time they use their vehicle.

The speaker's three main points are embedded within the thesis.

I. Smart automobile operators know the importance of wearing their seatbelt.

II. Smart automobile operators inspect their seatbelt for wear.

III. Smart automobile operators properly don their seatbelt every time they use their automobile.

The speaker chose as their proposition the three main points stated. You can see a specific and logical order in the process. If the presenter were to choose a different arrangement of the three main points, the audience may become confused.

The organizational pattern of your body's information varies based on which type pattern you use. The pattern you choose is dependent on what you wish to accomplish with your information. Presentations that are designed to inform may have a specific pattern based on your topic. Look at the following partial list of often-used information patterns.

Causal – Showing how some events bring about other events

Chronological – Discussing anything that occurs in sequence (by time or process)

Problem/Solution – Does not involve persuading but rather states a problem or issue and provides information on how it will be resolved

Topical – A topic that has main points of equal value (a particular order may or may not be critical)

One can see how it would be inappropriate to discuss a solution before stating the problem (problem/solution pattern) or discuss the elements of a specific process by starting with the final product and randomly stating the process in a non-sequential order (chronological).

The organizational pattern in persuasive presentations utilizes a unique process called Monroe's Motivated Sequence. This pattern is used in everyday communication through commercials and non-profit appeals for contributions. Monroe's Motivated Sequence has a specific pattern (Table 2.3).

TABLE 2.3 Elements of Monroe's Motivated Sequence

Attention
Establish a Need
Satisfy the Need
Provide Visualization
Call to Action

Within Monroe's Motivated Sequence the presenter initially grabs the audience's attention as with an informational speech. After the attention grab, the presenter states the need and then tells what the audience should do to satisfy the need. Once the need has been established and information to satisfy the need has been explicated, the presenter will paint a picture of what the audience's world will be like if they adhere to the principles stated in the satisfaction step. Conversely, it is also appropriate to state what the audience's world will be like if they *do not* adhere to the recommendation in the satisfaction step. Lastly, the presenter tells the audience specifically what they would like them to do or think. In other words, "call them to a specific action." Monroe's Motivated Sequence and the persuasive presentation will be discussed in greater detail in subsequent material, but it is mentioned here to help the reader understand that the body of your presentation can take on different organizational forms, and how you develop and organize the body of your presentation is dependent on your purpose.

The Conclusion

The final element in the presentation triumvirate is the conclusion. To restate, the introduction is where you "tell them what you are going to tell them," the body is where "you tell them," and the conclusion is where you "tell them what you just told them." As simple as this sounds, it's very effective.

The well-crafted conclusion has three components that should be completed as you wrap up your presentation. Notice the similarities of these components to those of the introduction (Table 2.4).

TABLE 2.4 Elements of the Effective Conclusion
Signal the End of the Presentation
Review the Main Points
Issue a Strong Closing Comment

Having completed the delivery of the information contained in the body, you want to ensure a smooth transition into the conclusion. This is accomplished by the first element of your conclusion "signaling the end of your speech." Be creative in your phrasing as you develop the words for your transition to the conclusion. Most often an audience will hear phrases such as "In conclusion," or "As I conclude." These sentences certainly accomplish the intent; however, they are used so often they may become trite and lose their impact. Examples of creative transitions are:

In the past few moments I have given you three keys of automobile safety.

We can see by the three guidelines illustrated, wearing seatbelts can change your world!

Notice how these statements implicitly indicate the leaving of the body and the transition to the conclusion. Also, the phrases gently reintroduce your three main points.

The second element of your conclusion is the review of your main points. By this time it may feel as if the speaker has been redundant in repeating their main points. But, repetition is not redundancy. The effectively crafted summary of your main points in the conclusion will embed your presentation in the minds of those who hear it. Summarizing your main points will also increase your credibility, as it displays your consistent organization throughout the presentation. The summarizing of your main points lends itself to a natural restatement of your thesis. Just as the previewing of the main points and thesis in the introduction sets the table for a successful presentation, the review of the same brings closure. Consider the following main point summarization and thesis review:

We can see by the three guidelines illustrated that, wearing seatbelts can change your world! Be a smart automobile operator by knowing the importance of wearing a seatbelt, inspecting it for wear, and properly donning it each time you use your vehicle.

An effective review completes the dispensation of your well-developed information and prepares the audience for the final element of your conclusion, the strong closing comment.

You will recall that a strong audience attention grab was important in establishing a good "first impression" at the beginning of your presentation. Subsequently, a strong closing comment serves an equally important function in bringing your presentation to a memorable close. Public speaking professors frequently hear students close their speeches with a "thank you" or a brief pause and latent "that's it."

In the professional presentation, these diluted finishes would diminish speaker credibility. Consider using a closing remark that stimulates thought, appeals to the audience's emotion and in the event of a persuasive presentation, incites the audience to action. Just as there are attention-grabbing devices in the introduction, there are strong closing devices in the conclusion. Let's consider three of them: the *quotation*, the *dramatic statement*, and the *rhetorical question*.

The rules for an effective quotation in the conclusion are the same as in the introduction. Be sure to use a quote that has relevance to your topic and is given the proper attribution. Your credibility is increased if your quote originates from a renowned person or one of historical significance.

Likewise, the dramatic statement is designed to have a positive impact on the audience's lasting impression. The dramatic statement also must be relevant. You may use a statement that the audience is familiar with, yet apply it to different topics. The phrase, "The life you save may be your own!" is a generally recognized phrase in the United States. The presenter could use this statement if he/she were discussing the wearing of seatbelts, getting annual physicals, or not smoking cigarettes.

Finally, the rhetorical question is another tool to memorably finish your presentation. As earlier defined, the rhetorical question is designed only to stimulate thinking and not for information gathering. Imagine how disastrous it would be if you finished your presentation with a response question and no one responded . . . to avoid this, use a rhetorical question. As an example, think about the question "Isn't saving a life worth five seconds of your time?" The presenter is not looking for a response, but the question is effective in causing the audience to think about how little time it takes to buckle a seatbelt and the possible rewards associated with this action.

Like the introduction, the conclusion occupies a smaller portion of your presentation, but its impact cannot be understated. You will want to preview your material in the introduction, detail your material in the body, and review your material in the conclusion while finishing with a strong close. When you master these concepts, you are on your way to delivering a professional presentation.

Organization through Outlining

Many students reveal that after the fear of public speaking, the organizing of their material is the most distasteful activity in giving presentations. "Why can't I just get up there and wing it?" is often their cry.

For any presentation to be effective, it must have strong content and be organized in a way that the audience can "follow" the presenter's thinking. For this to happen, the presenter must structure his/her material in a logical flow. The best way to accomplish this is to use the *preparation outline* and *delivery outline*. An entire chapter is devoted to this process later in the textbook; therefore, our purpose for now will be only to introduce the general concepts of outlining.

Preparation Outline

First, a **preparation outline** is a formal and complete sentence document. A preparation outline maintains a higher degree of thoroughness than the delivery outline in that a preparation outline's focus is directed toward an interested reader not having necessary prior knowledge of your topic (Grice and Skinner, 2001). In other words, the literate stranger should be able to read your preparation outline and have a general understanding of your presentation.

There is a specific format that is used in the preparation outline. Zeuschner (1997) refers to this format as a Standard Outline Symbol System (Subordination and Grouping) (Table 2.5). In this method there are a specific set of rules for creating the "skeleton" of your outline and plugging in the information.

Image © AVAVA, 2009. Used under license from Shutterstock, Inc.

TABLE 2.5 Zeuschner's Template for Standard Outline Symbol System (Subordination and Grouping)

- Start with capital Roman Numerals for main ideas
- Use upper-case Arabic letters for subordinate ideas
- Use numbers for supports related to each subordinate idea
- If necessary use lower-case letters to support subordinate ideas

---

A standard subordinate outline template would be configured similar to the following:

I. Main Idea X
  A. First subordinate idea related to X
    1. First support for A
    2. Second support for A
    3. Third support for A
      a. First support for 3
      b. Second support for 3
      c. Third support for 3
  B. Second subordinate idea related to X
  C. Third subordinate idea related to X
II. Main Idea Y
  A. First subordinate idea related to Y
  B. Second subordinate idea related to Y
  C. Third subordinate idea related to Y
III. Main Idea Z
  A. First subordinate idea related to Z
  B. Second subordinate idea related to Z
  C. Third subordinate idea related to Z

There are other accepted outlining formats that are utilized in different applications, but the concept remains the same; with each main idea, there can be subordinate ideas, and for each subordinate idea, there can be supports. Zeuschner adds these general rules when crafting a subordinate format outline:

A Logical Construction Should Be Evident

Ideas exist in relationship to each other (grouping) and there must be a direct link among the items in the group (for example there must be a direct link between Roman numeral I and A, B, C. There must be a direct link between the Letter A and numbers 1 and 2 and 3 etc.).

Main ideas should be stated in complete, concise sentences.

Subordinate ideas should be stated in complete, concise sentences.

Supports may be stated with key words.

You do not have to have an A, B, or C as subordinates to the Roman numerals, but if you have an "A", you must have a "B"; if you have a "1" you must have a "2" and so on.

The Delivery Outline

More simplistic in form is the **delivery outline**. This is the "speaker friendly" outline that the presenter keeps in his/her possession while speaking. Although less formal than the presentation outline, the delivery outline maintains the same order as its formal counterpart. Sometimes called a "key word" outline, this tool is designed to readily aid the speaker in his/her delivery. Instead of complete sentences, the delivery outline uses key words to prompt the presenter, utilizes a larger font size for quicker reference, and highlights words that the speaker wants to emphasize (by use of color, underlining, italicizing, etc.).

Delivery outlines also have creative notations for the presenter's benefit. Some have written prompts (delivery cues) in the margins that state, "breath here," "smile," or "make eye contact." Whatever the presenter needs to aid them in the presentation is fair to include in the delivery outline, as long as the information follows the order of your preparation outline.

Initially, the organization of your material may feel tedious. But as you perfect the process, you will realize how the information develops a logical flow that will aid the audience in their understanding and enhance your credibility as an effective presenter.

The Presentation Aid

Today's effective presenter has many more tools at their disposal for enhancing their presentation than did their predecessors. In the past, presentation aids (formally called visual aids), may have consisted of a poster board with photos pasted and handwritten letters. Certainly, with the development and evolvement of multimedia, presentations are more polished and professional. Computer technology (hardware and software), Internet video, video projectors, audio systems, smart boards, and peripheral technologies give the 21st century presenter remarkable tools for presentation success.

Even with all the advancements in visual and audio aids, the effective presenter knows that the presentation aid is only to be used as an enhancement to the information presented and is not the presentation itself. A presentation aid is thus anything that repeats, substitutes, or complements the verbal message.

As stated earlier there are numerous forms of presentation aids and these will be itemized in another chapter. But it is essential to note that no matter what your aids are, there are certain rules that govern their use.

Reasons Why Presentation Aids Enhance the Presentation

Presentation aids clarify, enhance, and give concrete meaning to your words: In the communication world, we communicate meaning by using symbols. Words are symbols and many times we disagree on what symbols mean. You may hear the word "base" and think you understand what "base" means. But what if the presenter showed a picture of a "bass" guitar? Would this have been your first assumption? The use of a visual aid in this instance would clarify the meaning of the word.

Presentation aids make your point memorable: Imagine giving a presentation on the tragedy of war. It may be difficult to use adequate verbal language to "paint a picture" for the audience to fully understand the ravages. However, if during your discussion you displayed a graphic image of a war-torn area, this would embed in the audience's mind the point you were illustrating. A caution here is to know who your audience is comprised of so that your material is effective, not offensive.

Presentation aids minimize lengthy explanations: This is the "a picture is worth a thousand words" analogy. In attempting to detail what an automobile looks like after a head-on collision, a simple image may minimize the amount of verbal equity the presenter has to commit. Also, per the reason stated before, a visual image may make your point more memorable than your words.

The reasons stated are but a sampling of the benefits of using presentations aids. Before we leave the topic, let's look at a few guidelines for using aids.

Guidelines for Using Presentation Aids

- Be sure you need the aid and it is relevant to your topic and the audience.

- Less is best! Do not make your aid busy or flashy to the point where the audience must "pull out" the information you are conveying.

- Ensure any text or images are large enough for everyone to see. Create the presentation for the person in the back of the room.

- Use your presentational aid only when you are ready for the audience to see or hear it. Posting a photograph before your point is made will only occupy the audience's attention and may possibly confuse them.

- Lastly, always cite the source of the aid. Photos, audios, and video clips must be attributed if they did not originate with you.

Much more will be discussed about presentational aids later. This section should give some initial direction on how visual and audio aids can send your presentation over the top!

Know Who You Are Talking To!

Standing before an audience and presenting your claim is parallel to having a conversation with an individual. In order to be effective in your communication, you need to know who you are talking to. What does the audience value, what do they know about your topic, what is their age, gender, ethnicity? As a presenter, knowing this information about your audience will increase your presentational success. As a general rule, audience members can be placed in one of four categories:

> **The Confused** – These are audience members who may not have formed a prior opinion on your topic due to their lack of knowledge or experience on your subject.
>
> **The Skeptic** – These are audience members who have prior knowledge or experience on your subject, but in principle do not agree with your claim.
>
> **The Apathetic** – These are audience members who may or may not have prior knowledge about your subject, yet they have no interest or emotional investment.
>
> The "Choir" – These are audience members who have knowledge about your subject, agree with your claim, and are emotionally vested in your topic. The term "choir" is an analogy to faithful church congregants who are always in attendance and have "bought in" to the ideology.

Knowing who comprises your audience aids in determining how you research, develop, and present your material. The confused may need background material to bring them up to speed, and the skeptic may require stronger emotional appeals to be persuaded. The apathetic will require information that speaks to the "what's in it for them," or how will they benefit by adopting your claim. The choir will need information to encourage them to "stay the course" and maintain their current position.

The Audience Analysis

How do you determine who comprises your audience? What do they value and what do they know about your topic? Collecting this information is accomplished through an audience analysis. An audience analysis allows the presenter to know three types of information about his/her audience; information about the *demographic* of the audience, information about the *attitude* of the audience, and information about the context or *situation*.

Demographic information is information about characteristics or traits the group represents. These are measurable characteristics such as age, gender, socioeconomic level, ethnicity, education, etc. Often companies ask for this information when you purchase one of their products. Have you ever filled

out a product registration card that included questions about your demographics? The company is gathering demographic information about those who buy their product for developing marketing strategies. Likewise, knowing the demographic of the audience will aid the presenter in determining the topic relevance and appropriateness.

Attitudinal information is the second type of information the presenter wants to gather and possibly the most important. This is where the presenter assesses the overall disposition of the audience. What do they value, what do they know about the subject, or how do they feel about the subject? This is essential information in refining the outcome statement and developing the content of your presentation. By adapting your information based on the beliefs, attitudes, and values of the audience you increase your probability of delivering relevant information to a receptive audience.

Situational information is the third type of analysis information. This includes everything from logistical information (the venue, the time of day, audience size, etc.) to context information (a solemn, formal environment or light and interpersonal). The use of humorous anecdotes may be inappropriate if the context is formal. On the other hand, a stoic delivery during an after dinner presentation may not be appropriate if the event is expected to be light-hearted. Based on this information the knowledgeable presenter will tailor his/her presentation according to the environment or situation.

Four Methods of Presentation Delivery

At this point of your presentation development, you should have a clear view of the mechanics of developing your material. This section will briefly discuss four methods of delivering your material. These methods are: reading you manuscript, memorizing and reciting your material, extemporaneous delivery, and impromptu delivery.

Reading Your Manuscript: This is the least desirable manner to deliver your material and may lessen your credibility immensely. Reading your presentation may negate your presentation in the following ways:

- Gives an impression of inappropriate preparation, and/or lack of confidence
- Minimizes eye contact with the audience
- Appears lifeless and static

However, there are occasions within a presentation that reading your material is acceptable. When the material has a high degree of complexity/detail or when accuracy is critical, then reading the content is appropriate. Examples of this are sections of reports, quotes, legal information, etc.; any information that has to be exact may be read. It is important to note, in reading this information, the presenter should only read the necessary information and not the entire presentation.

Memorizing and Reciting Your Material: Memorizing and reciting a presentation can be effective if properly done. However, the drawbacks outweigh the positives in the following ways:

Advantages	Disadvantages
Consistent content delivery	Requires more development time
Maximum audience eye contact	Potential memory loss during delivery
	May appear "scripted"
	Long pauses in delivery
	Loss of dynamism

There may be times that a memorized and recited delivery is accepted: acceptance speeches, introductions, any presentation that is brief where content accuracy is important. But as with reading your manuscript, you must be certain to make your presentation lively and engaging for the audience.

Extemporaneous: Extemporaneous speaking is the preferred method of delivery in most presentations. This is where the presenter speaks from a delivery outline . . . but not by reading or reciting the material. An extemporaneous presentation is where the deliverer has a command of the material and delivers the content in a conversational, dynamic, and engaging way. Extemporaneous speaking is a delivery from an outline, but not delivering the exact wording. It is internalizing the main ideas (which are organized and outlined) and adapting/expressing the content to the audience. Extemporaneous presentations do require extensive preparation with respect to content development, organization, and delivery practice. Usually, those involved in an extemporaneous presentation will have adequate time for preparation.

Impromptu: Impromptu presentations are those which afford little or no time for development and organization of content. Sometimes referred to as "off the cuff" speaking, impromptu deliveries must still have organization but are delivered in a dynamic manner. There may be a time in the past where you have been recognized as a friend of a bride or groom, or you may have knowledge about someone who is to receive an award. In these situations you may be asked to "say a few words" on the behalf of the celebrated. In this circumstance there will be no time to research and little time to prepare. However, impromptu opportunities such as these still require structure. As the speaker, you would consider the person you are to speak about and develop a brief "introduction, body, and conclusion" that acknowledges their accomplishments. In most of these events you are speaking to build goodwill for the individual(s). Brevity and appropriateness are essential in impromptu presentations.

Informative and persuasive speeches will almost always fall under the category of reading, memorizing, or extemporaneous presentations whereas special occasion presentations can often but not always be impromptu.

The special occasion presentation is normally associated with social events, but should also be associated within the business "world of work" setting. Often in business there is occasion to present awards, acknowledge good performance, and introduce new employees. Whether inside or outside of business the overall purpose of special occasion presentations remain the same: to create goodwill between entities.

By category there are five purposes of special occasion presentations and these purposes may apply to the social or business context:

Agenda Setting: At the beginning of a meeting or seminar, a master of ceremonies will establish the goals for the activity and establish or reinforce the values of the organization that is sponsoring the event. They will do this while creating appropriate focus and energy within the audience.

Celebrate: To honor or praise someone or something publicly.

Commemorate: To keep alive the memory of someone or something.

Inspire: To encourage or embolden others to a specific thought or action.

Entertain: To hold the interest of and amuse others. These occasions are usually informal and light-hearted.

It is evident that these purposes would comfortably fit in a social or business context. In almost every purpose there is a desire to create a positive atmosphere. If you are delivering a toast to a groom, you will deliver comments that are positive. If your task is to wish good luck to a retiring employee, you will again present the individual in a positive way.

The Ethos, Logos, and Pathos

Building on the definition of rhetoric from Chapter 1, Aristotle would have invoked the continued definition of rhetoric as the "available means of persuasion" (Beebe, 2000). Inclusive in the definition is the concept of the ethos, logos, and pathos; these are the "available means" that help persuade an audience. Let's briefly examine these three concepts in light of the professional presentation.

The *ethos* reflects the credibility of the speaker. We discussed the three forms of credibility earlier. Aristotle and rhetoricians since his initial learning understand the importance of the speaker having credibility with the audience. Ethos is built by having established a reputation for credible delivery and a commitment to accurate and relevant information, applied in a way that benefits the audience. Ethos is one of three essential components of a successful presentation.

Logos is the second component of a successful presentation that represents the logic of the presentation. More accurately it represents the "words" or the information shared. Is your information current, accurate, relevantly applied, and presented for ethical reasons?

Pathos is the third and final component. It considers the emotion of the audience and the use of emotional appeals to influence. Our society is inundated with emotional appeals from TV, radio, and the Internet. Entities that want us to buy their products or donate to their cause use pathos (emotional appeals) to influence us. Coupled with a strong message (logos) and speaker credibility (ethos), the use of effective emotional appeals completes the triangle of developing and presenting the perfect presentation.

The Audience as Your Customer and Evaluator

No matter the context of your presentation, the desired results are the same: to persuade, inform, and entertain your audience. With this responsibility comes the likelihood that your audience will evaluate specific elements of your presentation. Rhetorical scholarship suggests that there are five ways presenters are evaluated. The following highlighted information explains this principle:

The Five Areas of Evaluation

Everyone loves to hear a good presentation! And what do people love more than to listen to a good presentation? *Answer: To critique someone's presentation!* Even those who have no formal training in presentation skills instinctively understand what to look for:

1. **Thought:** This involves everything related to the development of ideas – evidence, organization, logic, persuasive appeals, etc., to form the substance of the presentation. Every presentation must "make sense" to the listener.

2. **Language:** This includes the specific words that were spoken. Were the words vivid, current, compelling, memorable, creative, familiar, and/or accurate? Were the words carefully selected to maximize the value and effect of the message?

3. **Adaptation:** This includes how well the message fit the audience, occasion, and the setting. Were the development of ideas and selection of words appropriate and fitting? Did they adapt their content and delivery prior to and during the presentation?

4. **Voice:** This includes how the voice was used to maximize the message. Volume, rate, tone, pitch, pauses/silence, enunciation, etc, all convey a variety of emotions (excitement, empathy, pity, disgust, envy, joy, bewilderment, honesty, urgency, conviction, etc.). The appropriate use of vocal variety puts "life" and "energy" into mere words.

5. **Action:** This includes everything done with the body, face, and eyes to maximize a message. Facial expressions, gestures, movements, postures, stances, and physical appearances/clothing all affect how a presentation is evaluated.

Lastly, great presenters can see the big picture. They know their presentation has relevance and they know how their audience can benefit from their information. The relevant, effective presentation entails five components that every speaker must master: These are called the Five P's of Great Presentations.

The Five P's of Great Presentations

Learning how to give great presentations is a key element of your professional development in college! But what makes a great presentation GREAT? To help you become a successful presenter, practice the **Five P's of Great Presentations**.

Purpose: Great presenters speak with a clear sense of purpose – they are on a mission! Thoroughly explain why you are presenting and what you will accomplish. Listeners always ask "What's in it for me?" Tell listeners why they should listen and what the payoff will be if they do. Clearly articulating a purpose and a payoff builds confident expectations.

Personality: Great presenters speak in a natural, conversational (extemporaneous) style. Do not be a lifeless "talking-head!" Showing your personality causes listeners to connect with you. Listeners want content but they also want to know the "real" you.

Passion: Great presenters are passionate and enthusiastic about their content/topic. Speak with conviction, energy, and emotion so the audience will listen and care. Use gestures, body movement, facial expression, and vocal variety to demonstrate that you are excited and serious about sharing this message with your listeners.

Power: Great presenters are powerful because they feed off of the energy of the audience! When you present great content, your real personality, and sincere passion about your topic, it energizes your listeners. They return the favor by giving you their eye-contact, smiles, attention, applause, and laughter. This makes you very powerful . . . the audience is under your control. But if you bore them, ignore their feedback, or fail to engage their hearts and minds, they will withdraw their attention and you lose your power and influence over the audience.

Pleasure: Great presentations create a pleasurable experience for everyone. By presenting with purpose, personality, passion, and power, you have accomplished your goal of "selling yourself and your ideas." You go away feeling energized and confident. Likewise, when you reward listeners with "the very best," they also experience a sense of pleasure and appreciation ("Wow, that was great . . . very informative . . . fun . . . eye-opening . . . motivating . . .").

◼ Chapter Review

As responsible citizens it is almost certain that there will be a presentation in your social, civic, or business future. What can you do to be prepared when it comes your time to present? It is important to develop the skill sets to conceptualize, develop, and deliver the effective presentation in an engaging manner that will be well-received by the audience. These skills include: topic selection, supporting your idea with credible information, and structuring your presentation in a purposed and systematic manner.

Knowing who comprises the audience aids the presenter in determining what to research and the approach to take in the delivery. Audience analyses gather information about your audience's demographics, their attitude toward your subject, and the context of the situation.

All of this is important because the audience will want to know what's in it for them and a savvy presenter will address these needs of the audience. The presenter gains confidence and credibility as he/she gains skills in effective communication. Certainly, the study of rhetorical thought merits your commitment during this class and the future application of the skills you develop will serve you throughout your life.

■ Thought Questions

1. Why might using only your opinion to support your ideas be ineffective in a presentation? How might using your opinion or experience along with other supportive material enhance your claim?

2. Think about speeches or presentations you have heard in the past. What topics did you find interesting? Which topics were irrelevant or inappropriate? Why do you think you perceived the topics in the way you did? Would these topics be appropriate in other settings or with different audiences?

3. Consider the students in your classroom. What demographic attributes do you share with them? How are you different demographically? How might these variables affect your choice in topic selection?

4. Think about a presentation you have heard in the past. Did you find the presentation interesting and engaging? What characteristics did the presenter display that made the presentation memorable? Or did you find the presentation irrelevant and stale? What characteristics did the presenter display that made the presentation boring or uninteresting?

5. How might a speaker with low credibility increase their credibility before, during, or after their presentation?

Developing and Presenting the Message

1. Utilizing Internet search engines create a search for presentation topic ideas. Experiment with different search titles such as "presentation topics" and then include keywords like "persuasive" or "informative." How many and what quality of topics could you find? Did seeing some of the examples generate any topic ideas of your own?

2. Connect to the American Rhetoric webpage at *http://www.americanrhetoric.com/*. Click on the link "Top 100 Speeches" and select one of the speeches that appeals to you. Examine the speech in light of the components of an effective presentation mentioned in the chapter. See if you can identify the following elements:

   The topic

   The general purpose

   The outcome statement

   The thesis

   The attention grab

   The main points

   The review of main points

   The strong close

   Are the components of the presentation easy to determine? Was there an effective attention grab and close? What are the main points? Are the main points easy to identify?

3. Individually or in a group create a strong attention grab for the topic "Cholesterol" using one of the methods discussed in the chapter (dramatic statement, quote, question, or narrative). If completed in the classroom, your professor may ask you to present your composition.

4. Look at the following example of a "broad" topic. Notice one method of narrowing it down to a more specific and manageable subject.

   GOLF → THE MASTERS → CHAMPIONS → TIGER WOODS

   Take the topic suggested below and narrow it to a more manageable subject that would be appropriate for the demographics in your classroom.

   LOVE

5. Explain how you would develop and present the topic of "going green" to the following audiences: The Sierra Club and OPEC. How would you differ your content and delivery for each audience?

References

1. Agnes, M. (Ed.). (2007). *Webster's New World College Dictionary* (4th ed.). Indianapolis, IA: Wiley.

2. Bebee, S. A. & Beebe, S. J. (2000). *Public speaking: An audience-centered approach.* (4th ed.) Boston: Allyn and Bacon.

3. Zeuschner, R. (1997). *Communicating Today.* (2nd ed.) Boston: Allyn and Bacon.

3

Communication Apprehension

Lou Davidson Tillson, Ph.D.

CHAPTER OBJECTIVES

At the end of this chapter, you will be able to:

- Recognize common symptoms of communication apprehension,

- Identify anxiety triggers,

- Explain why delivering presentations makes many people anxious, and

- Select appropriate stress management techniques to reduce your speech anxiety.

> That the birds of worry and care fly above your head,
> this you cannot change, but that they build nests in
> your hair, this you can prevent.
>
> ✍ Chinese proverb

> Nothing in life is to be feared. It is only to be
> understood.
>
> ✍ Marie Curie

Do you remember when you learned how to ride a bicycle? You weren't born with that ability . . . someone had to encourage you, push you, teach you. You probably began on a tricycle. I had an oversized red one that I proudly pedaled down the street to the post office with my mother each afternoon. It didn't require much skill. I just had to make sure I stopped pedaling when my mother stopped walking so I wouldn't ride up on her heels, which really annoyed her!

When I was 5 or 6 my parents bought me my first bicycle. It was a beauty . . . mirror-finished chrome and metallic blue paint, with handlebar streamers and a shiny blue and white, banana-shaped seat that sparkled in the sunlight. One of the most vivid childhood memories I have is of the day my dad took off the training wheels. My heart, pounding out a deafening rhythm in my chest, partially blocked out the frightened voice in my mind, which was whispering, "you can't do this . . . you're going to wreck . . . the other kids will see you and laugh when you fall . . . all of your friends can do it, but you'll never learn how . . . "

Nonetheless, my dad shouted words of encouragement above the sound of my thundering heart, gave me a final shove, and I was off. I pedaled with all the speed a 5 year old could muster, forgot about the bass drum thumping in my chest, and successfully, albeit a bit wobbly at first, flew down Oakwood Avenue demonstrating my newfound independence to the other kids in the neighborhood. Skinned knees and bruised elbows were forgotten as my father ran alongside me, coaching, "You can do it . . . keep pedaling . . . that's it . . . balance . . . balance . . . keep pedaling . . . you're doing it . . . you're doing it . . . keep pedaling . . . I told you, YOU COULD DO IT!"

Making a presentation is similar to riding a bicycle. You aren't born with this ability. You aren't even born with the ability to articulate words or speak in complete sentences. You have to learn how, just like you had to learn how to ride a bicycle. Along the way, you might have begun with the most simplistic delivery method (remember giving book reports in elementary school, barely speaking loud enough for the teacher to hear and NEVER glancing up from your notebook?).

Perhaps you've moved up to the bicycle with training wheels. You've made other presentations and taken some delivery risks, perhaps added more dynamic vocal inflection or better eye contact. Some of you might have taken a speech class in high school or competed on a debate team. Now, you're in college and preparing for your professional lives. It's time to remove the training wheels altogether and become a competent and dynamic speaker. It's going to require a lot of practice, but you can do it. You'll have to learn how to balance content with delivery and how to support your ideas with facts and examples . . . but you can do it! You'll have to learn how to organize your thoughts and present them creatively . . . but you can do it! You'll have to learn how to engage your audience with animated gestures and a dynamic voice . . . but you can do it! You'll have to practice, practice, practice, but you CAN DO IT!

Image © Ipatov, 2009. Used under license from Shutterstock, Inc.

This chapter will help you present with confidence, with a "can-do" attitude. The remaining chapters will teach you specific techniques and strategies for creating successful presentations for work and life. So hop on, let's get started. It's going to be a great ride!

Why Do I Need to Know How to Present in Public?

Riding a bicycle is challenging and fun. It fosters independence and can take you places that you couldn't get to otherwise. Presentations are much the same. Being able to share your ideas with others, persuade a group to agree with your point of view, or entertain an audience with a good story are presentation experiences every one of you is likely to encounter throughout your life. Being able to speak effectively is empowering and rewarding.

Most of you will have to make presentations in other classes during your college studies. Most of you (if you haven't done so already) will deliver presentations on the job, in social groups, or in civic organizations. "Presentation skills play a role in opening doors, influencing others, and in career development" (Baron, 2008, p. 1).

Unfortunately, most of us, as we prepare to enter the professional workforce, are still wearing our training wheels! We need to develop and

What do you expect to be doing in the future? Working for a major corporation or a non-profit organization? Going into the military? Raising a family? Participating in civic organizations? Teaching Sunday school? Going into the family business? Volunteering at a local school or hospital? Regardless of which path you walk down, good communication skills will be instrumental in helping you achieve your goals.

Employers consistently identify communication skills as a basic requirement. As a matter of fact, communication competence is necessary for your academic and personal success and helps to facilitate upward mobility and professional achievement (Morreale, Osborn, and Pearson, 2000).

Students enrolled in an introductory public speaking class were asked to identify the types of communication they anticipated engaging in based upon their major area of study and future career plans. Take a look at their list and highlight any that might match up with your course of study and future plans. Record additional presentation opportunities related to your specific career choice.

- Delivering platoon commands and orders
- Holding press conferences
- Delivering classroom lectures
- Presenting ideas to a school board
- Making speeches during band concerts
- Speaking to a curriculum committee about the importance of music in public schools
- Making presentations to college campus organizations
- Describing processes to clients
- Reporting to my supervisor
- Persuading companies to buy my product
- Persuading an organization to fund a project
- Informing groups about particular medical procedures
- Presenting legal arguments
- Delivering commencement addresses
- Speaking to Parent-Teacher Associations
- Making informal presentations on special occasions
- Recruiting organizational members
- Speaking at faculty meetings
- Making presentations at school programs
- Speaking to parents on "parents' night" at my school
- Leading meetings of professional organizations
- Selling a product or a service
- Leading staff meetings at work
- Presenting ideas to international clients or employees
- Presenting research findings
- Defending conservation efforts to the public

- Addressing employees
- Giving a talk at church
- Making progress reports at work
- Telling stories to young children
- Motivating athletes

- Lobbying politicians
- Conducting training seminars
- Other _____
- Other _____
- Other _____

fine-tune our presentation skills in order to move ahead. At this point you may be convinced of the need to develop your communication skills, but still apprehensive about doing so. The next section of this chapter will help explain why so many people are apprehensive (okay, downright scared!) about giving presentations and will give you some ideas to help manage that anxiety.

Why Do I Get So Anxious?

I have major stress and anxiety concerning public speaking. I know what I want to say and how to say it, and can say it just fine . . . until eyes are on me – I HATE the spotlight!! My stress greatly interferes with the quality of my speaking. It is crucial that I overcome this problem due to my future career field.

✍ *Buffy*

Mark Twain once said, "There are two types of speakers. Those who get nervous and those who are liars." Why are so many people anxious about public speaking? Hundreds of articles have been written about the subject and it's been labeled in myriad ways: bashfulness, timidity, stage fright, shyness, reticence, (un)willingness to communicate, presentational anxiety, communication apprehension, social anxiety, and **glossophobia**.

GLOSSOPHOBIA is the fear of public speaking. The word *glossophobia* comes from the Greek γλῶσσα *glōssa*, meaning tongue, and φόβος *phobos*, fear or dread.
("Do You Suffer from Glossophobia?" 2001, para. 1)

Image © Zsolt, Biczó, 2009. Used under license from Shutterstock, Inc.

Regardless of what it's called, most of us recognize the symptoms. Do any of these sound familiar to you?

- Pounding or racing heart
- Hot flashes
- Clammy or sweaty hands
- Dry mouth
- Butterflies in the stomach
- Nausea
- Breathlessness
- Trembling
- Muscle tension
- Shaky voice
- Blushing

All of these "symptoms" are physiological in nature and stem from what Harvard physiologist Walter B. Cannon initially described in the early 1900s as the "fight or flight response." He determined that when an animal senses a physical threat to its survival, it is faced with two options: fight off the attacker or flee from the threat.

> **What symptoms do you experience?**
>
> _____
> _____
> _____
> _____
> _____
> _____
> _____

Either option requires the body to prepare for intense activity in order to respond to the threat. The brain initiates 1400 different responses, including dumping **adrenaline** into the bloodstream producing an increase in heart rate, blood pressure, muscle tension, and breathing rate ("Stress," 2002). Interestingly, Cannon's research indicated that an animal would not differentiate between a real threat and a perceived threat. For example, an attacking dog and a movie depicting a vicious dog could elicit the same physiological response in a kitten exposed to both. In either case, the mind would stimulate the body to prepare to run away from, or to fight its way out of, the threatening situation (Allen, 1983).

What does the "**fight or flight response**" have to do with public speaking anxiety? Many people view public speaking as a threatening situation. They may be afraid that they will make mistakes or stumble, be evaluated negatively by the audience, or reveal insufficient presentation skills. For some, the stress is so profound that they postpone enrolling in a required 100-level basic public speaking class until the last semester of their senior year! Hopefully, they decide that completing the course is less of a threat than not graduating from college, so they enroll and "fight" their way through the assignments. Others repeatedly enroll in the class, but "flee" (drop) it before the first speaking assignment.

Research, however, suggests that it is "normal to experience a fairly high degree of anxiety about public speaking" (Richmond & McCroskey, 1985, p. 35). You are probably familiar with the results of a nationwide survey in which adults reported that speaking before a group was the greatest fear among the respondents (Wilder, 1999). It has been estimated that more than 70% of the general population experiences communication apprehension in the public speaking context (Richmond & McCroskey, 1985). In one study on speech anxiety, 64% of the respondents feared doing or saying something embarrassing, 74% feared their mind going blank, 63% feared being unable to continue talking, 59% worried about sounding foolish or not making sense, and 80% worried about trembling, shaking, or showing other signs of anxiety to their audience (Stein, Walker, & Forde, 1996). Clearly, stage fright is a common malady.

> *One of the fears that I have about public speaking is that of going completely blank and losing my train of thought right in the middle of my speech.*
>
> ✍ *Aaron*

The anxiety that you feel, caused by your brain's perception of a threat, mobilizes your body for the fight or flight response. Too much adrenaline can interfere with your ability to deliver a presentation by causing the symptoms listed earlier. Too little adrenaline can result in a "flat," uninspiring delivery that fails to engage your audience members' attention. A reasonable amount of this "adrenaline rush" can actually improve your speaking performance by stimulating creativity and adding energy and enthusiasm to it, much as it enables an athlete to succeed in his or her sport. Just like the children's story about Goldilocks and the Three Bears, a moderate amount of adrenaline is "just right" in most speaking situations.

Symptom	Cause
Pounding or racing heart Hot flashes	Breathing rate increases and the heart supplies more blood to the lungs to absorb the extra oxygen. Blood flow may increase 300% to 400% (Reuters Health, 2001).
Perspiration	Blood flow is diverted away from the skin to support the heart and muscle tissues, resulting in cool, clammy, sweaty skin (Reuters Health, 2001).

Symptom	Cause
Dry mouth	Fluids are diverted from nonessential locations resulting in dry mouth and difficulty talking or even swallowing (Reuters Health, 2001).
Butterflies or nausea	Digestive activity shuts down (Reuters Health, 2001).
Breathlessness	Breathing rate increases causing breathing to become more shallow (Oxford Brookes Medical Centre, 1999).
Trembling, pacing, swaying, rocking back and forth Muscle tension (stiff, motionless posture)	Extra energy is diverted to the muscles. If it is not worked out through physical activity, it results in muscle tightness, cramps, or feeling "shaky." (Rothwell, 2004).
Shaky voice	Muscles in the throat may tighten or spasm, and, when combined with breathlessness and/or dry mouth causes shaking vocal delivery (Rothwell, 2004).
Blushing	Blood vessels in the face (and sometimes throat and chest) are prompted to open wide, which floods the skin in these areas with blood (Better Health Channel, 2002).
Disfluencies (um, uh, like, you know)	Blood flow is restricted to the brain causing confusion of thought (Rothwell, 2004).

How Can I Manage My Speech Anxiety?

Tips for handling stress are as varied as suggestions for stopping the hiccups! The best strategy for you depends upon why you get anxious about presentational speaking in the first place!

The following are "tried and true" anxiety-reducing strategies and guaranteed to work better

PRESENTATION TIP:

For more information on all aspects of stress and how it affects the human body, visit The American Institute of Stress Online at *http://www.stress.org*

If you're anxious because . . .	then focus on:
■ you lack experience	skills training
■ you anticipate performing poorly	skills training and positive self-talk
■ your body seems to go into overdrive	deep breathing exercises and imagery
■ you tend to blow the public speaking experience out of proportion (e.g., I'll die if I have to give a speech!)	positive self-talk and reframing
■ you fear criticism from your audience	reframing

than the ineffectual suggestion to "imagine the audience naked."

Skills Training

For some students, speech anxiety occurs because they have never been taught how to deliver an effective presentation. If that describes you, then the introduction to public speaking class is the best place for you to be right now! This class will teach you how to select a topic, organize your thoughts, develop support for your ideas, and present them dynamically. Read ahead in the textbook. Talk to friends who have already completed the class. Observe skilled speakers on television or the Internet, in the classroom, or other live venues. Note what makes these speakers stand out and incorporate some of their techniques into your own presentations.

I am becoming much more relaxed and confident with each speech I give. The more I practice, the better I get. Also, I am starting to get to know my classmates, and this makes me much more comfortable in front of them.

✐ Anne

Once you have developed a solid outline, read through it. Ensure that you fully understand your main ideas and are comfortable saying them aloud. Stand up and deliver your presentation in your living room or other private place. Next, persuade your friends and family members to listen to you and

When I practice my speeches, I sometimes practice in front of the mirror. Other times I say my speech to my roommate or to my mom or boyfriend over the phone. It sounds silly, but it works. I practice especially any words and phrases that I wish to emphasize.

✐ Ashley

Billionaire Warren Buffett realized in college that he had to overcome his fear of public speaking. He said, "You've got to be able to communicate in life and it's enormously important. . . . If you can't communicate and talk to other people and get across your ideas, you're giving up your potential."

ask them for constructive criticism. Thoroughly understanding your topic and repeatedly rehearsing your speech will increase your confidence and help reduce your anxiety.

Deep Breathing

A former acting coach taught me to use this method before theatre productions to help reduce my stage fright. I've been passing the technique on to public speaking students for the past 30 years – it really helps! First, close your eyes and focus on your breathing. Breathe in through your nose and out through your mouth. Inhale and exhale as deeply and slowly as is comfortable for you. As you breathe begin to focus on the number "1." Say it and visualize it in your mind. Practice for at least five minutes every day for two weeks prior to your speech. This strategy works because engaging in deep breathing triggers a relaxation response in your body, thus slowing down the fight or flight response. Concentrating on the number "1" helps you to become more mentally focused and less distracted by the noises and events going on around you and the stressful feelings going on inside of you. As you practice this strategy, your mind and body will learn to respond with feelings of relaxation more readily. After you have mastered this technique, try doing it while waiting for your turn to deliver a speech in class. If you've been practicing it for several weeks, you should be able to generate a more relaxed state in only a minute or two!

Image © Andrejs Pidjass, 2009. Used under license from Shutterstock, Inc.

Imagery

After completing the deep breathing exercise described above, consider engaging in an **imagery** exercise. This isn't an opportunity for you to "visit your happy place," as some might suggest. Instead, it's an opportunity for you to "pre-wire" your brain for success! While your mind and body are relaxed, envision yourself successfully delivering a presentation. Include all of the sensory details to make the scene vivid in your mind's eye. *See yourself confidently walking to the front of the classroom – take note of the clothes you are wearing. Notice how you carefully organize your notes on the podium. See yourself look out at your audience, smiling as you make eye contact with your classmates. Picture how you will begin your introduction. Hear yourself speaking enthusiastically. See individual members of your audience smiling and nodding as you speak, clapping loudly as you conclude.* In other words, create a complete and detailed mental scenario of you delivering an A+ speech! Try to engage in this imagery exercise at least once a day for a week before you deliver a speech in class.

Professional athletes, like Tiger Woods and Lance Armstrong, frequently use these techniques to create a more relaxed mental and physical state, which improves their physical performance. In a study of Olympic athletes, Russian scientists examined the impact of mental training on the athletes' performance. They divided the participants into four groups:

Group 1: 100% physical training
Group 2: 75% physical training + 25% mental training
Group 3: 50% physical training + 50% mental training
Group 4: 25% physical training + 75% mental training

The scientists discovered that the last group of Olympic athletes, which devoted the majority of their time to mental training (including imagery), actually outperformed the others! (Scaglione & Cummins, 1993). In essence, visualizing success served as a template for actual success. If positive imagery can help Olympic athletes improve their performance, then surely it can help you decrease your speech anxiety and assist you in improving your presentational skills!

PRACTICE NOTE:

Create your own imagery script, complete with all of the sights, sounds, and movements needed to visualize delivering your perfect speech.

▌ *Reframing*

This strategy, also known as **cognitive restructuring**, helps you to redefine your thoughts and create more positive, or, at the very least, neutral labels for stressful situations. The assumption here is that if you don't label or define the event as stressful, then your mind, and hence your body, won't undergo the fight or flight response because it won't be experiencing stress. For example, if you describe a presentation situation as scary, your mind tells you that you are frightened and your body goes into fight or flight mode. If, however, you label the same presentation situation as challenging, your mind tells you that you are energized and excited and your body can function at a heightened pace, but not an abnormal one!

Another way to **reframe** a stressful situation is to simultaneously acknowledge negative aspects and actively seek out positive elements of the same event.

> *Delivering a presentation is intimidating, but it is not life-threatening.*
>
> *Delivering a presentation makes me nervous, but I know I can write a good speech.*
>
> *I have never delivered a formal presentation before, but I know I'm a good storyteller.*

Image © Stephen Coburn, 2009. Used under license from Shutterstock, Inc.

Another reframing strategy is to adopt a communication orientation instead of a performance orientation. A performance orientation suggests that you view the experience as "putting on a show." When an actor performs, he or she pretends to be someone else and interacts primarily with fellow actors, NOT the audience. The actor is concerned with having lines and movements memorized and executing both exactly the way they have been rehearsed countless times before. This strategy is appropriate on stage where precise repetition is needed to cue other actors and prop handlers, as well as lighting and sound technicians. While this type of approach is needed for theatrical performances, it doesn't typically promote effective presentational speaking.

A communication orientation, on the other hand, encourages you to conceptualize the experience as an interaction between you and your audience members where you maintain a focus on creating shared meaning. Think about a conversation you had with someone earlier today. Perhaps you told your friend about what you did last weekend (informative speaking) or encouraged this person to see a particular movie (persuasive speaking). Chances are you were focused on making sure the other person understood your message, not on whether you gestured at just the right moment, or delivered a line with perfect vocal intensity. In this case, you framed the experience as being other (audience)-centered, not self-centered. Your goal was to create understanding. In his book on overcoming anxiety associated with public speaking, Michael Motley (1995) explains, "I have never encountered an anxious speaker who did not have a performance orientation, or one whose anxiety was not substantially reduced when the communication orientation replaced it. Very simply, changing your overall approach to public speaking is the key to reducing and controlling the anxiety" (p. 49).

PRACTICE NOTE:

Describe your next presentation from a performance orientation and a communication orientation. Compare the two different perspectives.

▌Positive Self-Talk

As a child, I was terribly afraid of the dentist and managed to survive my visits to his office by talking myself through it: *I can do this; it will be over within the same amount of time it would take to watch my favorite TV show; other people do this, I can, too.* Without realizing what I was doing, I was replacing my fearful and self-defeating thoughts with positive messages.

Sometimes we let our minds talk us into feeling nervous or more frightened than a situation truly warrants. You might recall getting worked up over an upcoming examination only to discover that it was really a piece of cake. All of that needless worrying caused you to feel more and more anxious. Left unchecked, it could have even prevented you from studying and actually lead to a failing grade on the exam (i.e., negative self-fulfilling prophecy). Your thought process influenced your feelings of anxiety. With positive self-talk, we reverse the process. We send ourselves coping messages that help to decrease our anxiety instead of increase it. We create positive self-fulfilling prophecies! To engage in positive self-talk, you need to analyze your anxiety and create positive messages to replace your negative thoughts.

Practice thinking positively! Each time you catch yourself engaging in negative self-talk, quickly change your thinking. Replace the self-destructive thought

PRACTICE NOTE:

1. Describe what you think makes you feel anxious about a particular public speaking event. (e.g., first presentation, don't know classmates, presentation is graded).

2. Describe your thoughts about this situation. Anxiety producing thoughts are examples of your negative self-talk. (e.g., you might think, "What could I possibly talk about for three to five minutes that others would be interested in" or "I just know I'll lose my train of thought and start stumbling.").

3. Create positive self-talk messages to replace your negative thoughts. For example:

   – *What could I possibly talk about for three to five minutes that others would be interested in?*
   + *I have a lot of ideas that would be of interest to others.*
   – *I just know I'll lose my train of thought and start stumbling.*
   + *I can stay focused and speak fluently for 3-5 minutes. I've done it in alot of other situations.*

with a positive message. You might even consider putting a loose rubber band around your wrist and snap-
ping it each time you catch yourself engaging in
negative self-talk. The idea is not necessarily to inflict
pain, but to provide you with an attention-getting,
physical reminder to stop your negative thinking and
replace it with positive self-talk!

Chapter Review

CONGRATULATIONS! The training wheels are
off. I told you, you could do it! You may still be a bit
wobbly or feel a little unsure of yourself, but the rest
of this textbook will help develop your confidence
and capabilities so you can cruise through the
toughest of presentations. You realize that a little
anxiety will actually energize and enhance your
delivery. You understand that there are strategies
you can use to help manage extreme apprehension.
This knowledge and skill, coupled with your
"can-do" attitude, show you no longer need the
training wheels!

This chapter has explored the answers to three
questions: Why do I need to know how to present in
public? Why do I get so anxious? How can I manage
my speaking anxiety? The next chapter will help
you create a solid foundation for your presentations
through audience analysis, research, and supporting
material. The ride is not over with yet. There is
much more to be discovered. While most of us do

not need to know how to ride a bicycle like Lance
Armstrong, or deliver a presentation like Martin
Luther King, Jr., mastering the basics of either
activity can be rewarding and empowering
throughout your life.

Questions to Consider

1. What are some potentially negative
consequences for having low communication
apprehension? What are some potentially
positive consequences for having moderate
communication apprehension?

2. What public figures do you consider to be
excellent public speakers? Why? What delivery
skills do they have that you would like to
emulate?

3. What public figure do you consider to be a
really poor public speaker? Why? How do you
think these poor public speaking skills impact
other's perceptions of him or her?

4. Ask family members or friends if they've ever
experienced stage fright. Find out what coping
strategies they used.

5. What makes you the most anxious about
delivering a presentation? Given this cause,
what strategies would be the most effective at
reducing your apprehension?

ACTIVITIES

Communication Apprehension

1. Building Community and Reducing Communication Apprehension: A Case Study Approach

2. Personal Report of Public Speaking Anxiety (PRPSA)

3. Communication Apprehension Research Project

Building Community and Reducing Communication Apprehension: A Case Study Approach (Tillson, 1995)

Directions: Read the case study and answer the questions. Be prepared to discuss your responses.

Public Speaking 101: A Case Study

It was the first day of graded speeches in Public Speaking 101. Scott, the football team captain and a 4.0 student, was nearing the end of his speech on the use of steroids in high school athletics. He efficiently reviewed his main points and concluded his speech with a poignant story about a teenager who died because he wanted to play football as best as he possibly could, even if that meant taking drugs to do so.

"...Jason Robinson died in pursuit of excellence. There is no need for other youngsters to follow in his footsteps to an early grave."

His words ended on a quiet note and his classmates tentatively began to applaud before breaking out into a loud ovation. Breathing a sigh of relief, Scott gathered his notecards from the podium and began walking back to his desk in the third row of the classroom. His classmates were obviously impressed.

"Way to go, man! Where'd you learn to talk like that?"

"Geez, I'm glad I don't have to go next."

"Was that a true story or did you just make it all up?"

I asked the students to write down their comments on Scott's presentation while I finished writing my own evaluation. A couple of minutes passed and students began talking among themselves. I checked my sign-up sheet to see who would be delivering the next speech. It was Lisa. My heart went out to the timid girl sitting two seats away from me. Lisa had registered for my section of Public Speaking 101 last semester, but had dropped it before she had to make any oral presentations in the class. I knew she was nervous – probably more so than any of the other students. As she dropped her stack of 4X6 notecards and busily tried to reorganize them, a niggling little voice spoke in my mind, "Maybe you should have touched base with her last week to see if she was ready for the assignment." And then the voice of reason and practicality spoke up, "You don't have time to spoon feed every scared student."

"OK, Lisa. You're up next," I said in what I hoped was an encouraging tone of voice.

A petite, blonde girl wearing wire-rimmed glasses and clasping notecards, stood, took a few audible gulps of air, and walked toward the front of the classroom. Twenty-seven pairs of eyes looked in her direction. Lisa cleared her throat and placed the notecards on the podium as the class had been instructed to do. Her hands immediately grabbed onto the edge of the podium in a white-knuckled, death grip. A flush slowly inched its way from her chest to her throat. As her cheeks turned a blotchy, fire-engine red, she cleared her throat again and began to talk in a faltering, timid voice.

"My speech is on . . . why children who commit violent crimes . . . should be tried as adults in the court system," she stumbled. "There are three reasons why children who commit violent crimes should have to face adult penalties for their actions . . ."

Lisa got off to a rough start. "How many times had I told the class not to introduce a speech with 'my speech is on' or 'today I want to talk about'," I asked myself. "Where was the clever attention getter no speech should be without?"

She continued, "The first reason why children who commit violent crimes should be tried as adults is because . . ." Lisa fumbled through her preview. As she arranged her notecards, one fell off the podium and slid under a nearby desk. No one else seemed to notice – except Lisa. She appeared to freeze in time as she apparently wondered whether to retrieve the card or try to continue without it. Her eyes looked scared and wild, like an animal caught by surprise in car headlights on a dark road. . . . Several seconds passed before Lisa decided what to do. . . . As she stepped out from behind the podium she bumped into it and the rest of the cards fluttered to the floor. That mishap was the proverbial last straw. With a dumbstruck expression on her face, Lisa abandoned her search for the lost notecard, turned, and ran out of the room. Tears of frustration and embarrassment already stained her blotchy cheeks. The classroom was uncomfortably quiet except for the haunting sound of Lisa's footsteps running down the tile hallway. With a sinking feeling in my stomach, I looked away from the empty doorway and faced twenty-seven pairs of eyes looking at me.

1. What might have caused Lisa to feel/react the way she did?

2. Pretend you were one of her classmates. How would you have felt?

3. What was the instructor's reaction? How could s/he have prevented Lisa from "falling apart?"

4. What could Lisa have done to prevent reacting the way she did?

5. What advice can you give Lisa to help her prepare for the next speech assignment?

6. How can the instructor and/or the students show support for Lisa when she returns to class?

Personal Report of Public Speaking Anxiety (PRPSA)
(Richmond & McCroskey, 1985)

Instructions: This instrument is composed of thirty-four statements concerning feelings about communicating with other people. Work quickly; just record your first impression. Indicate the degree to which the statements apply to you by marking whether you:

1=Strongly Agree
2=Agree
3=Are Undecided
4=Disagree
5=Strongly Disagree

_____ 1. While preparing for giving a speech, I feel tense and nervous.

_____ 2. I feel tense when I see the words speech and public speech on a course outline.

_____ 3. My thoughts become confused and jumbled when I am giving a speech.

_____ 4. Right after giving a speech I feel that I have had a pleasant experience.

_____ 5. I get anxious when I think about a speech coming up.

_____ 6. I have no fear of giving a speech.

_____ 7. Although I am nervous just before starting a speech, I soon settle down after starting and feel calm and comfortable.

_____ 8. I look forward to giving a speech.

_____ 9. When the instructor announces a speaking assignment in class, I can feel myself getting tense.

_____ 10. My hands tremble when I am giving a speech.

_____ 11. I feel relaxed while giving a speech.

_____ 12. I enjoy preparing for a speech.

_____ 13. I am in constant fear of forgetting what I prepared to say.

_____ 14. I get anxious if someone asks me something about my topic that I do not know.

_____ 15. I face the prospect of giving a speech with confidence.

_____ 16. I feel that I am in complete possession of myself while giving a speech.

_____ 17. My mind is clear when giving a speech.

_____ 18. I do not dread giving a speech.

_____ 19. I perspire just before starting a speech.

_____ 20. My heart beats very fast just as I start a speech.

_____ 21. I experience considerable anxiety while sitting in the room just before my speech starts.

_____ 22. Certain parts of my body feel very tense and rigid while giving a speech.

_____ 23. Realizing that only a little time remains in a speech makes me very tense and anxious.

_____ 24. While giving a speech I can control my feelings of tension and stress.

_____ 25. I breathe faster just before starting a speech.

_____ 26. I feel comfortable and relaxed in the hour or so just before giving a speech.

_____ 27. I do poorer on speeches because I am anxious.

_____ 28. I feel anxious when the teacher announces the date of a speaking assignment.

_____ 29. When I make a mistake while giving a speech, I find it hard to concentrate on the parts that follow.

_____ 30. During an important speech I experience a feeling of helplessness building up inside of me.

_____ 31. I have trouble falling asleep the night before a speech.

_____ 32. My heart beats very fast while I present a speech.

_____ 33. I feel anxious while waiting to give my speech.

_____ 34. While giving a speech, I get so nervous I forget facts I really know.

To determine your score on the PRPSA, complete the following steps:

1. Add the scores for items 1, 2, 3, 5, 9, 10, 13, 14, 19, 20, 21, 22, 23, 25, 27, 28, 29, 30, 31, 32, 33, and 34.

2. Add the scores for items 4, 6, 7, 8, 11, 12, 15, 16, 17, 18, 24, and 26.

3. Complete the following formula:

$$PRPSA = 132 - (total\ from\ step\ one) + (total\ from\ step\ two)$$

Your score should range between 34 and 170. If your score is below 34 or above 170, you have made a mistake in computing the score.

SCORES BETWEEN	INDICATE
34 and 84	Low anxiety about public speaking (5%)
85 and 92	Moderately low level of anxiety about public speaking (5%)
93 and 110	Moderate anxiety in most public speaking situations (20%)
111 and 119	Moderately high level of anxiety about public speaking (30%)
120 and 170	Very high level of anxiety about public speaking (40%)

*MOST people score in the moderate to high categories!

Note: Complete one of these forms at the beginning of the semester and one after your final speech. Compare your total scores as well as your responses to individual items.

Communication Apprehension Research Project

Conduct a Google search to locate testimonials from four famous people (or stories about them) who have experienced communication apprehension. What symptoms did they report experiencing? How did each overcome his or her anxiety?

References

1. Allen, R.P. (1983). *Human stress: Its nature and control*. NY: Macmillan Publishing Co.

2. Baron, J.K. (2008). Public speaking: A critical success skill. *The Leadership Journal of the Centre for Organization Effectiveness, 1*(11), 1-4.

3. Better Health Channel. (2002). *Blushing explained*. Retrieved June 1, 2009, from *http://www. betterhealth.vic.gov.au/bhcv2/bhcarticles.nsf/pages/Blus hing_explained?*

4. *Do you suffer from glossophobia?* (2001). Retrieved June 1, 2009, from http://www.glossophobia.com/

5. Gallo, C. (2013, May 16). How Warren Buffett and Joel Osteen conquered their terrifying fear of public speaking. *Forbes.com*. Retrieved from http://www. forbes.com/sites/carminegallo/2013/05/16/how-warren-buffett-and-joel-osteen-conquered-their-terrifying-fear-of-public-speaking/

6. Morreale, S., Osborn, M., & Pearson, J. (2000). Why communication is important: A rationale for the centrality of the study of communication. *Journal of the Association for Communication Administration, 29* (1), 1-25.

7. Motley, M. T. (1995). *Overcoming your fear of public speaking: A proven method*. NY: McGraw-Hill.

8. Oxford Brookes Medical Centre. (1999). *Managing stress*. Retrieved June 1, 2009, from *http://www. brookes.ac.uk/student/services/health/stress.html*

9. Reuters Health. (2001). *What is stress?* Retrieved July 29, 2003, from *http://www.reutershealth.com/ wellconnected/doc31.html*

10. Richmond, V. P., & McCroskey, J.C. (1985). *Communication apprehension, avoidance, and effectiveness*. Scottsdale, AZ: Gorsuch Scarisbrick.

11. Rothwell, J.D. (2004). *In the company of others (2nd ed.)*. Boston: McGraw-Hill, (p. 405).

12. Scaglione, R., & Cummins, W. (1993). *Karate of Okinawa: Building Warrior Spirit*. NY: Tuttle Publishing.

13. Stein, M.B., Walker, J. R., and Forde, D. R. (1996). Public-speaking fears in a community sample: Prevalence, impact on functioning, and diagnostic classification. *Archives of General Psychiatry 53*(2), 169-174.

14. Stress: The silent killer. (2002). Retrieved June 1, 2009, from *http://www.holisticonline.com/stress/ stress_GAS.htm*

15. Tillson, L.D. (1995, Summer). Building community and reducing communication apprehension: A case study approach. *The Speech Communication Teacher, 9*(4), 4-5.

16. Wilder, L. (1999). 7 *Steps to Fearless Speaking*. New York: John Wiley & Sons

4

Audience Adaptation, Research, and Supporting Materials

Stephen A. Cox

CHAPTER OBJECTIVES

At the end of this chapter, you will be able to:

- Explain the relationship among audience adaptation, research, and supporting materials.

- Describe how effective audience analysis and research processes are used to build ethos, logos, and pathos.

- Differentiate between demographic, situational, and attitudinal analyses.

- Design and utilize methods of audience analysis to develop effective presentations.

- Explain why personal knowledge and experience, although very valuable, must be combined with additional research from credible sources.

- Explain the necessity of conducting diverse and thorough research to construct effective presentations.

- Conduct research by utilizing library, internet, organizational, mass-mediated, and interpersonal resources to construct effective presentations.

- Summarize the seven types of supporting materials for effective presentations.

- Explain criteria to use when selecting types and sources of supporting materials.

- Demonstrate the four steps of building main ideas and citing sources in effective presentations.

> **There are no bad speech topics . . . just bad ways of developing them.**
>
> ✍Dr. Jim Gibson, University of Missouri-Columbia

Don't forget this principle! Any topic can be made to seem "exciting" or made to seem "boring." It's your choice. It all depends on how you choose to develop your presentation.

When delivering a presentation, we all want to make a good impression. Unfortunately, most people try to find a topic they believe the audience will find "exciting" or "interesting." Let's face it, 90 percent of all topics you can think of would bore most people. What is "exciting" about deodorant, car tires, carpeting, or breakfast cereal? For most of us, NOTHING! But advertisers find ways to make each of these products interesting and desirable to consumers. You too can take any product, process, problem, service, or issue and find a way to hold the audience's attention, extend their knowledge, and convince them that you are right. By using a variety of images, examples, facts, stories, and testimony, you can build an exciting, interesting, and effective presentation.

When making presentations, you never want to bore the audience by only telling them what they already know or by being so sophisticated or technical that the audience loses interest. While you cannot prepare a presentation that satisfies everyone, the goal is to extend the knowledge of the majority of audience members.

▌ Adapting Your Presentation to Your Audience

Who is more important? (select one)

Yourself _____ Others _____

While you are in the midst of preparing your presentation, it is very easy to see yourself as the most important element in this process. After all, you are the one who has brainstormed the topic, determined a purpose, and crafted a thesis for the presentation. You're the one constructing it, you're the one doing the research to support your ideas, and ultimately, you're the one delivering it. It's yours.

Although it is easy to understand your role this way, it is more helpful to understand that the presentation you are constructing is for the benefit of someone else – a little like a gift you are presenting to someone. Did you ever receive a gift you didn't want, like, or need? While you may have said, "Thank you," did you also wonder if the gift-giver had you in mind at all when choosing or making it? Did the person give you the gift you wanted, liked, or needed, or the one he/she wanted to give?

Even though it cannot be accomplished all the time, we should always work to place the needs of others ahead of our own desires. Good spouses, parents, employees, and bosses conduct themselves in such a way to make "others" feel important and appreciated. Successful companies develop products that are customized to meet the unique desires of consumers (e.g., automobiles are produced in a wide variety of styles, classes, and colors to satisfy different consumers).

▌ *Adapting Your Ethos, Logos, and Pathos*

Your audience is the "consumer" of your ideas. Not all presenters are equally effective at getting audiences to consume presentations because some fail to adapt their message to meet the needs of audience members. In the 4th century B.C., Aristotle taught that speakers create effective (e.g., "easy to consume") presentations by adapting three elements: **Ethos, Logos,** and **Pathos.**

- **Ethos:** The character and credibility of the speaker.
- **Logos:** The logical appeals in the presentation (e.g., evidence, facts, or reasoning).

■ **Pathos:** The emotional appeals in the presentation (e.g., appeals to love, pride, or power).

You will conduct research to enhance the ethos (credibility), logos (logic), and pathos (emotion) of your presentation. Let's first look at why ethos, or credibility, is so important.

▌ *Ellen, Dr. Phil, and Your Credibility*

Students often ask, "Why should I conduct research? Isn't my personal opinion and experience

---

TIPS

Ways to enhance your credibility

■ Speak of your personal experience and learned knowledge.

■ Express awareness of and concern for the consequences of your information and ideas.

■ Use direct eye contact and smile.

■ Reference your positions of authority within organizations or the community.

■ Speak with enthusiasm, conviction, and sincerity.

■ Establish common ground with the audience by expressing points-of-view with which the audience can identify.

■ Support your presentation with engaging facts and testimony from respected sources.

■ Make the audience aware of any similarities between your background, beliefs, values, and attitudes and their own.

■ Establish goodwill for the audience. Demonstrate that you really and truly desire to provide benefits to your audience.

■ Demonstrate open-mindedness by respecting points-of-view contrary to your own.

---

enough?" The answer: NO. We live in the age of the talkshow: *Ellen*, *Dr. Phil*, and many others. These television shows prove one thing; everyone has an opinion and a story. Whatever opinion or experience you have, someone else has a different opinion or experience. Your opinions and experiences are a great start, but they are not enough to convince the audience that you are a credible speaker.

Begin establishing your **credibility** by telling of your experience, knowledge, training, and/or credentials. However, if the goal is to create an "iron-clad" argument, you will need the help of others. You need to discover other evidence to support your opinions and experiences. For example, find others who have written about their similar experiences, find documented facts that confirm your observations, and/or share the testimony of others who agree with your views. Citing the source or author of facts you share with the audience builds your credibility. For example, suppose you're giving a presentation on body piercing and you share a quote from a local tattoo/piercing artist. The credibility of that person makes your presentation seem more believable. Similarly, if Dr. Phil had an episode on body piercing, sharing a quote from one of his guests would add further credibility to your presentation. Whatever you can do to boost your ethos/credibility will aid your effectiveness as a speaker.

▌ *Overcoming the Audience's Skepticism, Confusion, and Apathy*

We often assume that our audience is highly motivated and interested in listening to our presentation. Unfortunately, every audience has members who fall into one of three categories:

■ The **Skeptics** – people who don't believe your message.

■ The **Confused** – people who don't understand your message.

■ The **Apathetic** – people who don't care about your message.

How do we overcome these problems? How do we get everyone to believe, understand, and care?

By conducting an **audience analysis**, you can custom build your presentation to fit your audience's unique characteristics. Audience analysis allows you to strategically select the best combination of credible fact, logical arguments, and engaging ideas. The *Skeptics* doubt because they don't believe you or your ideas are credible (i.e., poor ethos). The *Confused* don't understand because your facts or ideas are unclear (i.e., poor logos). The *Apathetic* don't care because you have not stirred their interest by relating your content to their lives (i.e., poor pathos). By analyzing your audience and discovering appropriate research, you will have the tools to build a solid presentation that is credible, clear, and interesting to your audience.

[handwritten: Skeptic— Ethos / Confused — Logos / Apathetic — Pathos]

Image © Michael Drager, 2009. Used under license from Shutterstock, Inc.

▌ What are the Audience's Attitudes and Behaviors?

An **attitudinal analysis** is the most important step in understanding your audience. An

---

"WII-FM" – The Audience's Favorite Station

Do you know what station every audience member listens to? *Answer:* "WII-FM" – The "What's In It For Me?" station. You must adapt your content to fit the audience because everyone is motivated by self-interest. The audience's personal knowledge, experiences, needs, wants, expectations, etc., will always influence the extent to which they listen to your presentation. You must motivate them to listen and hold their attention by presenting content that is relevant to their lives. If you are not "tuned into" them, then they will tune you out!

▌ How to Analyze Your Audience

To adapt your presentation, you need to size-up your audience so you have some idea about who they are, what they are like, and how they will respond. To thoroughly analyze your audience and the situation (or context) you will be presenting in, you need to ask three types of questions: (1) **demographic** (2) **situational,** and (3) **attitudinal.**

TIPS

Attitudinal questions to ask yourself

- Habits and behaviors – What related habits and behaviors do audience members practice?

- Knowledge – How much knowledge do audience members have of my topic?

- Attitudes – What likes and dislikes (or preference) do audience members have related to my topic?

- Values – How much importance does my audience place on issues or things related to my topic?

- Beliefs – What does my audience think to be true or untrue related to my topic?

- Ethics – What related behaviors or actions do audience members believe to be right or wrong?

- Motivations – What motivates the members of my audience? What needs and desires do they have (e.g., the need for power, success, love, creativity, or recognition)?

attitudinal analysis is an assessment of your audience's general disposition (e.g., attitudes, beliefs, and values), behaviors and knowledge level of your topic. Understanding what your audience likes, values, believes, and desires allows you to adapt your presentation to fit their lives, needs, hopes, habits, etc. Here are some of the key questions you'll want answered in your attitudinal analysis.

What are the Audience's Demographics?

A **demographic analysis** is a descriptive summary of the audience's objective characteristics or traits. Descriptive characteristics you may need to know include the age, income level, rank, race, gender, and/or educational level of your audience members.

TIPS

Demographic questions to ask yourself

- Gender – What percentage of my audience is female and what percentage is male?

- Age – What age groups are represented in my audience?

- Educational Level – What educational levels are represented in my audience?

- Group Affiliations – What political, religious, social, and/or professional groups are represented in my audience?

- Socio-cultural Background – What social and cultural backgrounds are represented in my audience (e.g., members' country or state of origin, economic background, ethnic or racial heritage, and/or marital status)?

- Work/Job Background – What work/job backgrounds are represented – employer, job classification/rank/title, job location/department, years of experience, shift, certifications/credentials, product/service line, specialty, etc.?

What is the Situation?

Always carefully consider the situation, occasion and setting in which you will be presenting. Here is a brief list of some key situational variables you should understand and adapt to when delivering a presentation.

TIPS

Situational questions to ask yourself

- Time – Time-of-day, day-of-the-week, month-of-the-year? How long can I speak?

- Place – Will I present indoors or outdoors? Will I present sitting or standing? What seating will the audience have available? How large is the room, how bright or dim is the lighting, and will there be a microphone and podium? What visual/audio equipment will be available? What sources of noise or distractions may be present?

- Size of the Audience – How many people will be in the audience?

- Context of the Presentation – What is the occasion of the presentation? What recent presentations has the audience heard? What recent events have occurred that may influence the audience's thinking?

Building Your Case and Selling Your Ideas

Conducting research is key to building a solid presentation. Just as a lawyer works to create a convincing courtroom case, you also must build an "iron-clad" argument (i.e., an argument that cannot easily be damaged or destroyed). In a criminal case, prosecuting lawyers must present enough compelling evidence to convince a jury or judge that the defendant is guilty beyond a reasonable doubt. If successful at presenting the right evidence in the right way, the prosecuting lawyer wins a conviction and the defendant is punished. What is the difference between an acquittal and a conviction? *Answer: the quality and combination of evidence and ideas presented in the courtroom.*

Likewise, when a sales representative goes to sell a product or service, the customer will always have a number of reasons not to buy (e.g., "It's too expensive . . . I don't need it . . . I buy from a different company . . . I don't know you"). A sales representative must convince the customer of the value, benefits, and advantages of his/her product or service. If the customer does not buy into the sales presentation, then no business is conducted and they go away empty handed. What is the difference between a successful and an unsuccessful sales presentation? *Answer: the quality and combination of evidence and ideas presented to the customer.*

Every speaker has the same goals as the lawyer and the sales representative. Speakers want to win over the hearts and minds of their audience by delivering the very best presentation. For this reason, you must conduct research to find the best combination of supporting materials to build a solid foundation for your presentation.

Conducting Research

You should now understand that by analyzing your audience and the speaking situation, you will have information to guide how you create the foundation of your presentation. As stated earlier, to give your presentation a *solid foundation*, you must find credible, logical, and interesting supporting materials. After all, a presentation's "foundation" must be solid if you are going to be effective . . . to win over the audience, sell a product, win a conviction, etc. The following will review both the sources of supporting materials and the different types of support you will want to consider using in your presentation.

Where Do I Research My Topic?

Building a solid presentation requires that you find a wide variety of **supporting materials** from a wide variety of sources. To create an accurate and credible presentation, find a vast number of expert opinions, examples, news reports, and/or facts to support your presentation. If your presentation were based on information taken from only two websites or

from three newspaper articles, your presentation would be very biased, underdeveloped, and poorly supported. Therefore, let's examine some of the various sources from which you can gather supporting materials for your presentation.

- Library
- Internet and Search Engines
- Corporate and Organizational Information
- Mass Media and Real People

Library

The best resource in any library is a librarian. Librarians love to search for information! They have extensive training and experience in how to help you find information from around the world. Realize that a library is not a *warehouse* for books. Rather, today's library is a *gateway* to valuable information that is stored both on-site and across the globe. Conducting research is like a "treasure hunt" and librarians possess the "map" to the "world of information." Librarians don't know what you'll find but they know where you should look to find related information. With the help of librarians, you can make the most of three key library resources: (1) library catalogs, (2) interlibrary loans, and (3) indexes and databases.

LIBRARY CATALOGS. Today, most libraries use electronic catalogs to list the books, journal titles, newspapers, microforms, DVDs, CDs, etc. owned by the library. These electronic catalogs generally allow you to search by author, subject, and/or title of the

Image © Johanna Goodyear, 2009. Used under license from Shutterstock, Inc.

work and provide the location within the library to find these resources. The variety of resources available through your library is extensive: dictionaries, yearbooks, encyclopedias, thesauruses, newspapers, anthologies, bibliographies, biographies, directories, catalogs, atlases, textbooks, government documents, journals, histories, genealogies, magazines, theoretical manuscripts, manuals, films, music, scientific reports, corporate/financial reports, fiction, and more! All of these resources may be potential sources for information on your topic located through the library catalog.

However, all libraries are limited in what they can afford to purchase. It may be necessary to search the catalogs of other community, university, state (e.g., Kentucky Virtual Library, *http://www.kyvl.org*), or national libraries (e.g., The Library of Congress, *http://www.lcweb.loc.gov*). Your library's homepage and/or librarians can assist you in locating the Internet homepages and electronic catalogs of these libraries.

INTERLIBRARY LOAN. Because your library has a limited collection of books, journals, newspapers, reports, CDs, etc., your library may offer "interlibrary loan" services. If you find citations to resources not locally available, the interlibrary loan staff can borrow these articles, books, reports, etc, owned by other libraries for your use. Be sure to check with your library to see if there are additional costs associated with borrowing the desired materials from other libraries.

INDEXES AND DATABASES. While there are still numerous *print* indexes and databases being published, searching through electronic indexes and databases is quick and convenient. These password-protected indexes and databases (e.g., EBSCOHost, FirstSearch, and PsycINFO) allow library patrons to search through a variety of information sources (e.g., journal articles, book chapters, news reports, conference papers, government documents, corporate and financial reports). These indexes and databases allow you to find and sort through the most recent articles, reports, book chapters, etc, related to your topic. Electronic searches provide the citation (e.g., author, date, source, page numbers, etc.) and often provide a brief abstract of the information. Some databases provide the citation plus the full-text, allowing you to read through or print the entire document.

Your library subscribes to these indexes and databases which have annual fees ranging from several hundred to tens-of-thousands of dollars per year. Keep in mind that all databases are limited due to the costs associated with publishing and indexing. Publishers sell to libraries direct access to their information or they sell it to database companies who then index and store full text versions of the information. Not every helpful resource will be listed in every index. For example, EBSCOHost will index thousands of the most respected and widely circulated journals, but you won't find all the journals indexed that relate to your topic. Also, electronic indexes and databases start with the most recent information and gradually add earlier information over time. For example, you may be able to find a 2010 article from *Fortune*, but the same database may not list *Fortune* articles published prior to 2005. Be sure to check on the limitations of any index or database when conducting research. Due to limitations in electronic databases. Librarians can help guide you through this maze of indexes and databases.

The Internet

The Internet is the information superhighway! This resource has changed the way the world communicates, shares information, markets products, promotes ideas, and entertains itself. We turn to the Internet for the latest information, news, opinions, and trends. The Internet is also a tremendous vehicle for democracy, allowing anyone with access to participate in sharing opinions and ideas. Clearly, the Internet has the potential to greatly enhance the quantity and quality of information you find to support your presentation.

Like any trip on a superhighway, you should know where you want to go and how to get there safely. The challenge of the Internet is to find accurate, unbiased information from credible sources. Because there are no regulations on Internet postings, people and organizations are virtually unlimited on the opinions and information they can choose to include on their sites. You have to carefully evaluate the credibility and accuracy of that information.

You will need to determine the author of the information, when the information was posted, and if it may be biased due to the sponsorship or organizational affiliation of the website. Older information may be uncovered during an internet search that may or may not be more accurate than information posted

Image © Stephen Coburn, 2009. Used under license from Shutterstock, Inc.

more recently, so be careful to confirm the accuracy of information by reading several related items. Because a **"wiki"** is a collaborate website that allows individuals to freely contribute or edit content, how reliable is it? Wikipedia (*www.wikipedia.org*) is a very popular online encyclopedia; however, is the information credible, accurate, or biased? Likewise, a web search could uncover information about global warming posted by Exxon/Mobil Corporation, the U.S. Environmental Protection Agency, and former Vice President Al Gore, but which is most credible and why?

Keep in mind that all Internet search engines (e.g., Yahoo or Google) will have strengths and weaknesses. Search engines will have the most popular topical areas divided into subject areas (e.g., news, entertainment, travel, business, sports, health), but each uses different processes for finding, prioritizing, and listing results. Finding the best information often depends on which search engine you use with which key words (or combinations of key words). Your best bet is to use a variety of search engines and related key words as you begin your Internet research. The search engines will take you to the free information posted by organizations, individuals, companies, etc.; however, some of the best information may cost you money to access.

Corporate and Organizational Information

Corporate and organizational information may be found through the library's catalog, indexes, and databases, or you may go directly to these corporations and/or organizations for information. Although organizations or corporations are obviously biased, they are very valuable sources of publications and resources that may not make it into your local library. Corporations and organizations often have individuals or entire departments (e.g., Public Relations or Public Affairs) devoted to generating and distributing information about the goals, successes, and actions of the company or organization. Looking through the company's or organization's homepage will often provide you access to a wide variety of information. Annual reports, position papers, press releases, informational videotapes, fact sheets, and other types of published materials are generally available upon request if not posted on their website.

To balance the bias of the information provided by the corporation or organization, you may ask their competitors and customers their observations and opinions. For example, competitors can provide additional information about the competitive environment, how the companies perceive one another, and the key strengths and weaknesses of each. Likewise, customers can tell us their impressions of how well the organization or company lives up to their mission, why they use the company or organization, and specific examples or stories about the company or organization that may help you support your main ideas.

Mass-Media and Real People

So far you can turn to the library, the Internet, and the company/organization for information. However, a couple other sources may also aid your research efforts. First, don't forget other forms of mass-media and entertainment as potential information sources: internet/television news, documentaries, broadcasts, podcasts, speeches, concerts, special reports, films, plays, sporting events, music, talk shows, educational programs, comedies, dramas, cartoons, billboards, magazines, advertisements, how-to shows, reality shows, etc. All of these are full of examples, stories, statistics, illustrations, and facts that can be used to help support your presentation.

Second, interviewing "real people" who have special knowledge or experience related to your topic may help your presentation (e.g., local experts, coworkers, customers, neighbors, business owners, or friends). Your community includes medical professionals, educators, lawyers, ministers, managers, bankers, technicians, government officials, business owners, and a host of other "experts" who can provide you information. If you are giving a persuasive presentation on the need to update highway infrastructure, interview the local "experts" on road and bridge conditions (e.g., the owner of a local paving company or the director of the county highway department). If you are giving a presentation on small business development, interview the president of the local Chamber of Commerce. Likewise, do not overlook interviewing your neighbors and friends. While we may not know them personally, the fact that you do and they have related experience or knowledge makes them an ideal resource. For example, if you are giving a presentation on cancer prevention and you share the story of your neighbor who's spouse died of cancer, the reality and credibility of your presentation dramatically increases. Remember, experts, neighbors, and friends are all valuable sources of support.

T I P S

When conducting research interviews

- Interview last – Do your other research first so you know exactly what information you hope to get from the interviewees.

- Sell them on the interview – Tell them why you want to interview them and what type of questions you will ask.

- Time limit – Tell them how much time the interview will take.

- Recording the interview – If you want to record the interview, ask permission first.

- Don't improvise – Formulate a short set of clear interview questions.

- Take the list of interview questions with you.

- Take thorough notes during the interview and review your notes to add missing details after the interview.

- Respect anonymity – If they ask to remain anonymous, do not identify them by name.

■ What Types of Supporting Material Could I Use?

When looking for types of **supporting materials**, follow the principle of "The more the merrier!" The more types of **support** (e.g., definitions, facts, examples, statistics, opinions, and stories), the more "building blocks" you'll have with which to construct your foundation. But remember, you'll be selecting the most appropriate building blocks based on your audience analysis. Therefore, some supporting materials you find will work and other information would be inappropriate for your audience. This is why the greater the variety of supporting materials, the better presentation you can potentially construct. Let's quickly review a variety of helpful forms of supporting materials.

1. *Facts and examples.* Everyone wants to hear concrete facts and examples. If you were making a presentation on dieting, giving examples of new laws that regulate these facilities is a concrete way to support your presentation. Saying, "My neighbor lost 15 pounds in three months by eliminating fried food from his diet" would be a concrete fact the audience can understand. The more vivid and specific the facts and examples, the easier it will be for your audience to understand and retain your ideas.

2. *Explanations.* Explanations get beyond the simple fact of *what* something is to specifying the *how and why* something works. For example, it is not sufficient to say to a customer, "My company's products will save you money and time." The customer will want to hear *how and why* it will save both money and time. Audience members would want to know *why* eliminating fried food from their diet is the key to losing weight. Saying, "Research states that fried foods are bad for your health" is a good start, but individuals want to know *how bad it is* and *why it is bad*. Explanations help create deeper understanding by describing the relationships and connections between causes and effects.

3. *Analogies.* An analogy is either a literal comparison or a figurative comparison between two things. To draw a comparison between two laws, towns, people, or events would be a literal

analogy (e.g., "Last year's hurricane season was the same as the 2012 season. They both had mild, wet summers followed by turbulent August and September weather patterns."). However, a figurative analogy draws comparisons between two dissimilar things to highlight unexpected similarities (e.g., "It was a disaster! Last year's hurricane season was as unpredictable as a room full of 7th grade boys.").

4. **Definitions.** A definition, either from a dictionary or in your own words, helps to provide clarification and a common starting point from which to educate your audience. Abstract terms and technical jargon often need to be defined for audience members. For example, if you were going to give a presentation on "The American Dream" or "The Challenge of Stem Cell Research," either of these phrases would need to be clearly defined to ensure the audience members shared a common point of reference to understand your presentation.

5. **Opinions and testimonies.** An opinion or testimony is a statement of the experiences, beliefs, or feelings of an individual. Brief opinions or more developed testimonies can be taken from either literary figures (e.g., a quote from a character in fiction . . . Tom Sawyer, Scarlet O'Hara, Mickey Mouse), experts (e.g., statements from historical or current experts on a subject), or even from your peers and friends. Citing the opinions or testimonies of literary figures, respected experts, and/or your peers is a memorable, effective, and credible way to support your presentation.

6. **Stories.** Everyone loves a good story. If you say to an audience full of adults, "Let me tell you a story," they will all begin listening as if they were children back in elementary school. People will rarely listen to 30 minutes of facts, examples, definitions, and statistics without losing interest. However, 30 minutes of "storytelling" is sure to keep them engaged (just like a 30 minute episode of your favorite television show). We are all familiar with the basic structure of a story – a situation, characters, conflict, dramatic climax, and a resolution of the problem leading to some insight about life. Likewise, stories can help you frame the introduction of your presentation, help illustrate key ideas in the body of your presentation, and assist you in concluding the presentation. When looking for relevant stories, you are free to draw from your personal life, professional/work experiences, factual stories about others you may or may not know, or fictional stories to illustrate a point (but always let the audience know it is fictitious). Clearly, good stories, either brief or thoroughly developed, can add life to your presentation by making your topic vivid, engaging, and memorable.

7. **Statistics and numbers.** As you can now see, statistics and numbers are only one form of supporting material. The use of statistics and numbers tends to bring an air of credibility and objectivity to your presentation. For example, saying that "Four out of five dentists recommend chewing sugar-free gum" sounds impressive. However, how many dentists did they survey? You may also be able to find four dentists to say that the amount of sugar in chewing gum is so small that it makes no difference what type of gum people chew. If you blindly claim "the numbers speak for themselves" or use too many numbers, your audience is likely to become confused and is not likely to believe you. Here is a set of

guidelines to assist you in the use of statistics and numbers.

a. *Less is best when using statistics and numbers. Using too many statistics will overwhelm, confuse, and bore your audience.*

b. *Round off statistics and numbers. Telling the audience that "632,014 U.S. children were born last year in poverty," is too confusing. It is best to say, "over 600,000." It is better to say, "75 percent of all our customers . . . " rather than saying "Exactly 73.67 percent of our customers . . . ." Numbers that are rounded off, without being "misrepresented," are easier to retain and are more effective.*

c. *Interpret statistics for the audience. Because numbers don't speak for themselves, your job is to interpret statistics for your audience. For example, a 25 percent payroll tax increase sounds huge! How much is "a 25 percent payroll tax increase" in real dollars per taxpayer? If a 25 percent tax increase resulted in an extra $50 dollars, per taxpayer, per year that sounds much more reasonable than if a 25 percent increase resulted in an extra $500 in annual taxes per taxpayer. Find ways to make these statistics understandable and relevant to the audience.*

d. *Use representative, reliable statistics and numbers. Using earthquake statistics from California would not apply to an audience from Kentucky. Be sure to check if your statistics are representative of all cases or apply to only to specific groups, areas, or industries. Furthermore, you must check to see if the statistics are from a reliable source. The National Inquirer may not provide as reliable economic data as would The Wall Street Journal.*

e. *Use visual aids to show statistics and numbers. A picture truly is worth a thousand words when it comes to statistics and numbers. Due to the complexity of numbers and statistical data, visuals will help you display your numbers more clearly, increase your audience's understanding, and increase audience retention of numerical information.*

ETHICS: Am I telling the truth?

The ethical dilemma of conducting research is to ensure that you have thoroughly researched the topic, accurately interpreted that information, truthfully represented these ideas, and cited the sources from which you gathered it. Telling "the truth, the whole truth, and nothing but the truth" is the outcome of good research. To help ensure you are being ethical, ask yourself . . .

- Am I taking supporting materials out of context?
- Am I exaggerating or misrepresenting facts?
- Am I using single facts or examples to make sweeping generalizations?
- Am I finding enough relevant information to fully represent my topic?
- Am I citing the sources of my supporting materials?
- Am I omitting important information the audience should know to make an informed decision?
- Am I presenting all sides of the issue?

Which Supporting Materials Should I Use?

Where the previous section followed the principle of "the more the merrier," your new dilemma will be sorting through your collection of supporting material to select the very best supporting materials. At this point, you now need to adopt the philosophy that, "Less is best!" Provide enough foundation and support to fit the audience and situation but don't try to include all that you have found. In fact, you will only be using a small percentage of everything you discovered. You are transitioning from an extensive understanding of *"what could be said"* to a more focused and refined sense of *"what should be said."*

Here is a list of criteria to use when selecting which sources and types of supporting materials to include in your presentation.

TIPS

Criteria for selecting supporting materials . . .

- How relevant is your supporting material to your purpose and main ideas?

- How vivid and interesting is your supporting material?

- How appropriate is your supporting material for your audience?

- How difficult will it be to explain your supporting material to this audience?

- How timely is the supporting material? Is it too dated or is it timeless?

- How credible and reliable is the source of your supporting material?

- How biased is the source of your support?

- How accurate is your supporting material?

- How representative is the supporting material? Does it apply generally or is it a limited example? Is it consistent with other supporting materials?

Building Main Ideas and Citing Sources

One of the major questions students in this class ask is, "How do I include all this supporting material and cite sources in my presentation?" Remember that you need to cite the sources of your material to enhance your credibility. Keep in mind that not every fact, definition, example, statistic, and story must be fully cited with source, year, page, etc. Writing the outline of a presentation is not the same as writing a well-supported and appropriately cited essay. However, you must include enough supporting materials and cite enough sources to create a credible, understandable, and interesting presentation.

The following four-step process will illustrate how to integrate supporting materials and cite sources in order to create a solid presentation.

Four Steps of Building Main Ideas and Citing Sources[2]

I. State your main idea

II. Cite your source(s)

III. Present supporting material
Repeat steps II and III until the main idea is sufficiently proven

IV. *Restate main idea*

As you can see, the first step is to clearly state your main idea. Once the main idea is sufficiently introduced, you can begin citing sources and presenting supporting materials. Keep in mind that every piece of support may not need a citation. It can also be that some citations are vague reference to the sources (e.g., "Other recent news reports have confirmed that new treatments for the disease are being tested.") other times you can skip citing a source. However, the audience will begin questioning your ideas if they feel you are making too many statements without citing credible sources. Once enough supporting material and credible sources are established to prove your main idea, it is then time to repeat and summarize the main idea one final time before moving onto the next main point. Look at the following example of how a speaker could integrate each of these steps into building a well-developed main idea.

(**I. Main idea**) The first step to improving our state's economy is to get more adults to attend and graduate from college. (**III. Support**) We can all agree that the highest paying jobs generally require the most advanced training, such as jobs in engineering, medicine, finance, or law. Unfortunately, our state is not producing enough college graduates to work in these high-paying career fields. (**II. Source**) Daryl Denham, State Commissioner for Higher Education, (**III. Support**) reported that less than 25 percent of the state's high school seniors applied to attend a college and technical school last year. A recent (**II. Source**) *Time* article (**III. Support**) reported that over half of all new U.S. jobs require some college or technical training. How can our state's economy improve with so few citizens prepared for these jobs? Sadly, (**II. Source**) the 2010 U.S. Census reported that (**III. Support**) our state ranked 47th in the nation in "adults with college degrees" and 45th in the nation in "per-capita income." **(III. Support)** Contrast our numbers with Missouri, which ranked 28th in "college degrees" and 26th in "per-capita income" or Indiana, which ranked 22nd in "college degrees" and 25th in "per-capita income." **(IV. Restate Main Idea)** The relationship between a state's percentage of college educated adults and the income level of its citizens is strong. If our state's economy is going to improve, we must get more adults to pursue higher education.

Summary

Clearly, there is a foundation for a good presentation. The previous pages reviewed a number of key ideas essential for building a solid foundation for a presentation.

- You must be an audience-centered speaker rather than a self-centered speaker.

- You must realize that a solid presentation is credible (ethos), clear (logos), and interesting (pathos).

- You must adapt your presentation to the demographics, situation, and attitudes and beliefs of the audience.

- You must realize that finding supporting materials may require you to gather library resources, Internet information, corporate/organizational resources, mass-media and entertainment sources, and interviews of people.

- You must use more than just statistics and numbers to support your presentation. You should also gather facts, examples, analogies, explanations, definitions, opinions/testimonies, and stories as forms of potential supporting materials.

- You must carefully evaluate which supporting materials can be used and which will not facilitate building a solid presentation.

- You must intentionally and purposefully integrate supporting materials and cite related sources to show the audience that you have effectively developed a credible, logical, and interesting presentation.

Regardless if your goal is to sell your product, motivate your workers, win a court case, or persuade citizens to vote, you must first lay a solid foundation for your presentation. Clearly, good research is the key to creating a solid presentation in every speaking situation.

ACTIVITIES

Audience Analysis and Research

Increasing Speaker Credibility

1. One hurdle for the beginning speaker is to increase his or her credibility. In small groups, first create a list of 10 speech topics the entire group considers to be "good" topics. Look back at the "Tips" box in the chapter that described ways to enhance your personal credibility. For each topic, discuss the "collective credibility" your group possesses for each of these topics (e.g., knowledge level, related experiences, social or professional affiliations, enthusiasm, etc.).

Ten Speech Topics

1.

2.

3.

4.

5.

6.

7.

8.

9.

10.

2. By this time you should know who is the most and least credible speakers related to these ten speech topics. Decide which group member has the "most speaker credibility" related to one of your ten topics (e.g., "Ann has the most credibility on the topic of architectural design."). Likewise, select the one group member who seems to have the "least speaker credibility" related to a second topic (e.g., "Doug has the least amount of credibility on the topic of pledging a sorority.").

   ■ As a group, brainstorm about how the **"high credibility"** member can go about further a) establishing and b) enhancing his/her credibility on his/her topic. Be as specific as possible. Record your ideas:

   ■ As a group, brainstorm about how the **"low credibility"** member can go about a) establishing and b) enhancing his/her credibility on his/her topic. Be as specific as possible. Record your ideas:

Name: _____ Date: _____

Gathering Supporting Materials

To create a logical, interesting, and credible presentation, you must gather a variety of supporting materials beyond those readily available through your own personal knowledge and experiences.

What is the topic of your next presentation? _____

1. Log onto the library main homepage and locate the list of available electronic "indexes and databases." Using one of these indexes/databases, locate a full-text journal article (one where the entire article could be printed or downloaded) related to your topic. You may need to read the description of each database to determine which would be of greatest help related to your topic.

   Name of the database/index used: _____

   Keyword(s) used to find the article: _____

   Write the bibliographic citation of the source of this article:

   _____

   _____

2. Use the electronic library catalog (e.g., RACERTRAC) to find one resource (print or audio/visual) on your topic available in the library. Use either a "Keyword" search or a "Subject" search. Provide the following information:

   Call number: _____

   Author: _____

   Title: _____

   Publisher and date: _____

3. Using an index or database, find one "periodic article" (e.g., newspaper, magazine, or scholarly journal – not a book) related to your topic that is not available in your library. Go to the library reference desk or the library homepage to find the Interlibrary Loan (ILL) form. Fill out the request for the article and attach the form to this assignment. DO NOT PROCESS an ILL form unless you really need the article.

   Name of the DATABASE used to find the article: _____

   Title of article: _____

   Author: _____

   Title of periodical: _____

   Volume: _____ Date: _____ Pages: _____

4. Using the Internet, locate one web resource or site related to your topic. Write the name of the site and the URL (Uniform Resource Locator) of the site:

Name: _____

http:// _____

Using the Internet, locate the homepage of an organization, corporation, or government agency that would provide information for your topic. Write the name of the organization/corporation, their mailing address, and the URL of the site:

Name: _____

Mailing address: _____

http:// _____

5. Identify the names of three potential interviewees that could provide you additional information about your subject. Explain why they would be helpful sources of information.

Name: _____

Name: _____

Name: _____

Variety of Supporting Material

Clearly, a wide variety of supporting materials can be used to support any speech. This chapter reviewed seven types of supporting materials: facts/examples, explanations, analogies, definitions, opinions/testimonies, stories, and statistics/numbers.

1. Using your library catalog, periodical databases, or the Internet, locate the text of a speech. Go through this speech locating at least one example of each type of supporting material. Attach a copy of the speech where you have **highlighted** and *labeled* the speech text to show each of the seven types of supporting materials. Indicate if any of the seven types of support are not present in your speech's content.

   From the speech, provide one example of each of those seven types of supporting materials:

   Facts/examples: _____

   Explanations: _____

   Analogies: _____

   Definitions: _____

   Opinions/testimonies: _____

   Stories: _____

   Statistics/numbers: _____

2. Using the same speech, evaluate how well the speaker supported his/her presentation. Review the "tips" on the "criteria for evaluating supporting materials" and the information on the effective use of statistics. Also, look at the four steps of "building main ideas and citing sources." Apply all these guidelines to evaluating the speech content. Type a two-page critique where you evaluate how well he/she followed these guidelines and supported his/her presentation. Give examples of both the strengths and weaknesses of the speech. How could the speaker have improved his/her speech content? What did you learn about creating a solid presentation by analyzing this speech?

References

1. Berger, C. & Calabrese, R. (1975). Some explorations in initial interaction and beyond: Toward a developmental theory of interpersonal communication. *Human Communication Research, 1,* 99-112.

2. Bebee, S. A. & Beebe, S. J. (1994). *Public speaking: An audience-centered approach.* (2nd ed.) Englewood Cliffs, NJ: Prentice Hall.

5 Putting It All Together: Organization and Outlining

Frances L. M. Smith

CHAPTER OBJECTIVES

At the end of this chapter, you will be able to:

- Understand and delineate the general purpose, outcome statement, and thesis of your presentation.
- Choose main points for your presentation and organize those main points in a clear pattern.
- Use appropriate connections to move the audience from one section of the presentation to the next.
- Understand and practice creating a thorough preparation outline for the presentation.
- Properly edit and create a useful delivery outline for the presentation.

Getting Started...

There you are, sitting at the computer ready to write your presentation. You have a topic. You have some research, but now what? You may be asking yourself, how do I take this massive amount of information – all these ideas floating around in my head – and turn it into something interesting for the audience? How do I put it all together in such a way that it is clear and understandable? Where do I even begin? Most of us at one time or another have wished that a presentation would just write itself. That somehow we would sit down at the keyboard and the ideas would flow magically out of our fingers onto the keys. However, presentations do not just appear. It takes work and practice to learn how to create a well-organized presentation. Through good preparation and clear organization, you can craft a well-written presentation that will captivate your audience. This chapter will show you how.

Organization

Good presentations start with good organization. Until you have a clear purpose, goal, key ideas, and a solid direction for your thoughts, your presentation will float in the air like a feather in the wind. Your audience will not be captivated by you if you do not succeed in presenting a clearly organized message.

Presentation Objectives

One of the most important keys to developing your presentation is considering your audience. The audience is the group you are working to influence. Whether you are trying to teach them, change their ideas about something, or simply entertain them, you must keep them in mind as you think about your presentation objectives. What are the goals you want to achieve through this presentation?

First, you must think about the purpose of your presentation. Without a clear purpose in mind, your presentation does not have a foundation. Your **general purpose** is the overall purpose of your presentation. There are three types of general purposes: to inform, to persuade, and to entertain. In a presentation to inform, your goal is to teach the audience about a particular topic. In a presentation to persuade, your goal is to influence the audience's attitudes, beliefs, or values about a particular topic. In a presentation to entertain, your goal is to provide an entertaining experience for the audience. In this chapter, the examples used will be from informative speeches.

Second, you should consider the reaction (or outcome) you want from your audience after they have listened to your presentation. You should write this in the form of an **outcome statement**. An outcome statement should specifically state the behavior you want your audience to be able to do or begin doing at the end of your presentation. This statement should be clear and concrete. The audience should be able to argue, explain, critique, defend, list and describe, or demonstrate something as a result of your presentation. In a persuasive presentation, the audience should take further action and may choose to donate, vote, quit, start, sell, or buy something as the result of your presentation. The outcome statement should specify how the audience will demonstrate their new knowledge, emotions, or feelings they gained from your presentation. Consider the following outcome statements. The first example is written too generally. The second example is written correctly.

Informative Presentation

Incorrect: At the end of my presentation, the audience will know about the four stages of child development.

Correct: At the end of my presentation, the audience will be able to explain the four stages of child development.

Incorrect: At the end of my presentation, the audience will feel good about the art of Monet.

Correct: At the end of my presentation, the audience will be able to describe how Monet's art founded the impressionist art movement.

Notice how in both of these examples, the incorrect example is very broad and does not describe the behavioral outcome of the audience. The correct example provides a concrete, measurable outcome to determine what the audience will be able to do when the presentation is complete. Even when the goal of your presentation is to change the audience's feelings, as in the second example above, you should consider what the audience should do with those feelings. The same concrete wording should be used for outcome statements in persuasive presentations.

Persuasive Presentation

Incorrect: At the end of my presentation, the audience will feel sorry for children suffering from poverty.

Correct: At the end of my presentation, the audience will pledge to sponsor a child through Compassion International.

It is particularly important to move the audience to action in a persuasive presentation. Unless you have achieved the goal of moving your audience to action, you have not achieved the goal of persuasion. You will learn more about persuasion in chapter 10.

By creating a strong outcome statement, you have a specific goal to work towards as you continue to create your presentation. When your presentation is complete, you should be able to ask an audience member if they have met the goal stated in your outcome statement and they should be able to do what you have specified. If your audience cannot demonstrate the behavior outcome you specified, you have failed to

meet your goal. An outcome statement can also help you to see if the goal you are trying to reach is too broad for the length of your presentation. For example, if your outcome statement indicates that your audience will be able to explain the twelve steps of being a successful bank teller then your goal is probably unrealistic. Evaluate your outcome statement to be sure that you have developed an obtainable goal for your audience and then create your presentation so that it focuses on meeting that goal.

Third, you must draft a **thesis**. If you have taken writing classes before you have probably written thesis statements. In a presentation, your thesis should be a declarative sentence summarizing the presentation. In other words, a thesis is your presentation in one sentence. Writing a one-sentence summary of your presentation will help you in clearly narrowing the topic so that it is understandable for the listener. Your thesis should also include the main points that will be the key ideas within the presentation. We will discuss main points next.

Here is an example of a general purpose, outcome statement, and thesis for a presentation on the topic of listening styles.

General Purpose: To inform

Outcome Statement: At the end of my presentation, my audience will be able to describe the four styles of listening.

Thesis: Listening is an important skill which has four styles: people-oriented, action-oriented, content-oriented, and time-oriented.

Main Points

After you have identified your general purpose, the goal of your presentation, and developed a thesis, you must choose your key ideas or **main points**. Main points are the key ideas you want your audience to remember about your topic. Choosing main points may seem like a daunting task. If your topic is too broad, you may have several options for main points that seem equally important. If your topic is too narrow, you may have too few main points, or main points with very little support. Therefore, as you organize your presentation you may find that you need to adjust your topic in order to properly adapt your presentation to your audience.

As you choose your main points, consider key ideas that appear within your topic. Does your topic have logical divisions[1]? For example, if you are giving a presentation on the top three Fortune 500 organizations, there are three logical main points in that presentation – one for each major organization. Another way to choose main points is to determine if there is a series of steps within your topic[1]. For example, if you were giving a presentation on the topic of being a server in a restaurant, you might choose to discuss how to serve a table of guests from the time they are seated until they leave. If you do not choose main points based on logical divisions or based on a series of steps, you may have to dig a little deeper into your topic in order to discover the main points. Good research can reveal main points[2]. Use your research skills gained in chapter 4 to gather appropriate knowledge on your topic and determine the most important key ideas that you want your audience to remember about your topic.

Main points are the foundation of the body of your presentation. Since these are the ideas you want the audience to remember, it is important that you choose your main points carefully. Remember these tips for main points:

- Only use 3-5 main points in your presentation. Your audience does not have the benefit of going back to re-read your presentation. They must commit your ideas to memory. Therefore, limit your number of main points to 3-5.

- If you have too many main points, consider grouping some smaller points together under a broader main point. For example, consider the presentation about how to be a server at a restaurant. You may be able to think of 10 steps to being a good server. Rather than having 10 main points, group them into categories such as: serving the customer before their meal arrives, during their meal, and after dessert.

- If you have a main point that has no support material, it should not be a main point. Think about each main point and how you will use your research and support material to back up that key idea. If you have a main

point that is not backed up by research and support material, it does not deserve to be a main point.

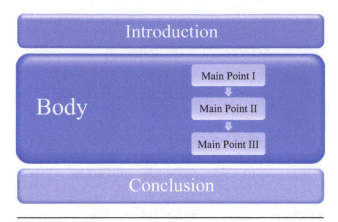

General Presentation Structure

Organizational Patterns

Once you have main points for your presentation, you must put them together in some kind of order. To do this, you must use an organizational pattern. What do you do when you tell your friend about the date you had last weekend? You tell the story in some kind of logical way. The same needs to be true for your presentation. There should be a logical order to your thoughts. Your presentation should be carefully planned and strategically organized with the audience in mind. Sometimes your organizational pattern will be obvious, but sometimes it will not. If your organizational pattern is not obvious, you must carefully consider what organizational pattern will be the most clear to your audience and will help them to understand and remember your presentation. We will discuss five types of organizational patterns: chronological, spatial, causal, topical, and mnemonic/gimmick.

Chronological

Use a **chronological** pattern when organizing your main points by time. This pattern is used most often when you give a presentation on a topic related to an event in history or some other sequential event. For example, if you were to give a presentation about the history of women in business, would be logical for you to organize your main points in a chronological pattern.

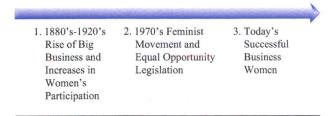

The History of Women in Business

Spatial

In **spatial** organization, the main points are organized by location or direction. A presentation organized spatially follows a logical path, usually through some kind of location[1]. Spatial organization takes the audience on a tour, of sorts. The audience follows the speaker from one place to another within a specific location. Imagine you are giving a presentation about the Google headquarters, Googleplex, in Mountain View, California. Your main points would take the audience through the Googleplex by telling them about where the organization is located, the office spaces, recreation facilities, and snack rooms.

Working for Google in Googleplex

Causal

Presentations organized in **causal** order show a cause-effect relationship. Main points in this organizational pattern are designed to show the cause of an issue and its effects. While this organizational pattern has a clear persuasive application, it may also be used in an informative presentation. Topics that allow you to analyze a specific problem are particularly well-organized using a causal pattern. For example, if you were to give a presentation about the causes and effects of childhood obesity you might organize main points to discuss lack of good nutrition and physical activity in children.

The Causes and Effects of Childhood Obesity

Problem-Cause-Solution

While the **causal** order outlines the causes and effects of an issue, the **problem-cause-solution** goes a step further by organizing the body of the presentation into three main sections: (a) the nature and significance of the problem, (b) the causes and effects of the problem, and (c) the best possible solution to the problem. This organizational pattern starts by thoroughly illustrating the significance and prevalence of a problem and argues why the problem is related to the lives of the audience. Second, the problem's most likely causes and greatest effects (direct/indirect, short-term/long-term, etc.) are reviewed. Finally, a solution is presented and an argument is created to justify why the proposed solution is the "best" solution. For example, the topic of childhood obesity could be addressed by explaining the significance and relevance of the problem, reviewing the possible causes and greatest effects of childhood obesity, and then arguing why the proposed solution is best option and will stop all/most of the root causes of childhood obesity. Overall, the problem-cause-solution pattern is used when it is essential to motivate the audience to look deeper into an issue and accept the advantages of your proposed solution.

Topical

A **topical** organizational pattern divides the presentation into natural divisions based on the speaker's discretion. In other words, a topical pattern allows you as the presenter to choose how you want to organize the material and key ideas. A topical pattern allows you to give equal emphasis to each main point as it informs your topic.

The order in which you arrange your main points in a topical pattern is up to you. You may choose to organize your main points according to personal preference. Other options within the topical pattern include: primacy, recency, and complexity[1]. If you organize the main points according to primacy, put the most important or compelling main point first and progress to the least important or compelling point. If you organize your main points from the least important or compelling to the most important or compelling, you would use the principle of recency. Finally, if you are using a topical organizational pattern, you may find that your main points range from simplistic to complex. If that is the case, you may choose to arrange them in order of complexity. If you choose to arrange your main points in order of complexity, list your main points in order from the more simplistic to the more complex. This will allow the audience to understand the simplest main points first and understand the more complex main points later in the presentation.

Below is an example of a presentation arranged in topical order. If you chose a topic regarding jobs you could obtain with an organizational communication degree, you might talk about jobs in human resources, management, marketing, public relations, and non-profit organizing. Those main points should each receive similar attention and do not lend themselves to any other particular organizational pattern.

What You Can Do with an Organizational Communication Degree

Mnemonic/Gimmick

The final pattern you may choose to use for your speech is the **mnemonic/gimmick** pattern[3]. In the mnemonic/gimmick pattern, the main points are organized in such a way as to spell out a word or some other kind of memory device. Before you use a mnemonic/gimmick pattern, carefully consider your topic and your audience. Is your topic conducive to such a pattern? If your topic is very serious, for example, using a mnemonic/gimmick pattern may cause your audience to feel that you are being disrespectful of the situation. However, it is important to consider audience retention. Just as using a mnemonic device can often aid in your memory as you study for an exam, using a mnemonic device may help your audience remember your main points in a way that they would not have if you had organized them in another way. For example, if you were to give a presentation about "The Three F's of Buying a Cell Phone" you would use three main points that began with the letter F, such as funds, features, and freedom.

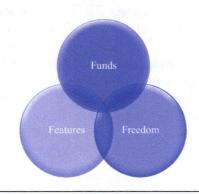

The Three F's of Buying a Cell Phone

▌ Connections

Now that your main points have been determined and organized, you can begin to put them together within the body of the speech. Although you have determined an order, you have not made connections between your key ideas. While connections may seem insignificant, they are an important part of helping your audience understand and follow your presentation. Connections help your audience to visualize where you have been and where you are going within the presentation. A presentation without connections can leave the audience lost and looking for direction. You should use connections between the introduction and the body of the speech, between each main point and sub-point, between each sub-point, and between the body and the conclusion. There are five types of connections we will discuss in this chapter: transitional statements, internal previews, internal summaries, signposts, and nonverbal transitions.[1]

Transitional Statements

A **transitional statement** is a phrase that tells the audience that you are finished with one idea and you are moving to another. Transitional statements are particularly useful when you move from one main point to another. They help the audience feel a sense of completion of one main point and remind them of the next main point that is to follow. Here are some examples:

"Now that we understand more about the weaknesses of wrought iron rivets that were used in building the Titanic, let's see how those rivets may have lead to the death of over 1,500 people on April 14, 1912."

"Preparing for the interview is only the first step you should take if you want to obtain your dream job – next, you must make a good first impression."

"Let us begin by considering how to prepare for interacting with someone from a culture that is different from our own."

Internal Previews

An **internal preview** provides the audience with a preview of the key ideas that are coming next in the presentation. Internal previews are much like the preview statement within an introduction, except they come within the body of the presentation. They are more detailed than transition statements and give the audience a clear picture of what is to come. The following are some examples:

"Since good nutrition is so important, I will discuss three ways we can begin to eat healthier which are: planning ahead, reading nutrition labels, and buying healthy foods in bulk."

You can also use the internal preview in combination with a transitional statement as in this example:

"(Transitional Statement) Now that we have a clear understanding of why gas prices have skyrocketed in the past few years, let's consider the effects these high prices have on low-income

families. (Internal Preview) Specifically, I will discuss the economic effects on low-income families related to work, school, and daily necessities."

Internal Summaries

When you have presented a complicated main point, you may choose to use an **internal summary** to connect your audience to the next main point. Internal summaries are the opposite of an internal preview as they review what has already been discussed in the previous main point or points in order to help the audience retain the information and move on to the next step. Internal summaries are well suited to be paired with transitional statements to move from one point to the next. Here is an example of an internal summary:

"(Internal Summary) I hope you now know the basic steps to using Microsoft Excel. We began by creating a file, inputting data, adding formulas, and formatting the style. (Transitional Statement) Next, I will teach you how to print your file so that you may share your data with others."

Signposts

Signposts are brief words or statements that tell the audience where to focus attention. Signposts are often simple, but they allow an audience to understand what the presenter sees as important or where the presenter is within the presentation. Some examples of signposts are:

- First…Second….Third…
- Never forget…
- Finally…
- In conclusion…
- Remember…
- Above all…

Nonverbal Transitions

Nonverbal transitions describe the way you use your gestures, facial expressions, and body movements to create transitions within your presentation[1]. Nonverbal transitions can take place in conjunction with any of the verbal transitions mentioned above. For example, if you were to give a presentation on the September 11th attacks in New York and Washington, DC, you might begin with an introduction about the number of casualties resulting from that event. Before you move into the main points, take a moment to pause and maintain eye contact with the audience. Then say, "Almost 3,000 people lost their lives that day in New York, Washington, DC, and Shanksville, Pennsylvania, making 9/11 the worst terrorist attack in U.S. history." Using facial expressions, pauses, and gestures in nonverbal transitions adds depth to your connections by emphasizing your connection not only through your words, but also through your nonverbal delivery. You will learn more about delivery in chapter 8.

Image © blueking, 2009. Used under license from Shutterstock, Inc.

work. However, an outline is vital to the success of your presentation. Outlining your presentation will help you as the presenter to clarify your ideas, organize your thoughts, and visualize your presentation in a way that you could not do without an outline. Learning how to properly outline your presentation and making a habit of proper outlining will benefit you as you continue to make presentations throughout your lifetime. In the following section of this chapter we will discuss two kinds of outlines: the preparation outline and the delivery outline. We will also discuss how to properly edit your presentation.

The Preparation Outline

Your **preparation outline** should be a detailed outline of the presentation. Overall, the preparation outline should include about 80% of what you plan to say in your presentation for an extemporaneous presentation. Therefore, the preparation outline should include all of the important keys in preparing your speech. Begin with a heading that includes your general purpose, outcome statement, and thesis. Including these elements in a heading will help you remember the goals you have created for your presentation as you continue to prepare.

After the heading, your preparation outline should include the introduction, body, and conclusion of the speech with all the transitions labeled. The introduction should be clearly labeled as the introduction and should include your attention-getter, statement of credibility, and preview statement. After the introduction is complete, a

---

Name: Pamela Smith
General Purpose: To inform
Outcome Statement: At the end of my presentation, my audience will explain how to train new employees within an organization.

Thesis: When training new employees within an organization, the trainer should welcome them, give them a tour of the organization, describe their work environment, and train them on one task at a time.

Outlining

You have selected a topic, researched it, and decided on your general purpose, outcome statement, thesis, main points, and organizational pattern. Now it is necessary for you to put those ideas down on paper in the form of an outline. You may be thinking to yourself that an outline is really unnecessary busy-

transitional statement should lead into the body of the speech.

After the introduction, you should write out the body of the presentation. The body should include each main point and sub-points with transitional statements. As you write out your main points and sub-points remember that if you have a main point

Introduction

I. [Attention-Getter] I'm sure most of you plan to get a job after you graduate from college. So imagine yourself working diligently at your desk, when your boss comes into the room with someone you have never seen before. He introduces you to the new employee and then informs you that you will be responsible for training her.

II. [Statement of Credibility] The example I just gave you happened to me at my current job. I was asked to train a new employee without any prior experience or training.

    A. Over a three year period, I have trained over one hundred new employees at Southeastern Book Company.

    B. After several training sessions, I realized that there was a distinct process in training new employees.

Preview Statement: When training new employees, the trainer should follow these steps: welcome them, take them on a tour of the facility, familiarize them with their work environment, and train them on one specific task.

Transitional Statement: First, let's look at welcoming the new employee.

---

that cannot be supported by sub-points then that main point should be reconsidered. Perhaps it would better fit as a sub-point to a larger main point. Main points without sub-points are not well supported. Also, as you include information from sources in the body of your presentation, be sure you state the source within the presentation as you present that information. Stating the sources within the presentation prevents plagiarism and adds to your credibility by showing that your presentation is well-researched and you are prepared.

Body

I. [Main Point] The first step in training new employees is welcoming them into your company.

    A. Introduce yourself with a smile, showing them they are important.

        1. You want them to feel comfortable.

        2. According to an article in *Business Journal* by Ingrid Murrow Betero, "if the first day is not structured and if attention is not paid to new employees, then they are likely to feel unwanted."

    B. Do not leave them alone for extended periods of time.

Transitional Statement: After establishing a positive training relationship, you should then focus on the organization.

II. [Main Point] The second step in training new employees is to take them on a tour of the facility.

    A. In this tour, the history of the organization should be discussed.

        1. Where or how it started.

        2. What is the purpose of the organization; why does it exist?

        3. What are they wanting to achieve – goals?

        4. What is important to this company?

        5. An article in *Personnel Psychology* stated that "employees cannot embrace an organization's goals or values if they are not made aware of them."

    B. You also want to go through the different departments so they can grasp the whole process of the organization.

Continued

C. You want to introduce them to key people throughout these departments.

D. Last, you want to make sure they know where the bathrooms, water fountains, and break areas are.

Transitional Statement: Following the tour of the facility, new employees should be brought back to their department.

III. [Main Point] The third step in training new employees is to familiarize them with their department.

A. Walk them through the entire department.

1. Introduce them to their co-workers along the way.

2. Familiarize them with how the department is set up.

B. Make sure they understand the language of the department.

1. According to an article from the Spring 2000 issue of *Personnel Psychology*, the language is "the technical language, acronyms, slang and jargon unique" to an organization, job, or profession.

2. One way to help them with unfamiliar terminology is to provide them with a handout of related terms and definitions.

C. Show them how the department is run.

1. Task involved.

2. Line of authority.

3. Who can be depended on for help.

4. Job responsibilities.

Transitional Statement: Once employees have a good understanding of their department, you should then start them on a specific task.

IV. [Main Point] The fourth and final step in training new employees should be to start them on one specific task at a time.

A. You want to make sure they have a clear understanding of each task before they begin on the next.

B. One of the most important things for a trainer to do at this stage is to stay with the new employee.

1. Answer questions.

2. Correct mistakes.

3. Provide positive reinforcement.

C. Last, evaluate their progress and modify training to suit their individual needs.

Transitional Statement: Let's conclude with a review.

After you have written the body of your outline, finish with your conclusion. Your conclusion should include your review statement and a closing statement. Be sure you have written your conclusion completely so that you end your presentation with a strong finale.

Conclusion

I. [Review Statement] I have discussed four steps in training new employees: welcome them, take them on a tour of the facility, familiarize them with their department, and start them on one specific task at a time.

A. [Closing Statements] It is your responsibility to make sure new employees have a clear understanding of the organization and their responsibilities.

B. Remember, to these new employees, you represent the company; therefore, you should step up to the occasion and be the best trainer you can possibly be.

C. New employees benefit and so does the company!

The final important element to the outline is your bibliography. You may be familiar with a number of ways to format a bibliography – MLA, Chicago, APA, or others. The most commonly used formatting style in the social sciences is APA style, so that is the format that will be shown here. If you want to use APA style, there are many resources you can use to help you. Purdue University has an excellent online resource at: *http://owl.english.purdue.edu/owl/resource/560/01/*. You may use whatever formatting style you find appropriate. The important thing is that you have a bibliography with formatted references so that you and others who may see your outlines know what your sources are and how to find them.

References

1. Botero, I.M. (2005). The secrets of effective employee training for new employees. *Business Journal, 210*, 150-151.
2. Effingham, A.K. (2004). Tying goals into employee training. *Personnel Psychology, 84*, 24-44.
3. Reader, C.M. (2000). The importance of language in the workplace. *Personnel Psychology, 44*, 108-110.

When you have completed your preparation outline, you should have approximately 80% of what you plan to say in your hands. It is expected that you will expand on your points and that you may not say these sentences exactly the same as you have them written, however you now have a thorough outline from which you can clarify your ideas and begin to practice. Here are some keys to remember about your preparation outline:

■ **Label all the parts of your outline clearly** to give you a visual representation of each part of your presentation. If you notice that your introduction encompasses more than 10% your presentation, perhaps the introduction is too long and should be shortened.

■ **Use consistent symbols and indentation.** Roman numerals are the preferred symbols to use during your preparation outline, but whatever symbols you choose be sure they are consistent throughout the outline. Using symbols and indentation helps you to visualize the relationship between main points, sub-points, and other components of your outline. Seeing this relationship will help you to determine if you have given adequate support to main points and attention to each section of the presentation.

■ **Main points and sub-points should be written in full sentences.** Write your main points and sub-points in full sentences so that you can construct your sentences as you prepare. Although your goal in the presentation is not to memorize a manuscript, writing out full sentences will allow you to prepare your words and think through your key ideas completely.

■ **Each main point should have at least two sub-points and any sub-point with divisions should have at least two sub-divisions.** This coincides with the rule you may have heard before: if there is an "a" there should be a "b," if there is a "1" there should be a "2." Make sure your divisions are appropriate to support their main point.

Editing Your Presentation

Before we move on to your delivery outline, let us spend some time talking about editing. As you prepare your presentation and develop your preparation outline, you may find that you need to edit your presentation. In some cases, editing needs to be done because the outline is too long and your presentation is going to exceed the time limit. Other times, you need to edit because your presentation lacks consistency and your thoughts are not coherent. Either way, editing is an important process and one that should take place after you have completed your preparation outline.

Steven and Susan Beebe offer excellent advice on editing a presentation.[1] Here are some of their thoughts:

- **Think about the audience.** Go back through your outline and think about what material will be most interesting and useful for the audience to know and understand. If there is a piece of support material that will not enhance the audience's understanding of the main point, remove it.

- **Be simple.** Check your writing for extraneous words that do not add to the meaning of your message. Phrases such as, "and all that," "when all is said and done," "as a matter of fact," and "before I begin," add little if any meaning to what is being said and really serve no purpose in your presentation. Cut them.

- **Ask for help in cutting from a listener.** As someone who has written the presentation, you may be too close to the material to really see what can be cut or modified. Ask someone else to read your outline or, even better, listen to you practice. A listener can often help you cut material or tighten main points because they can see areas of improvement that you may miss.

- **Consider the introduction and conclusion.** The introduction should only comprise about 10% of your presentation. Likewise, you should only spend about 10% of your time in the conclusion. If you find that your introduction and conclusion exceed those percentages, consider where you can take away from those sections. While those sections of the presentation are extremely important, the body is the substance of the presentation and must be given the most time.

Delivery Outline

After you have completed your preparation outline and edited it, you are ready to develop your delivery outline. The **delivery outline** is a shorter version of your preparation outline used for delivering your presentation. Your delivery outline should have the same visual representations as the preparation outline as far as symbols and indentations; however unlike your preparation outline the delivery outline should include only key words or phrases and delivery cues for your use. The purpose of a delivery outline is for you to have notes to use during the presentation as an aid, but not notes that will cause you to read word-for-word, sentence-for-sentence. After you have prepared and rehearsed using your edited preparation outline, you should be able to use a delivery outline to present the

presentation and still maintain appropriate eye contact with the audience.

Here are some tips for creating a delivery outline from your preparation outline:

- **Keep it brief.** Delivery outlines should be limited to one page. Having multiple pages in front of you as you speak to an audience can be a distraction for you and for the audience. If you keep your delivery outline to one page, you will not have the distraction of turning pages while you present.

- **Use key words or phrases.** Unlike the preparation outline which should be written in full sentences, the delivery outline should only include key words. You should be familiar enough with your material by the time that you present that a key word or short phrase is all you need to remind you of what you wanted to say. The only exception to this rule is if you are quoting from one of your sources. In that case, you may want to include the whole quote so that you do not risk misquoting your source.

- **Include delivery cues.** Delivery cues can include statements like, "smile," "pause," "change slide," "breathe," and "take two steps." Cues like this in your delivery outline can help you remember important aspects of your delivery while you present.

- **Use colors or highlighters.** As you prepare and practice you may find that there are particular areas of the presentation in which you struggle to remember what you want to say next. When you find those areas, take time to highlight those or mark them in some other way to draw your attention to them quickly. That way when you are in front of the audience, you will not have as much difficulty finding those places.

You may also want to take your delivery outline and create note cards with it. Note cards can be useful for speakers who want to move away from the podium. There are a few important strategies to remember if you decide to use note cards for your delivery outline:

- **Number your cards.** It will probably be impossible to put your entire delivery outline on one note card which means you will have multiple cards during your presentation. Clearly marking each card with a number will allow you to put them in order easily should one fall out of place.

■ **Consider the size and color of your cards.** Note cards come in a variety of sizes and colors so choose a size and color that will not be distracting to your audience. Standard 3 x 5 inch white note cards are the most common and probably the least distracting note cards to use. Larger cards, such as 5 x 8 inch, may provide you with fewer cards to handle, but may also be a distraction to the audience as you carry them away from the podium. Ultimately, the less you can draw your audience's attention to your note cards, the better. Their attention should be on you and your message – not your notes.

■ **Only use one side of the note card.**[4] Using multiple sides of one card will cause you to have to flip the card over or if you are holding the card in front of an audience, they may try to read the card instead of pay attention to you.

Chapter Review

Proper organization and outlining is essential to the preparation of a strong presentation. You must consider your general purpose, outcome statement, and thesis as you begin. Next, it is important to determine your main points and how you will structure those main points through organization. You may choose to organize your main points through chronological, spatial, causal, topical, or mnemonic/gimmick organizational patterns. Then, you should think about how you want to connect your key ideas through transitions such as transitional statements, internal previews, internal summaries, signposts, and nonverbal transitions.

After you have organized your ideas, you should begin to prepare a preparation outline. The preparation outline should comprise about 80% of what you plan to say in the entire presentation and should be clearly labeled throughout from the heading to the bibliography. After your preparation outline is complete, edit the outline to make sure

you have the appropriate amount of information included and that information is clear and concise. Finally, prepare a delivery outline to facilitate a smooth delivery of the presentation.

With appropriate organization and outlining skills you will master the ability to create an effective presentation. Well organized presentations are an important part of achieving your goal with the audience.

Application Questions

1. Consider each of the following presentation topics. What would be the most appropriate general purpose, outcome statement, and thesis for each topic?

   How to interview for a job
   Broaden your horizons! Why you should study abroad
   The three C's of successful customer service
   The importance of effective brand management
   Silent thieves: The effects of illegally downloading music
   Going global: How to conduct a meeting via webcam

2. Consider the six presentation topics in application question 1. Create main points for each topic. How might you organize those main points into an organizational pattern? Justify the reason for the organizational pattern you have chosen.

3. What important elements of a presentation should be included in a presentation outline? Why is the presentation outline such an important part of presentation preparation?

4. What is the purpose of a delivery outline? How does a delivery outline prepare the presenter for the presentation?

Putting It All Together: Organization and Outlining

Activity 5.1

Use the organizational pattern listed below to create a sample speech for the topic given. Write a basic preparation outline for each speech.

Chronological: Choose a movie you have seen and give an informative speech about it.

Spatial: Organizing an office.

Causal: The effects of sleep deprivation on work performance.

Problem-Cause-Solutions: Illegal drugs

Topical: The high school experience.

Mnemonic/gimmick: The three P's of a successful job interview.

Activity 5.2

Analyze the following preparation outline. Mark all of the mistakes.

General Purpose:

To inform my audience about dogs.

Outcome Statement:

Dogs are cute.

Thesis:

I enjoy having a dog. They are fun to play with and you can get them from the humane society.

Introduction

    I. How much is that puppy in the window? If you choose to get a dog from the human society, you don't even have to ask that question.

    II. I like dogs.

        A. I've had 3 dogs and 2 cats.

Preview Statement: You should get a dog from the humane society to protect them from being killed.

    I. The first thing you should do is determine what kind of dog you want.

        A. You can look at pet stores or look at dog websites.

            1. Different dogs are different.

    II. Go to the humane society.

            1. If dogs are left at the humane society and not taken to good homes they are put to sleep.

            2. Give a dog a good home.

            3. You can volunteer to play with dogs at the human society even if you can't take one home.

Transitional Statement: So go get a dog.

Conclusion

    I. I have told you how important it is to get a dog from the human society.

        A. Know what kind of dog you want.

        B. Have fun with your dog.

References

http://www.dogs.com

Activity 5.3

The following are pieces of a preparation outline. Cut the pieces apart and reconstruct the outline in order.

Transitional statement: Let's look first at getting a shot.

Preview statement: Having a cavity in your tooth filled is an almost painless and easy process with three steps: you must get a shot, you must get the decay drilled out, you must get your cavity filled.

Transitional statement: Once the decay is removed from the tooth, it is time to replace the lost tooth surface.

    a. First, the decayed area must be sealed with Dycal to prevent further decay.

III. You must have the cavity filled with amalgam (am- al- gaam) which is the silver material you see in a filled tooth.

    d. Fourth, the amalgam is carved to fit the natural line of your bite.

II. Let's face it; no one likes to go to the dentist. I even had one patient tell me that she would rather have a baby than go to the dentist. The bottom line is if you will take care of your teeth by brushing after every meal and going for regular check ups with the hygienist, you probably won't have to have any major work done.

Conclusion

    I. I would like for everyone to close his/her eyes. Now imagine that you are in your dentist's office sitting in the chair. When you hear this sound, what images does it bring to your mind? (Play drilling sounds)

Name: Maria Kuykendall

    b. I have had at least 15 cavities filled and most of those refilled.

    a. First, nitrous oxide, better known as laughing gas, is given to relax you.

Transitional statement: After the epinephrine has had time to numb the tooth, the dentist will then move on to the next step – drilling.

Body

    I. Having cavities filled is something that I can relate to.

  II. You must have the decayed part of the tooth drilled out.

    b. Second, topical gel is applied to numb the gums around the tooth.

        i. Flavors

        ii. Appearance

    a. I work in a dentist's office.

General Purpose:

To inform

    I. Going to have a cavity filled is an almost painless process that involves multiple steps: you must get a shot, you must have the decay drilled out of your tooth, you must have the cavity filled.

Ehrlich, A. & Torres, H. (1990). *Modern Dental Assisting.* Philadelphia, PA: Saunders

Introduction

    c. I can alleviate your fears about having a cavity filled by explaining what actually takes place.

Outcome Statement: At the end of my speech, my audience will know the three steps in filling a cavity.

    c. Third, the shot is given.

        i. Location

        ii. Amount

    I. According to the book, Modern Dental Assisting, by Ehrlich and Torres, you must get a shot of epinephrine (epp – in- ef – reen) to numb the nerves of the decayed tooth.

References

    a. The decay in the tooth is caused by the collection of bacteria on the tooth surface.

    c. Third, the space is filled with amalgam material.

        i. Mixing

        ii. Packing

    b. Second, the hole is made sticky with Copalite so that the silver will adhere to the surface.

    b. The decay may be shallow. But…

        i. If not filled – extends far into the pulp.

        ii. Further dental work may be necessary

Thesis: Getting a cavity filled is an almost painless and easy process with three steps which include getting a shot, getting the decay drilled out, and getting the cavity filled.

Activity 5.4

Editing

Consider the following preparation outline sections. Edit the pieces to make them clearer and more succinct.

I. Actually, the sales process is kind of a spiral, each step feeding back and influencing the others as the process overall moves forward toward the close, assuming that it is carried out correctly. You see, you must carry out the sales process correctly in order for the sale to be completed in a proper way. If you don't carry out the sale correctly, the customer may not be satisfied. If the customer lacks satisfaction, they may never return to your store which could cause you to lose sales in the long-run.

II. As soon as the customer walks in the door, the very first thing you want to do is size them up. This means that you should notice every aspect about them. Pay attention to everything they say and do. Notice their age and what kind of clothes they are wearing – head to toe. In other words, consider everything about the customer. Try to learn as much as you can about them from their appearance. This will give you their sense of style, and help you pick out items they might like. Perhaps they would like a certain kind of necklace, earrings, shirt, or jeans. Consider every possible thing that they might like.

III. After the sale is complete, you must leave the customer pleased with the experience. If they are unhappy, they may not return to your store. Make sure they have left the store satisfied. Smile and offer to help them find anything else that they need. If they do not need anything else, wish them a good day. You can wish them a good day in multiple ways such as good evening, have a good day, come back soon, or hope to see you again. In my opinion, have a good day is the best way to end a customer interaction. Never forget to smile as you hand them their merchandise.

Example Outline-Informative Speech

Name: Pamela Smith

General Purpose: To inform

Outcome Statement: At the end of my presentation, my audience will be able to explain how to train new employees within an organization.

Thesis: When training new employees within an organization, the trainer should welcome them, give them a tour of the organization, describe their work environment, and train them on one task at a time.

Introduction

I. I'm sure most of you plan to get a job after you graduate from college. So imagine yourself working diligently at your desk, when your boss comes into the room with someone you have never seen before. He introduces you to the new employee and then informs you that you will be responsible for training her.

II. The example I just gave you happened to me at my current job. I was asked to train a new employee without any prior experience or training.

    A. Over a three year period, I have trained over one hundred new employees at Southeastern Book Company.

    B. After several training sessions, I realized that there was a distinct process in training new employees.

Preview Statement: When training new employees, the trainer should follow these steps: welcome them, take them on a tour of the facility, familiarize them with their work environment, and train them on one specific task.

Transitional Statement: First, let's look at welcoming the new employee.

Body

I. The first step in training new employees is welcoming them into your company.

    A. Introduce yourself with a smile, showing them they are important.

        1. You want them to feel comfortable.

        2. According to an article in *Business Journal* by Ingrid Murrow Betero, "if the first day is not structured and if attention is not paid to new employees, then they are likely to feel unwanted."

    B. Do not leave them alone for extended periods of time.

Transitional Statement: After establishing a positive training relationship, you should then focus on the organization.

II. The second step in training new employees is to take them on a tour of the facility.

    A. In this tour, the history of the organization should be discussed.

1. Where or how it started.

2. What is the purpose of the organization; why does it exist?

3. What does the organization want to achieve – goals?

4. What is important to this company?

5. An article in *Personnel Psychology* stated that "employees cannot embrace an organization's goals or values if they are not made aware of them."

B. You also want to go through the different departments so they can grasp the whole process of the organization.

C. You want to introduce them to key people throughout these departments.

D. Last, you want to make sure they know where the bathrooms, water fountains, and break areas are.

Transitional Statement: Following the tour of the facility, new employees should be brought back to their department.

III. The third step in training new employees is to familiarize them with their department.

A. Walk them through the entire department.

1. Introduce them to their co-workers along the way.

2. Familiarize them with how the department is set up.

B. Make sure they understand the language of the department.

1. According to an article from the Spring 2000 issue of *Personnel Psychology*, the language is "the technical language, acronyms, slang and jargon unique" to an organization, job, or profession.

2. One way to help them with unfamiliar terminology is to provide them with a handout of related terms and definitions.

C. Show them how the department is run.

1. Task involved.

2. Line of authority.

3. Who can be depended on for help.

4. Job responsibilities.

Transitional Statement: Once employees have a good understanding of their department, you should then start them on a specific task.

IV. The fourth and final step in training new employees should be to start them on one specific task at a time.

A. You want to make sure they have a clear understanding of each task before they begin on the next.

B. One of the most important things for a trainer to do at this stage is to stay with the new employee.

1. Answer questions.

2. Correct mistakes.

3. Provide positive reinforcement.

   C. Last, evaluate their progress and modify training to suit their individual needs.

Transitional Statement: Let's conclude with a review.

Conclusion

I. I have discussed four steps in training new employees: welcome them, take them on a tour of the facility, familiarize them with their department, and start them on one specific task at a time.

   A. It is your responsibility to make sure new employees have an understanding about your organization and their responsibilities.

   B. Remember, to these new employees, you represent the company; therefore, you should step up to the occasion and be the best trainer you can possibly be.

   C. New employees benefit and so does the company!

References

1. Botero, I.M. (2005). The secrets of effective employee training for new employees. *Business Journal, 210,* 150-151.

2. Effingham, A.K. (2004). Tying goals into employee training. *Personnel Psychology, 84,* **24-44.**

3. Reader, C.M. (2000). The importance of language in the workplace. *Personnel Psychology, 44,* 108-110.

Informative Outline Template

Name: _____

General Purpose: _____

Outcome Statement:

_____

_____

Thesis:

_____

_____

Introduction

Attention Getter:

_____

_____

_____

_____

Establish Credibility:

_____

_____

_____

_____

Preview Statement:

_____

_____

_____

_____

Transitional Statement:_____

Body

Main Point I.

_____

_____

    Support Material A._____

    Support Material B._____

Transitional Statement:_____

Main Point II.

_____

_____

    Support Material A. _____

    Support Material B. _____

Transitional Statement: _____

Main Point III.

_____

_____

    Support Material A. _____

    Support Material B. _____

Transitional Statement: _____

Main Point IV.

_____

_____

    Support Material A. _____

    Support Material B. _____

Transitional Statement: _____

Conclusion

Review Statement:

_____

_____

_____

_____

Closing Statement:

_____

_____

_____

_____

References

_____

_____

_____

_____

Example Delivery Outline

(EYE CONTACT! EYE CONTACT! EYE CONTACT!)
(BREATHE!)

Introduction

I. She was scared . . .

II. Pets are the best when . . .

III. I have had pets . . .

IV. I'd like to share three reasons why pets . . .

Body

I. First . . . comforting

   A. Example of Susan

   B. According to TIME magazine in an article taken on June 10th, 2004, "over 16 million people have pets."

   C. When I was sick . . .

Transitional Statement: Now that I've told you . . .

II. Secondly . . . protection

   A. My grandfather was 75 when . . . . . burglars came in . . .

   B. My friend Bob . . . . we ran down the street . . . . we ended up with two dogs . . . . .

   C. There are agencies here in town that train . . . . .

      1. Trainers are Us . . . . Concentrates on family protection

      2. Obedience USA . . . . . heavily involved in discipline . . . not expensive . . .

Signpost: This last point is very . . . . .

III. . . . . . . not difficult to maintain

   A. Groomers are available

   B. When I have to, I take Charlie . . . . (SHOW PICTURE HERE!)

Conclusion

I. Remember the three reasons . . .

II. Having pets . . . .

III. . . . . . please go right now and . . . . you won't regret it.

(WAIT FOR APPLAUSE_————— DON'T WALK AWAY UNTIL LAST WORD)

*Outline courtesy of Crystal Rae Coel Coleman

References

1. Beebe, S.A. and S.J. Beebe (2006). *Public Speaking: An Audience-Centered Approach* (6th ed.). Boston: Allyn and Bacon.

2. Lucas, S.E. (2001). *The Art of Public Speaking* (7th ed.). Boston: McGraw Hill.

3. Grice, G.L. and J.F. Skinner (2001). *Mastering Public Speaking* (4th ed.). Needham Heights, MA: Allyn and Bacon.

4. Griffin, C.L. (2003). *Invitation to Public Speaking.* Belmont, CA: Thomson Wadsworth.

6

Introductions and Conclusions

David M. Gesler

CHAPTER OBJECTIVES

At the end of this chapter, you will be able to:

- Understand the importance of introductions and conclusions

- Define the elements of an introduction and conclusion

- Define the purposes for having an introduction and conclusion

- Create effective introductions and conclusions

Introduction

By now, you've read and learned about the importance of communicating, the elements of an effective presentation, how to conduct research to gain information for your presentation, and how to organize and outline your presentation. Without question, these are important topics you need to know in order to deliver a successful presentation. However, without the information contained in this chapter, your presentation will have no beginning and no end. It will neither start nor stop in the eyes of your audience, and that will cause your audience to stop listening to you. If your audience stops listening to you, there is no reason for you to be giving a presentation. Like a beautifully wrapped gift box, the introduction entices a person to want to know more about your presentation, just as the wrapping paper on the gift entices people to want to open the box and see what's inside. The conclusion takes the "open package," your content, and re-wraps the information so that the audience is left with another package; one that reminds them and can help them remember what was just presented. Thus, every successful presentation must have an effective introduction and conclusion.

Image © Feverpitch, 2009. Used under license from Shutterstock, Inc.

Starting Your Presentation – The Introduction

The introduction is the most important part of any presentation. Before you show your fabulous visual aids, before you wow the audience with your supporting material, even before you present your interesting main points, your audience will hear your introduction. The introduction of your presentation is the most important element of the presentation because it will be the first thing your audience will hear from you. It is also important because the introduction of a presentation must fulfill four functions. Your introduction must 1) Set the tone of the presentation, 2) Gain the attention of the audience (get the audience to want to listen to you), 3) Establish your credibility and sincerity toward the audience, and 4) Preview the rest of the presentation. As you learned in Chapter 5, about 10% of your presentation should be devoted to your introduction, and as such, delivering an excellent presentation in the eyes of your audience hinges upon delivering a good, solid, and confidence-boosting introduction. It is that important! Let's look at each of the four "introduction functions."

Introduction Function 1: Setting the Tone of the Presentation

There is a lot riding on the introduction, as without a good, solid, and effective introduction, delivering an excellent overall presentation becomes very difficult. The first introduction function is to set the tone of the presentation. Like the old saying goes, "you never get a second chance at making a first impression," and you want that impression to be stellar, to instill confidence not only within yourself and in what you're saying, but also to create confidence in the audience members about you and your topic. If you get started off "on the wrong foot" in a presentation, you will then have to focus your energy on bringing the level of the presentation back to being successful. This takes energy away from delivering an outstanding presentation, you get out of the "flow" of the speech, your confidence is shaken, and you end up delivering the presentation in "survival mode." You may survive the presentation and get through it, but it will not be successful in the eyes of your audience. This situation is very similar to a figure skater competing in a free skate program.

A free skate program lasts from four minutes (for the ladies) to four and a half minutes (for the men), which is a long time to be skating at a top level, performing leaps, spins, and jumps. Commonly, skaters will perform jumps in the beginning of the free skate program, as jumps require much energy, and skaters have the most energy in the beginning of their program. If a skater, in these first seconds of her program, attempts a jump and falls, most times the skater ends up not having as good a program as when the jump is made. The skater ends up not only thinking about the missed jump for the rest of the program, but her confidence is weakened, and she ends up trying to bring the rest of the program up to a high caliber level, instead of being able to focus on the "flow" of the program and focusing energy into delivering an awe-inspiring program. When this happens, skaters end up skating in "survival mode" to "just make it through the program," and thus, are scored lower by the judges. Just as you wouldn't want to be that figure skater who falls in the first couple of seconds of their program, you don't want to be that presenter who stumbles and falls in their introduction. Establish a positive tone for the rest of the presentation through the delivery of a good introduction.

Introduction Function 2: Gain the Attention of the Audience

As mentioned before, if you don't gain the attention of the audience, they won't listen to you. If the audience does not listen to you, there is no reason to give a presentation. The introduction needs to be used to get the audience to *want* to listen to you, through gaining their attention. You can gain the attention of the audience in numerous ways.

Relate Your Topic to the Audience

This first technique of gaining the attention of the audience is to relate your topic to the audience. If you can tell your audience why your topic is important to them, how it effects them, and how it is connected to other things important in their lives, then you will gain their attention. People want to know "what's in it for them" when listening to a presentation. By relating your topic to the audience, you satisfy the audience's question of why they should listen to you. In fact, even when you use the other techniques listed to gain the attention of the audience, you should still strive to relate your topic to the audience.

Using this technique to gain the audience's attention requires at least a minimal knowledge of your audience, so that you can tailor your introduction to them, thereby gaining their attention (review Chapter 4 and look ahead to Chapter 9, which both describe how to conduct an audience analysis). Once you have knowledge of your audience, you can then better relate your topic to them, as you'll know some basic demographic information about them, such as average age, race, gender, and education level. For example, let's say your audience is 20 of your classmates. You estimate the average age of this audience to be 20 years old, from a variety of places, about half male and half female, and all are in college. From this information, you could create an introduction for a presentation about healthy eating that begins:

Eating healthily is probably not high on your list of things to do. As college students we have little extra money, little extra time, and being young, are in good health generally, so why would we need to worry about eating healthily right now? I know that eating healthily costs more money than going out for fast food and takes more time to prepare than popping a frozen dinner into the microwave. However, being college students, we also don't get enough sleep, we are under a tremendous amount of stress at times, and in general we don't take care of ourselves. By eating healthily, we can feel better, have more energy, think more clearly, and our bodies will handle stress more effectively, thereby allowing us to be more successful in college.

This introduction relates to this particular audience because it centers on the notion of the audience being in college and introduces the issues that are faced while in college and how to contend with those issues through healthy eating.

Shock or Startle the Audience

The second method you can use to gain the attention of the audience is to shock or startle them. This shock could be either from something shocking that you say, or it could also be from a startling action you engage in. People tend to listen more when shocked; they hear something they didn't expect or see something they didn't expect and that alerts them to keep listening. This technique is often used by television newscast commercials. To get people to tune into the nightly news, news anchors will record a commercial about the upcoming newscast, to be played a few hours before the newscast airs. The anchor will say something such as:

Coming up at ten . . . 14 things in your home . . . . that can kill you!

The hope is that viewers will be shocked at hearing that and want to tune in to listen for more information. Another example is from a professor in medical school, teaching a mass lecture class of about 300 students. In the first class session, she told the students to look to the person on their left, and then look to the person on their right. After the students did this, she said:

The people you just looked at will either drop out or fail out of this medical school before you graduate.

This was perhaps not the most accurate way to say that two-thirds of the entering medical school students would not graduate from this particular medical school, but it certainly was a shocking way to present that fact, and it certainly gained the audience's attention. An example of using a startling action in your introduction might be blowing a referee's whistle to start a presentation on how to be an intramural basketball referee.

However you choose to shock or startle the audience, you'll need to make sure the "shock" relates back to your topic as well as to the audience, otherwise it may have the opposite effect on your audience (they will be wondering what your shocking comment or startling action has to do with your topic at hand).

Use Suspense

The simple notion of not revealing your topic until close to the end of your introduction is very effective at gaining the audience's attention:

Almost everyone in this room will experience this at some point in their lives. The pounding heart, the sweaty palms, the queasy stomach, the headache. You wished you didn't have to go through it, but you know you have to. You'll never reach your goals in life until you go through this awful, stressful, and intimidating process. It's inevitable. You worry about it for weeks until the day finally comes. You haven't been able to eat or sleep, you've been so nervous. But you know, if you are successful, this could be the gateway to the good life. What am I talking about? Finding love? Running a marathon? Serving on jury duty? No . . . . I'm here today to talk to you about how to be successful in your first professional job interview.

Using suspense in gaining the attention of the audience works because they will be constantly wondering what you're talking about. In general, using suspense works best if you can describe what your topic is without revealing it, in a way that the topic usually isn't described, such as in this job interview example. The thoughts and feelings leading up to an important job interview may be reflected accurately in the example, however, people usually don't describe going on an interview in that manner. Thus, the example's description of going on an interview gets the audience engaged in guessing what you're talking about and gains their attention.

Ask the Audience Questions

When you ask someone a question, you engage their mind to what you're saying, as they have to think about an answer to the question posed. Asking questions and thinking of answers to those questions is an active communication process. Once you get the audience's mind active in this fashion, then you will have gained their attention. The questions you ask in the introduction can be questions that you want the audience to answer, such as:

By a show of hands, how many people here have ever gotten a parking ticket on campus?

The questions asked can also be rhetorical questions, in which you do not expect the audience to answer. An example of a rhetorical question might be:

How does the parking patrol know the exact five minutes that I'm parked in an illegal zone to give me a ticket?

With either type of question, when you ask the audience to think about something in the form of a question, you actively engage their mind to what you're saying and gain their attention.

Use a Quotation

Often, there is no better way to say something than to quote someone else's famous words. When using a quotation in an introduction, you will gain the audience's attention as people like to hear familiar sayings spoken in relation to different contexts. Using a quotation gives the audience something familiar to listen to and focus on. Those familiar and positive feelings the audience experience from hearing you present a quote from someone else will foster familiar and positive feelings toward you, the presenter, and your topic. The audience will, by association, place those good and familiar feelings from the famous quote toward you and your presentation. Let's say you wanted to give a persuasive presentation with the purpose of persuading your audience to become more civically involved. A good quote to use in the introduction might be the famous quote from John F. Kennedy's Inaugural Address given on January 21, 1961:

> *"Ask not what your country can do for you, but ask what you can do for your country." At no time in the history of the United States is this quote more relevant than today; the economy is at the lowest point it's been in decades, the jobless rate is also at an all-time high and there is constant unrest and instability throughout the world. Isn't it about time you got involved in the processes and procedures happening in your world to make it better?*

In using this quote, you will gain the attention of the audience as there likely is not a person in your audience who has not heard this quote at least once in their lifetime. Because this quote is familiar, the audience will want to listen to your presentation more to discover how you will tie in the quote to the topic you're talking about.

Use Humor

The sixth method to gain the attention of the audience is to use humor in your introduction. People like to laugh. Hackman (1988) states that humor is extremely beneficial to those giving a presentation, as the notion of using humor to gain audience atten-

tion in a presentation has been around since the teachings of Plato, Aristotle, and Cicero. Just as in the other methods of gaining the audience's attention, you'll need to make sure the humor you're using relates to your topic and to your audience, otherwise, what you're saying will be more confusing to the audience than funny. For example, don't start your introduction with a joke about dogs unless your topic somehow relates to dogs. People might laugh, but they ultimately will be confused as to why you told a joke that had nothing to do with your topic. When they become confused they will stop listening to you, and then you have no reason to be giving a presentation. Being funny and relevant is the key, such as in this example introduction from a presentation about going to yard sales:

> *I don't like to admit it. I'm very ashamed of it. I have a horrible addiction. I know I'm supposed to be strong. I know I'm supposed to resist, but I just can't help myself. I drive by a "supplier" and no matter how strong my willpower is, I always give in and spend money when I shouldn't have. As you've probably guessed by now, I'm addicted, yes, I'm not proud of it, to yard sales. Like the old joke goes, a man was taking his time browsing through everything at a yard sale and said to the hostess, "My wife is going to be very angry when she finds out I stopped at a yard sale." "I'm sure she'll understand when you tell her about all the bargains," the hostess replied. "Normally, yes," the man said. "But she just broke her leg, and she's waiting for me to take her to the hospital to have it set." That may be a funny joke to you, but to me, that was last Saturday. As I said, I'm addicted.*

There are a couple of precautions you'll need to be aware of before you use humor in the introduction of your presentation to gain the attention of the audience. First, don't use offensive humor, which is humor that could upset or hurt the feelings of certain groups of people. If you think your humor might offend just one person in the audience, leave it out of the presentation. It would not be worth offending anyone (even just one) in the audience, as then they'll stop listening to you. Second, be sure you use humor that is funny to a majority of people. Remember, just because *you* find something humorous doesn't automatically mean that the audience will find it funny. Be sure to double-check your humor with others before you give your presentation.

Tell a Story

The last method to gain the attention of the audience in an introduction is to tell a story. Everyone loves a good story. Listening to stories allow the audience to "escape" the present and use their imaginations to get involved with the presentation. Kuyvenhoven (2007) describes storytelling as not only a way to gain the attention of a whole group, but also to engage them, to motivate them, and to inspire them. Being able to tell a good story in the introduction of a presentation is powerful! Here is an example of a story told in a presentation about adopting a dog from the shelter:

When we walked into the shelter, "Admiral," the beautiful Newfoundland we were there to look at and potentially take home, was being led into an SUV by another family who had just adopted him! Imagine our utter disappointment and how the children's spirits were crushed. Admiral was going to be our oldest daughter's Christmas present and now, that wasn't going to happen. We decided to look at the other dogs in the shelter, as perhaps there was another dog that we'd like and want to adopt. We wanted a bigger dog, and with that limitation there wasn't much choice: Thunderbolt, a beautiful one year old black lab, and Fred, a very big and older yellow lab.

The kids and I checked out Thunderbolt first. He was a beautiful dog: shiny black coat, lean body, perfect proportions. However, when we got him outside on the grass, he did nothing but scare my two littlest children to death. Thunderbolt, true to his name, ran as fast as he could away from us, stopped, turned, and then came charging right at us all the while barking! Right as he would get back to us, the process would start over again. After picking up the kids and convincing them that Thunderbolt did not want to eat them, we got Fred outside. Fred, upon seeing our kids, leisurely walked over to them and gave each a big lick! Then Fred proceeded to flop on the ground, roll over, and insist we scratch his belly. Needless to say, Fred is now a member of our family.

This is a good example of how stories gain the attention of an audience. Not only is this story about a subject that most can relate to, but it also includes many descriptors of the dogs, as well as including action that has to be imagined by the audience, all of which gain their attention.

Remember, the story you tell in an introduction could be a real, true life story that actually hap-

pened, or it could be a made-up story in order to get your point across. All in all, telling a story gets the audience engaged in your presentation so that they want to hear more.

Overall, when gaining the attention of your audience through the introduction, don't be afraid to use these techniques in combination with each other. For example, you could tell a shocking quote, or a humorous story, or a shocking and humorous quote from a story. There is no limit to how creative you can be in gaining the attention of your audience.

▌ Introduction Function 3: Establish Your Credibility and Sincerity with the Audience

The third function of the introduction of your presentation is to establish your **credibility** with the audience. As you remember from Chapter 4, this type of credibility is called **derived credibility**. This is a very important subject in relation to getting your audience to want to listen to the rest of your presentation. If the audience doesn't perceive you as being credible, they will not trust you. If your audience doesn't trust what you're saying, they'll stop listening to you and you have no reason for giving a presentation. Therefore, you need to establish your credibility with the audience in relation to your topic and your presentation.

How do you establish credibility in your introduction? One of the most effective and easiest ways is to be sincere. Simply being genuine when you speak will do much to get people to see you as credible. If your audience perceives you as being sincere and "real" as you talk to them, they will give you more credibility than if they perceive you as being insincere or "fake." We are all human beings and as such, we generally have a good idea of when someone is not being sincere with us. Remember the Michael Nolan quote that says:

People are far more interesting and successful when they are less concerned about being normal, and more concerned about being natural.

Thus, to be sure to be seen as credible, be sure to be real.

Another way to establish your credibility in the introduction of your presentation is to tell your audience why you're an "expert" in the topic you're presenting. You may be an expert in your topic because you've participated in it for years, or you may be an expert in your topic simply because you've researched it and learned about it for the presentation. Either way, you'll need to let the audience know they should listen to you about the topic. The trick is to present this in a way that is neither bragging nor off-putting to the audience. As stated before, be sincere and be humble about what you know, but do let the audience know why you're an expert. Your statement to establish your expertise in your introduction may be as simple as:

> *In my ten years of working at an ice cream store, I've seen all combinations of flavors, toppings, and techniques to making sundaes. In my experience, there are three main ice cream sundaes that can be created: the traditional sundae, the fruit-based sundae, and the always popular "un-sundae," or the sundae that doesn't look like a sundae, but rather looks like some other kind of dessert, such as a brownie, cake, or cookie with ice cream on top.*

This example illustrates a very subtle way of letting the audience know why this person is an expert in ice cream sundaes. By simply stating, "In my ten years of working at an ice cream store" the speaker is sincerely and humbly telling the audience why they are an expert on this topic. This speaker did not brag about how much experience they had nor did they offend the audience by telling the audience how much more they knew about ice cream than the audience did. The speaker simply stated why the audience should listen to them regarding the topic of ice cream sundaes. Stating your expertise in this manner will establish your credibility with the audience, which will allow them to trust you and thus want to listen to you and your presentation.

Introduction Function 4: Preview the Main Points of the Presentation

The final function of your introduction is to preview the **main points** of your presentation. You must remember that your audience has nothing to go by in relation to your presentation except for the words you speak. They won't have an outline, they won't have an overhead or PowerPoint of your presentation, and thus you'll need to tell them specifically what you'll be talking about for the remainder of the presentation. Think about it as giving your audience a "roadmap" to where you're going to go in the presentation. Without this roadmap, they'll get lost. If your audience gets lost, they'll stop listening to you and there is no reason for giving a presentation. To ensure that you don't lose your audience, you've got to make it easy for them to listen to you. A good way to do this is to preview the main points of your presentation.

Previewing your main points should be done as a transition statement (for more information on transition statements, review Chapter 5) at the end of your introduction, transitioning into the body of your presentation. The trick is to make the preview flow from the end of your introduction to the beginning of the body of the presentation. In other words, your preview needs to "fit" with the rest of the presentation and enhance it. Again, taking the little bit of extra time to make sure your preview flows with the rest of the presentation will make your audience want to listen to you and the rest of your presentation. For example, you could preview the main points of your presentation by simply stating:

> *The rest of my presentation will inform you on what you should wear to a job interview, what questions you should be prepared to answer in the interview, and what to do when the interview is over.*

This example is not necessarily a bad preview of the main points, but it could be much better. It doesn't flow as well as it could or should from the introduction nor to the body of the presentation. The preview would be better stated:

> *You've just heard one of my humorous experiences in going on a job interview. As you remember from my story, I didn't wear the right clothes, I was not prepared to answer questions, and I didn't know what do to at the end of the interview. So, this presentation will focus on these three areas of interviewing: how to dress for an interview, questions you should be prepared to answer in an interview, and what to do when the interview is over. First, your potential employer will notice how you're dressed before all else, so let's discuss this first.*

This example of previewing main points is much better than the first example. The presenter was able to make it flow from the introduction to the body of the presentation seamlessly. This main point preview example gives a great "roadmap" to the audience, outlining the three main points to be discussed, and has good flow, which makes it easy for the audience to listen to the presenter, which will make them want to listen to the rest of the presentation. This presenter has made it easy for the audience to want to keep listening. Of course, if you get your audience to keep listening to you, and you keep presenting your topic, at some point you'll have to end your presentation. To do that, let's discuss conclusions.

Ending Your Presentation – The Conclusion

As stated in the beginning of this chapter, the introduction is the most important part of any presentation. However, that doesn't mean you can nor should forget about the rest of the presentation. In fact, other than the introduction, the conclusion of a presentation is the second most important element of your presentation. Before your audience stops listening to you, before they start applauding for you, and before they move on with their lives, your audience will hear your conclusion. In Chapter 5 you learned that your conclusion should be about 10% of your presentation. That 10% of your presentation is your last opportunity to retell the audience what you want them to remember from your presentation, and it is also your last opportunity to make the audience feel glad they took the time to listen to your whole presentation.

Not only is the conclusion of your presentation the second most important element of the presentation because it will be the last thing your audience

Image © Feverpitch, 2009. Used under license from Shutterstock, Inc.

will hear from you, but it is also important because the conclusion of a presentation must fulfill four functions. Your conclusion must, 1) Signal the end of the presentation, 2) Review the main points of the presentation, 3) Wrap up the presentation and create psychological unity for the audience, and 4) Leave the audience with a lasting and positive impression of you and your presentation.

Delivering an excellent presentation in the eyes of your audience not only hinges upon delivering a good, solid, and confidence-boosting introduction. You must also have a great conclusion so that the audience will walk away not only saying how great you and your presentation were, but also walk away being excited about and remembering what you said about your topic. Let's look at each of the four "conclusion functions."

Conclusion Function 1: Signaling the End of the Presentation

Earlier in this chapter, you read about giving your audience a "roadmap" of your presentation in the form of previewing your presentation's main points in your introduction (Introduction Function 4). That was a preview for the body of the speech. Through that preview in your introduction, the audience will know what your main points in the presentation will be. However, your audience will not know when you'll be done speaking about your last main point unless you consciously signal the end of your presentation into your conclusion. This is important.

It's important to signal the end of your presentation because, as stated before, you want to be audience centered, and in being audience centered, you want to make it easy for the audience to listen to you. You do not want the audience to have to work hard to listen to you because then they will stop listening to you. If your audience stops listening to you, then you'll have no reason to give a presentation. In signaling the end of your presentation, you are making it easy for the audience to know where you are in your presentation (building upon your "roadmap"). That gives them a sense of security and comfort. People like to know where they are, not only when driving somewhere, but also when they're watching a movie (how many times have you checked your watch during a movie to see how much time was left in the movie) or listening to a presentation. To satisfy the need of the audience to know where they are in your presentation, you need to signal the end of your presentation through your conclusion. There are a couple of ways you can do this.

The first way to signal the end of your presentation in the conclusion is by using transition statements or signposts (for more information, review Chapter 5) at the beginning of the conclusion. For example, this could be one way to signal the end of a presentation about hockey in a conclusion:

> *In sum, hockey is a fantastic sport. Although not as popular as the big three sports of football, baseball, and basketball, its fans and proponents are crazy with hockey fever. These people truly believe that no other sport exists. It is this loyalty to the sport of hockey that ensures that future generations will come to know and play the greatest sport on ice.*

A second way to signal the end of your presentation is to indicate the ending or closure through non-verbal cues. These cues are usually done unconsciously by most people, but you'll want to make sure you do this consciously to have an effective conclusion. Things like raising the pitch of your voice in the first sentence or two of the conclusion and slowing down just a bit in your rate both indicate to others that your presentation is coming to an end. This technique is quite apparent in the last story of a newscast on TV. The anchor will often start the last story with something like,

> *And finally tonight, a skateboarding bulldog riding his board down the street. Isn't he cute.*

The anchor raises the pitch of her voice on the "And" and then slows down for the rest of the sentence, so much so that the last part of the sentence ends up sounding almost choppy, "...isn't....... he.......cute" with long pauses in between each of those words. In doing this, the anchor indicates to the viewers that she is wrapping up the newscast, which lets the viewers know where they are in the newscast and know they should mentally prepare for the ending of the newscast.

Conclusion Function 2: Reviewing the Main Points of the Presentation

The second function of the conclusion is to review the main points of the presentation. This is a very important function with your conclusion at this point, you reiterate the few thoughts from the body of the presentation you want your audience to remember. You will always be fighting a losing battle when it comes to trying to get the audience to remember what you've presented, as your audience will only remember 50% of what you just presented. By telling the audience the main points of your presentation for a second (or perhaps third) time, there is a greater chance the audience will remember at least your main points after you speak. You are also helping the audience remember more of your presentation by doing this review in your conclusion, as this review of the main points will be one of the last things the audience hears from you. The more recent that information is given to people, the more likely they are to remember it.

Conclusion Function 3: Wrapping Up the Presentation and Creating Psychological Unity for the Audience

Part of a good, effective conclusion in a presentation is to use the conclusion to wrap up the presentation. There is nothing worse than to listen to an entire presentation and then be hit with the ending, out of nowhere, with no warning. Again, people not only like to know where they are within the presentation, but they also like to listen to an ending that wraps everything up and ties loose ends together.

For example, have you ever watched a movie and as you're watching the action unfold, you think to yourself that the ending of the movie better bring closure to the storyline, because as of right now, you don't see how the movie will wrap up or make sense? If the movie does a good job of wrapping the storyline up and the movie ends in a way that makes you think "Wow, that was a great ending!...I was worried the story wasn't going to make sense, but the ending of the movie really solidified the entire plot," then the writer of the movie created an effective ending to the movie that wrapped up everything. Compare that feeling of "Wow, great ending" to the feeling you get after watching a movie that did not do a good job of wrapping up the storyline in the ending. Usually your feelings from this type of ending run from "Wow, that was confusing" to "Wow, that was a terrible movie!" simply because there was no wrap up. This is also why people love a good mystery. A good mystery story is written in a way that makes the reader wonder how seemingly disconnected elements within the story will make sense and contribute to the telling of the complete story by the end of the book. When this happens, and the author wraps the book up nicely, the reader finds the conclusion satisfying and enjoys the book that much more, much like puzzle pieces that fit together to make a beautiful picture.

In addition to wrapping up the presentation in the conclusion, if you are able to reference back to something you said in your introduction you can create **psychological unity** within the presentation. Bringing a quote, concept, or story into the conclusion that was first introduced in your introduction allows you to connect with the audience one last time. It's much like putting a big beautiful bow on the package that is your presentation. For example, let's say you were giving a presentation on the history of the presidency of the United States, and you started your presentation with a quote from Abraham Lincoln to gain the attention of the audience. A way to create psychological unity in the presentation would be to use another quote from Abraham Lincoln in the conclusion. The final reference back to Lincoln in the conclusion will be psychologically satisfying to the audience in that their mind will have made a connection back to the introduction and overall they will get a feeling of "oneness" or "completeness" from your presentation. The audience will then have a lasting and positive impression of you and your presentation, which is the last function of your conclusion.

Conclusion Function 4: Leaving the Audience with a Lasting and Positive Impression of You and Your Presentation

The last function your conclusion should serve is to create a lasting and positive impression of you and your presentation. If you present your material well throughout the entire presentation, then you already have planted that positive impression "seed." However, presenting your material well, although needed and important, will not necessarily leave your audience with a lasting and positive impression of you and your presentation. To do this, you'll need to create a fantastic ending remark, one that leaves your audience awestruck and wanting

more. Like the saying goes, "End with a BANG, not with a whimper!"

Ending your presentation with a final, absolutely "killer" last thought will ensure that your audience will not only remember you and your presentation well after you stop speaking, but will also ensure that they will think positively about you and your presentation. It would be self-defeating if you had an ending remark that created a negative lasting impression of you with your audience. Therefore, your final thought to end your presentation needs to be something that will give the audience positive feelings toward you and your topic. A way to accomplish this is to be diligent, thoughtful, and to work hard to craft that final sentence that will be the very last thing your audience hears from you. Often it is too easy to come to the conclusion of your presentation, be "burned out," and not give your final remark any forethought at all. In this instance, you would not leave your audience with a lasting and positive impression of you, but rather, your audience would simply forget about you and your presentation as soon as you stopped speaking. Therefore, develop the last remark of your presentation to the same quality that you developed your very first remark in the introduction of your presentation, and you will always "leave them wanting more!"

Chapter Review

There is nothing more important in your presentation than creating and developing a good, solid introduction and conclusion. Taken together, these two elements of your presentation can "make or break" the audience's impression of you and your presentation. The introduction and conclusion literally begin and end your presentation, and as such, serve vitally important roles. If your introduction doesn't have enough power to set the tone of the presentation, gain the attention of the audience, establish your credibility and sincerity toward the audience, and preview the rest of the presentation, then, like a freight train engine that didn't have enough horsepower to pull the rest of its cars, your weak introduction will not be able to sustain the rest of your presentation. By the same token, if your conclusion fails to signal the end of the presentation, review the main points of the presentation, wrap up the presentation and create psychological unity for the audience, and leave the audience with a lasting and positive impression of you and your presentation, then like a caboose of a train that has derailed and pulled the rest of the train off the track, your weak conclusion will drag the rest of your presentation down in the minds of the audience.

Thus, work hard to create great introductions and conclusions. Make it easy for your audience to want to listen to you and your presentation, and make it easy for your audience to remember you and your presentation in a positive light. As countless coaches have told athletes throughout the years before games, "Start strong and finish strong." The fate of your presentation is dependent upon having a stellar introduction and conclusion.

Application Questions

1. Why is the introduction considered the most important part of a presentation?

2. About what percentage of the presentation should be your introduction?

3. What are the four functions of an introduction?

4. Why is it imperative that you set a good tone for your presentation in the introduction?

5. How many ways can you gain the attention of the audience? What are they?

6. Why do you need to establish your credibility in the introduction of a presentation?

7. Which function of an introduction is like a "roadmap" for your audience? Why is it important?

8. Why is the conclusion an important part of a presentation?

9. About what percentage of your presentation should be your conclusion?

10. What are the four functions of a conclusion?

11. Why do you need to signal the end of the presentation?

12. What are you helping the audience accomplish when you review your presentation's main points in the conclusion?

13. Why should you wrap up your presentation for the audience in the conclusion of the presentation?

14. What is psychological unity and how is it accomplished in the conclusion of a presentation?

15. How can you leave a lasting and positive impression of you and your presentation with the audience?

Introductions and Conclusions

Song Starters

Purpose:

To recognize and identify how the beginning (introduction) of a song is able to set the tone of the song as well as gain the attention of the listener, and to make the connection of how a presentation introduction needs to do the same.

Materials needed:

Access to songs and a way to play them.

Time:

15-20 minutes.

Directions:

1. Divide students up into small groups of 3-4 students per group.

2. Explain to the groups that you will play the beginning (introduction) of a popular song and they are to listen, discuss, and write down the ways in which the song sets the tone for the rest song and gains the attention of the listener.

3. Play 4-5 beginnings of songs.

4. Discuss and debrief. Some questions to ask the students: How did the song introductions set the tone for the rest of the songs? How did the song introductions gain your attention? In what ways are these examples like the introductions for your presentations? What can be learned from the beginning of songs in relation to your introductions?

Name: _____   Date: _____

Movie Conclusion Fusion

Purpose:

To recognize and identify how the endings (conclusions) of movies can signal the end of the movies, can wrap up and create psychological unity within the movie, and can leave the viewers with a lasting and positive impression of the movies. This activity should make the connection of how a presentation conclusion needs to do the same.

Materials:

None.

Time:

25-30 minutes.

Directions:

1. Divide students up into small groups of 3-4 students per group.

2. Explain to the groups that they are to select 4-5 popular movies, and they are to discuss and write down the ways in which the movies either do a good or bad job at signaling the end of each movie, wrapping up and creating psychological unity within each movie, and leaving the viewers with lasting and positive impressions of each movie.

3. Discuss and debrief. Some questions to ask the students: Why did each movie do a good or bad job in their respective endings? If bad, how could the movies have had better endings? How did you feel if the movie ended "well"? How did you feel if the movie ended poorly? What is the connection between movie endings and the conclusions to your presentations? Similarities? Differences?

The GAA (Gain the Audience's Attention) Game

Purpose:

To identify, create, and develop effective ways to gain the attention of the audience in the introduction of a presentation using the methods outlined in the chapter (relate topic to the audience, shock the audience, use humor, etc . . .).

Materials Needed:

None.

Time:

25-35 minutes.

Directions:

1. Divide students into small groups of 3-4 students per group.

2. Explain to the groups they are to come up with 5 topics for presentations. For each topic, they are to use at least one method of gaining the audience's attention to develop an effective introduction that gains the attention of the audience. Each of the 5 topics needs to utilize different methods of gaining attention. Once each group finishes developing a short introduction for each topic, have each group present their introductions to the class. The class must figure out which method of gaining attention was used for each topic.

3. Discuss and debrief. Some questions to ask the students: Was each group able to gain your attention? Why or why not? Are some methods of gaining attention more effective than others? Why or why not? Do the choice of topics influence which method of gaining attention should be used?

Websites for Further Investigation

Introductions:

1. *http://www.speechmastery.com/speech-introductions.html*

2. *http://www.toastmasters.org/Members/MemberExperience/MeetingRoles/Toastmaster.aspx*

3. *http://aresty.rutgers.edu/resources/Presentations_files/frame.htm*

4. *http://www.articlebiz.com/article/233130-1-how-to-deliver-a-killer-speech-introduction/*

Conclusions:

1. *http://www.colorado.edu/communication/courses/comm1300/selfexa.htm*

2. *http://faculty.riohondo.edu/jameen/class_speech_outline_examples.htm*

3. *http://homeworktips.about.com/od/speechclass/ss/writeaspeech_4.htm*

References

1. Hackman, M. Z. (1988). Audience reactions to the use of direct and personal disparaging humor in informative public address. *Communication and Research Reports, 5*(2), 126-130.

2. Kuyvenhoven, J. (2007). "What happens inside your head when you are listening to a story?": Children talk about their experience during a storytelling. *Storytelling, Self, Society, 3*(2), 95-114.

7

Powering Your Presentation with Presentational Support

Cami Pierce Duffy

CHAPTER OBJECTIVES

At the end of this chapter, you will be able to:

- Identify the purpose of presentational supports in presentations
- Identify the types of presentational supports available for use in presentations
- Avoid the pitfalls of not practicing with presentational supports
- Recognize the benefits and drawbacks of using each type of presentational support
- Appreciate the importance of practicing with presentational support

The Power of Presentational Support

We are visually oriented as a society and use visual aids in a variety of ways including but not limited to when we are:

- giving directions,

- explaining how an item works or functions,

- recounting the fun of the past weekend,

- pointing to historical events in our personal lives or in society,

- trying to persuade our parents for money or to support something that will cost them more money,

- exclaiming the wonders of a new product or service that we love,

- documenting our excitement, sadness, frustration or confusion during an event

The fact is that words are an integral part of communication but images and visual accompaniment enhance the spoken word to re-emphasize, bolster, clarify, and illuminate the content in ways that words alone or visual images alone cannot do. The launching of new concept technology such as YouTube® and Instagram® are societal responses to the growing need for visual stimuli. In short, visual aids provide precision for your communication interactions and your life.

While visual images tend to captivate the audience and enhance the verbal message being communicated, any presentation could benefit from any one or more of several types of presentational support (pictures, graphs, charts, multimedia presentations, drawings, etc.) Presentations can be enhanced using presentational support that repeat, substitute, or compliment the verbal messages used by the speaker. Good speakers understand the value of presentational support and recognize that presentational support and verbal messages are equally important and mutually necessary.

Image © iophoto, 2009. Used under license from Shutterstock, Inc.

The Purpose of Presentational Support

Vital Questions to Consider

There are a variety of reasons for using presentational support in an oral presentation. When thinking about how you might enhance an oral message with presentational support, your first consideration should be: What do I want the presentational support to do? What is its function?

And this leads us to a second vital consideration. Presentational support is used to strengthen a specific part of your presentation – a specific main point, a particular piece of evidence, a specific process.

Presentational supports are not last minute add-ons to a presentation after the content has been constructed; nor should the support type chosen be an afterthought or requirement. Presentational support should only be used when you can determine that it would add value to a point in the presentation – an idea being communicated orally – at the time. Presentational support is used for a specific purpose at specific times and places within your presentation. Microsoft has asserted that the motivation behind the PowerPoint© software is to give "power to your points." That is, it adds value to specific ideas in your presentation rather than serving as an attractive yet distracting transcript of the presentation. Remember, if everything is on the power point, there is no need for you.

▌ *Seven C's Method for Adding Value*

As you contemplate the use of presentational support, you will want to keep these methods in mind to ensure that inclusion of the support will assist the audience in understanding both the oral message and the visual message and their connection. There are seven (7) methods for adding value to your presentation: To provide clarity, create emphasis, carveout connections between the audience and the speaker's ideas, conjure up memorable ideas, give your presentation more concrete meaning, reduce speaker anxiety, and minimize lengthy explanations in presentations. Let's look specifically at each of the seven to illuminate the value of each.

1. Clarity

Presentational supports can provide clarity to a presentation when words alone cannot express the message in the exact way the speaker intended. For instance, if you were giving a presentation on how to complete a voter registration card, immediately you recognize the detail involved and how quickly a listener might become lost as you detail the process. To provide clarification for the audience during this segment of your presentation, you might choose to enlarge a sample voter registration card to assist your audience in following the steps. Your motioning to each portion of the card as you discuss the steps will make this presentational aid both memorable and helpful for your audience.

2. Create Emphasis

Presentational supports can emphasize key points of your presentation when the words you've chosen seem to fall short of the complete message you intend to share. In another example, to demonstrate your passion for intolerance for broken laws or other criminal activity you might decide to strike the podium with your fist as you deliver the content you would like to emphasize. Your simple assertion that you feel strongly for or against a particular idea does not send as strong a message as those exact words coupled with a timely knock on the podium as you speak.

3. Connections

Presentational supports can provide "links" between your spoken word and the message comprehension for your audience. These connections can mentally trigger common experiences for your audience members. For instance, a connection could be made for the audience by placing a picture of a baby on an overhead projector and then asking the audience two questions: "What are your initial thoughts when looking at this picture?" and "Is this baby worth saving?" The speaker can then transition into a moving persuasive presentation about how appropriately used car seats can save the life of a baby. Using connections common to most audience members can help draw in the interest of the audience at different points of your presentation.

4. Conjure Lasting Memories

Speakers craft their presentations with the hope that the audience will perceive the presentation as quite memorable. Presentational supports can certainly help the speaker achieve this goal. Since your audience will most likely forget a large portion of your presentation, having presentational supports that grab the audience's attention can increase the audience's retention of the material. If you were to use a computerized presentation software package to animate and automate your presentational supports as opposed to using the standard types of mediums (poster board, transparencies, handouts, etc.), your audience will remember the novelty of the presentational support as well as the message content you are presenting.

Keeping your presentational supports novel and different will also increase the likelihood that your audience will walk out and remember something more from your presentation than simply the title. If indeed one of your key goals is to be remembered for your presentation . . . diversify and be different!

5. Concrete

Presentational supports bring a certain level of solidarity to your presentation. Your words are in many ways very abstract to your audience. Presentational supports help to solidify your meanings in the minds of your audience and make your presentation both comprehendible and memorable.

For many of you, you have built a comfort level in speaking abstractly rather than concretely. For example, you might talk about the importance of dressing for success in a presentation about interviewing well. Every audience member has a different set of experiences and perceives "dressing for success" differently. However, having models wearing the clothes you are describing or using enlarged photographs of these clothes will increase the "common understanding" of your message.

6. Convey Certainty

Practice and preparation are key to reducing your anxiety. However, presentational supports can, for even brief moments, transfer the attention of the audience from you, the speaker, to the actual presentational support. This will provide an opportunity for you to gather yourself and mentally prepare for the next point as you are explaining the presentational support.

7. Concise Explanations

Presentational supports can minimize lengthy explanations in your presentations. At several different points in your speaking life, you will struggle for the exact words to use in your presentation to convey a particular message. In this instance, you are searching for a preciseness that words cannot achieve. For example, to show the impact of drinking and driving, a videotape of a drunken driver's car wrapped around a telephone pole might convey your message in a shorter time frame than an extra ten minutes of explanations.

In short, presentational supports must serve a purpose in a presentation. Presentational supports cannot stand alone in a presentation, nor should they detract the audience's attention from you for extended periods of time. You've reviewed the purposes for a presentational support; now, let's review the types of presentational supports available for your presentation.

Types of Presentational Supports

With so many types of presentational supports . . . which one should you use? There are several types of presentational supports available for use. Some presentational supports will yield better results than others, depending on the presentation situation. In any case, you will want to familiarize yourself with the following presentational support types:

- Objects
- Models
- Assistants
- Photographs
- Multimedia presentations and slideshows
- Posters
- Transparencies
- Graphs
- Charts
- Audio, video, and handouts
- Pictures
- Speaker's own body

Objects

Objects can provide clarity for your message especially when the object is unfamiliar to the audience. In the event that you deliver an informative presentation about the adventure of rock climbing, you quickly recognize that the gear used in this sport is important for the audience's understanding. You then make arrangements to secure the actual gear used to rock climb for display purposes during your presentation. Actually being able to see the object(s) will help the audience understand the tools much better than just simply speaking about the tool usage. Be very careful though; there are always some objects not suitable for the classroom or the speaking situation. Be sure to get permission from your instructor or from the person/entity who invites you to speak before preparing your presentational supports. The worst thing for your presentation is to display or use inappropriate presentational supports that put your audience in a negative frame of mind towards the subject matter and/or the speaker.

Models

Models are used as presentational supports when the actual object is too small or too large to be used during the presentation. For example, a student giving a presentation about examining a car prior to leasing would want to use a model of a scaled-down car as opposed to the life-sized version, which is too large for use in a presentation, especially in a classroom. Speakers should note that models can be both costly and time consuming. You will want to keep this in mind as you plan your presentation.

Assistants

Sometimes the speaker will want to use his/her body as a presentational support. However, there are presentational situations that complicate this possibility. In those instances, the speaker will want to use an assistant. If the speaker felt that a role play was best to illustrate a procedure or action, an assistant may be employed. The speaker and the assistant will certainly want to rehearse the role play multiple times to ensure a smooth integration into the presentation.

Photographs

Photographs give you the flexibility to display your presentational support when you may not have access to the actual object or a model. With the advent of digital cameras and one-hour photo processing, you can have pictures at your fingertips within hours or minutes of taking the picture. You should note that pictures must be large enough to be seen from all sides of the room. Photos that you carry in your wallet or that sit on your desk at home are not appropriate. Enlargements would be necessary, and for many pictures, enlargements, while increasing the size of the photograph, do not maximize the quality of the photo. Keep this in mind as a limitation as you decide if a photograph is among the best ways to visually share the information with

the audience. Additionally, the vantage point of the photograph is also important. For instance, a close-up of the impact point for the first plane versus a wide shot of both towers would allow the audience to see the devastation caused by both planes.

Speaker's Own Body

You may use your own body as a presentational support. If you were asked to give a presentation about sign language, you would use your hands to demonstrate the different signs. You may even use your own body as you are giving a presentation on CPR to demonstrate the exact placement of the hands. You will want to be careful to not turn your back on the audience.

With your back turned, you are blocking the line of sight for the audience. Turning your back on the audience subconsciously signals to the audience that it is acceptable to ignore the speaker.

Additionally, the speaker will also want to be mindful of the clothing worn on speech day if use of the speaker's body will be employed. Loud or extremely vibrant colors or patterns can be very distracting. Soft or muted colors and patterns are best.

Presentation Software: PowerPoint or Prezi?

Considering designing an exciting presentation but struggling to decide between the traditional Microsoft PowerPoint, and Prezi, the newer, non linear software tool? Which one will help you accomplish your goal? Which one will help you motivate the audience to take a desired action? While both have benefits, they both also provide some limitations. To help you, the speaker, make an informed decision, both offerings follow.

PowerPoint

What is it?

Microsoft PowerPoint® or PowerPoint is a presentation aid multimedia tool created by Microsoft in 1990. PowerPoint is a slide-based presentation software for presenting ideas in a linear format proceeding from one slide to the next. Then in 1997,

Microsoft added features that would allow transitions for each slide and nonlinear movie-like styled effects for the files created by speakers. The speaker, as they design the PowerPoint output, places media (pictures, graphs, text, video, audio files, and other presentation media) on a number of individual pages or "slides." The slide terminology is a reference to slide projectors that were once used and are now fairly obsolete or in rapid decline today. The output can be printed, displayed on a computer, or navigated based on the prerogative of the speaker. The output is generally projected onto a screen using a video/data projector. Today, many PowerPoint presentations are the basis of webcasts. PowerPoint features three types of moments: entrance, emphasis, and exit of items on the slide/page itself; transitions between slides; and custom animation. PowerPoint provides many features that offer flexibility and the ability to create professional quality presentations. The speaker also has the option of customizing the slides in a different way than was originally planned while preserving the original document. For instance, the speaker may want a particular slide to reappear several times throughout the speech and that option is readily available in PowerPoint. The presentation software allows users for to work offline and captures the speaker's work in a .ppt file format. Further, the software also provides Americans with Disabilities Act (ADA) accessibility features for enjoyment by the entire audience.

However, while popular, PowerPoint is highly abused by speakers around the world. Unfortunately, this software has lulled speakers into delivering painful, embarrassing, confusing, and lackluster presentations. If the presentation is poor in quality in the first place, PowerPoint will only highlight and enhance these weaknesses for the audience. Edward R. Tufte (2004), author of *The Cognitive Style of PowerPoint* echoes this sentiment in an entire book stating that "Presentations largely stand or fall on the quality, relevance, and integrity of the content. If your words or images are not on point, making them [words] dance in color won't make them relevant."

Tufte goes on to state the following about PowerPoint: ". . . rather than supplementing a presentation, it has become a substitute for it [presentation]. Such misuse ignores the most important rule of speaking: Respect your audience." PowerPoint presentational support should follow the same usage guidelines noted for other types of presentational support. PowerPoint can seem pretty overwhelming especially when the speaker has 100 slides for a four-minute presentation.

Advantages of PowerPoint

1. **User friendly** – technically PowerPoint is very simple to use. Microsoft Office programs (PowerPoint, Word, and Excel) are taught in school, so most people have at least some familiarity of how the software works.

2. **Control** – PowerPoint provides seemingly endless possibilities when it comes to slide design. You can choose from an endless amount of colors, fonts, graphics, and backgrounds.

3. **Builds, transitions, and animations** – you can use these visual enhancements to add to the explanatory power of the presentation and also enhance your visuals.

4. **Hyperlinks** – allow you to click on a link and be taken directly to the links location on the web or somewhere else in the presentation.

5. **Syncs with SlideShare** – lets you upload your presentation to the web so anyone can view your presentation online.

6. **Can print handouts of the slides** – allows audience to follow along without having to focus on writing notes on the presentation.

7. **Charts and tables** – help you present various sets of data.

Challenges in the use of PowerPoint

Despite the fact that PowerPoint has become the standard "go to" software when putting together presentations, everything has advantages and disadvantages, so PowerPoint is no exception.

1. Death by PowerPoint!

The benefit of delivering a presentation with interesting graphics, avoiding the time-draining efforts of drawing by hand, minimizing the amount of items the speaker will need to transport, is overshadowed often by the poor use of the software. Users often refer to this phenomenon as "Death by

PowerPoint" (coined by Angela R. Garber), "PowerPoint Poisoning" (coined by Scott Adams of *Dilbert*) or "PowerPoint death march." It is important that speakers understand that they are the instruments by which the speech is delivered NOT the PowerPoint. In other words, the PowerPoint cannot give speech itself. Remember that PowerPoint is a tool not a speech delivery mechanism.

2. Customization overload

While Microsoft PowerPoint® allows the speaker to take advantage of countless different font sizes, types, colors, etc., those offerings need not all be employed in one PowerPoint or it overwhelms the audience and creates an opportunity for the audience to disengage from the speech. This customization also creates large file sizes, especially when audio, images, and video are added, which makes e-mailing the file frustrating. Speakers can use cloud storage websites such as Dropbox® to share larger file sizes.

3. Convenient prop for speakers

PowerPoint is dazzling and attractive, but it should not serve as a prop for the speakers or a way to deceive the audience into believing you adequately prepared for the speech. PowerPoint makes it easy to simplify complicated messages into bullet points, which can elevate the style over the substance of the presentation.

4. Tedium

Too many slides is often an issue of tedium for the audience, causes boredom, and prompts the speaker to "just read from the slides." Too many slides is also a sign of unpreparedness on the part of the speaker.

5. Automation

Automation of the PowerPoint slides to advance after a preestablished time period is the subject of anxiety for many speakers who fail to recognize that no matter how you practice with a multimedia presentation, the live presentation will almost certainly demand that the speaker allow for variations to analyze and respond to the needs of the audience. For instance, should the speaker explain a concept and notice puzzled looks on the faces of those in the audience, the speaker should then recognize that a subsequent explanation or example is needed to help the audience understand the content. If your slides are automated, the slides will not align with the content you are discussing at the moment and serve as a distraction to the audience. Audience analysis is not the only reason that automation of slides is an issue, in fact, when speakers either increase or decrease the cadence in which they speak, the slides (timed/automated) will be out of sync with the speaker causing embarrassment and/or anxiety. It is recommended that you save the automation of PowerPoint for tradeshows or vendor booth setups which provide for an automated multimedia slide show that does not require a speaker and is repeated on a loop for those who pass by the booth.

Quick Guide to Creating a PowerPoint presentation

1. You start by clicking on the PowerPoint icon.
   a. Once the program opens up, choose a template (you can always switch it later if you don't like the template).
   b. Choose the New Slide button, then click "OK."
   c. Click in the title place holder and type in a title for your presentation.
   d. Click the New Slide button, and then double-click on a layout for the next slide.
   e. Add your content, then repeat steps c and d for each new slide.
   f. When you finish, save your presentation (Choose Save from the File menu).

2. *To edit a slide*: In slide sorter view, double-click on the slide you want to edit.

3. *To delete a slide*: In slide sorter view, click on the slide you want to delete and press the delete key.

4. *To add clip art or photos* from the built-in clip art gallery:
   a. Click on the Insert from the menu and choose pictures or the Clip Art button.
   b. Locate the clip you want to add and double-click on it. (You can also choose your own files at this point.)
   c. Drag the clip to the position you want.
   d. You can also use copy and paste in the usual way to add clip from another document.

5. *Adding slide transitions*:
   a. Select the slide or slides where you want to add the transition.
   b. Choose Slide Transition from the Slide Show menu.
   c. Choose the transition you want from the effect pop-up menu and then select any other options you want.
   d. Applying the transition features:
      i. To apply the transition to the selected slide(s): Click the Apply button.
      ii. To apply the transition to all slides: Click the Apply to all button.

6. *Changing slide order*:
   a. To move a slide: In the slide sorter view, drag the slide to its new position.
   b. Cut/copy/paste: You can also cut, copy, and paste slides in the slide sorter view.

7. *Showing the Slides*:
   a. Choose Slide Show from the View menu or choose the miniature projector screen in the bottom right-hand corner of the PowerPoint window.
   b. To advance to the next slide, click the mouse button or press the right arrow key. (To return to the previous slide, press the left arrow key.)
   c. To end the slide show, press the ESC key.

8. *Creating handouts*:
   a. Choose Master from the View menu and then click Handout Master.
   b. Click the buttons on the Handout Master toolbar to locate the handout you want.
   c. Add any text or other items you want to the Handout Master.
   d. Click close on the Master Toolbar.

9. *Printing slides*:
   a. Choose Print from the File menu.
   b. Choose the Settings feature.
   c. Choose Print All Slides option.
   d. To print Handouts version: Choose 3 slides handout option which yields three slides per page with lines to the right for notes, etc.
   e. To print miniature of slides: Choose 6 slides handout option which yields six slides per page.
   f. Then click Print icon.

10. It would be impossible to include all of the instructions for all of the different versions of PowerPoint available for use. If something is not working, choose the "Help" feature or "?" option for specific instructions on how to access these options on your version of PowerPoint.

Tips for the use of PowerPoint

1. Use the PowerPoint CheckUp Checklist to address many of the common errors found when speakers use the software. (The Checklist can be found in the Activities section at the end of the chapter.)

2. Make your titles headlines, not descriptions. Each slide is a valuable piece of real estate in that you are adding information to the story you are trying to convey, so don't waste a single slide. For instance, "2014 Revenue" is a description rather than "2014 Revenue Soared 32%."

3. Give your audience a roadmap. The audience will be more comfortable if you let them know where you are headed. An agenda slide can help provide some order to your presentation so that the audience always knows where you are in the presentation.

4. Don't give your presentation software center stage. This is a huge mistake since the presenter has clearly forgotten that PowerPoint is a tool designed to augment their presentation and not replace the speaker in the presentation.

CheckUp!—Checklist to remedy errors in PowerPoint

Using a checklist to audit your PowerPoint presentation during the preparation phase of crafting your speech is a great way to remove those hurdles to the success of the speech. The activity section of this chapter provides a checklist that you may photocopy for each speech in which you plan to use PowerPoint.

▌ *PREZI*

What is it?

Prezi is another presentation aid multimedia tool created in 2009. Prezi is a cloud-based presentation software for presenting ideas on a virtual platform instead of the traditional slide-by-slide format featured in Microsoft PowerPoint®. The product employs a zooming user interface which allows the speaker to zoom in and out of the presentation to display and navigate the content in a more fluid manner than its Microsoft PowerPoint counterpart. The speaker, as they design the Prezi output, places media (pictures, graphs, text, video files, and other presentation media) on a canvas and navigates between the media. The paths identified in Prezi are navigational sequences that connect the media for the purpose of designing a linear presentation. The cloud-based presentation software allows users for a fee to work offline and captures the speaker's work in a .pez file format. For those speakers who decline the fee-based offline option, the speaker's work is saved online and remains an open-source end product for others to see or use. Additionally, there are file size and other limitations to the use of Prezi online.

Challenges in the use of Prezi

1. Zoom, zoom, zoom, STOP!

The zooming user interface, although interesting because it provides motion and movement not present as a feature for its competitor Microsoft PowerPoint, can cause issues for those individuals with motion sickness and has been known to induce nausea. This side effect for the audience should be an important consideration for the speaker since the goal is to avoid inducing experiences for the audience that are unpleasant and will be long connected with the speaker in negative ways. Additionally, dynamism and a nonlinear structure work well for many presentations, but may not work well for all content or presentations. For a history presentation displaying a world map could benefit from the zoom in and out feature to focus on particular places on the map or a timeline; however, if the goal were to simply reveal one continent or a specific person's portrait, zooming in and out may not be a benefit. In fact, many audience members may find the zoom and spinning features quite distracting despite the merit of the content of the presenter.

2. Customization limited

While Microsoft PowerPoint allows the speaker to take advantage of several different font sizes, types, colors, etc., those offerings in Prezi are minimal and could limit the impact the speaker intended to have on the audience. Of course, for a fee, a speaker could

upgrade from the free or student discounted version of Prezi to the premium version, but for a fee the offering is for limited file space and storage.

3. Presentation Aids and Accessibility

Since Prezi is a flash-based zooming user interface tool, a majority of the presentation cannot interface with screen-reading devices utilized by individuals with disabilities. There are two tools that can be used to assist those individuals with disabilities who use Screen Reading software. The first tool is called "Image Alt Tags" which are invisible descriptions of images which are read aloud to users on a screen reader. The second tool is called "iframes" which allows one HTML document to be embedded within another HTML document and can be read aloud to users on a screen reader. For example, in Microsoft PowerPoint, the speaker can add alt tags to images which enables the accessibility for individuals with disabilities. Given that your audience can be made up of a diverse group of individuals, it is wise to employ a presentation aid that is accessible and permits the entire audience to enjoy your presentation aid tool. In many speaking situations, speakers have been required to provide an accessible Microsoft PowerPoint version of the presentation originally prepared using Prezi because it makes good business sense to think of those that represent the audience you serve.

4. Internet access required

Web based format is ideal to address computer compatibility issues when students jump from computer to computer or when working with a team on different sections of a presentation, however, there are downsides to Prezi's web-based format. Speakers must prepare an alternative means of delivering the presentational aid in the event that internet access is limited, unavailable or intermittent. One remedy has been to have the speakers create a PowerPoint presentation as a backup or to deliver the speech without a presentational aid.

5. No printable content

If you wanted to have a printout of your presentation so that you can practice with the material or provide handouts for reference later, you will be disappointed since that is not an option with Prezi.

6. Learning curve

While there is often a learning curve with any new software, in the event that you are short on time to self-teach, you may want to pass on Prezi and save its use for a later presentation after you have learned the features and usage. It is fairly simple in nature but will take some time to increase your comfort level with the platform. In fact, the software is in many ways not intuitive since the software lacks "standard" functions found in PowerPoint coupled with the Path function. It is important to note that users should set up the path according to how the audience will jump around the canvas. The manner in which the pathways are set can be difficult to figure out. Prezi is definitely outside the comfort zone for many nondesigners, but you can learn the software if you are willing to invest the time to put into practice.

7. Integration limitations

Unlike PowerPoint, graphs and flowcharts, as well as other images, have to be created external to Prezi and integrated into the presentation.

Quick Guide to Creating a Prezi

1. You start by opening your preferred Internet browser (Internet Explorer/Mozilla Firefox/ Chrome).

2. In the URL bar fill in http://www.prezi.com and press enter on your keyboard.

3. When you reach the Prezi homepage you'll be presented with a lot of pretty graphics, but don't get distracted, click "**Sign Up**" in the top right-hand side of your window.

4. Now you should be presented with three main options and two suboptions, don't jump straight to the free option (especially if you're a student), take your time to choose the right option for you.

5. If you choose the plain free option, proceed as follows (if you choose the student option skip to step 6):

   - Fill in the empty fields **first name, last name, email, and password** (don't forget to verify your password) **OR** you can sign up using Facebook (handy).

   - Tick the Terms and Conditions box.

   - Then click "Register and Continue" at the bottom of the page.

   - Boom! You can now start making your very first Prezi presentation (it's simple).

6. If you chose the student option (like me), then you're in for a few extras.

7. All you need to enter is your e-mail address in the empty field and press continue and you should be ready to go!

Benefits of the use of Prezi

Prezi works very well for those speeches that:

1. Contain complex visuals needed to completely understand the topic especially those with different elements that you will need to focus on varying points during the presentation. For instance, if you were talking about parts of a computer, you as the speaker may well want to return to the overall diagram of the computer throughout the presentation. Prezi makes that simple to do with the "path" feature, whereas with PowerPoint, you would have to recopy that slide with the diagram in each place it needed to reappear in the presentation.

2. Highlight the relationships between different visual or textual information.

3. Address issues of scale, both literal and conceptual.

Tips for the use of Prezi

1. **Use the Prezi CheckUp Checklist to address many of the common errors found when speakers use the software. (The Checklist can be found in the Activities section at the end of the chapter.)**

2. **Think of Prezi as a canvas and not a slide.** Prezi unlike PowerPoint is not a set of slides or pages. Consider a "big picture" approach where the full canvas conveys the message to the audience. Another way to think of Prezi is that similar to a "concept map."

3. **Be mindful of the motion sickness factor.** Slow down the speed of the zoom and turns. You may want to insert an intermediate point on the path to assist you with minimizing this "side effect." Use rotation and spinning to highlight key points only rather than for everything.

4. **Be creative.** Consider structuring your Prezi around a thematic concept, story, or metaphor which provides a visual framework for the audience to follow.

5. **Think simple!** Minimize the number of steps on the path and deal with only one concept at a time. Eliminating unnecessary information also helps.

6. **Aim for uniform design conventions.** If the audience cannot see it because of contrasting colors or too small text, the content is useless. Use the same font types and sizes and formats since it helps the audience quickly discern between headings and content or items you wish to highlight.

7. **Spend some time getting to know how to use Prezi.** The Prezi website www.prezi.com provides some great tutorials.

8. **Create your structure first.** Making it up as you go will lead to a disjointed Prezi. Jot down on a piece of paper what you want to appear in Prezi in terms of content and the order you want the content to be viewed. Draw, in effect, a concept map.

9. **Utilize frames and invisible frames.** You'll want to use something other than the standard brackets.

10. **Size.** Images will fill the screen when you zoom in on a graphic or item. If the item is originally smaller than the full screen size, it will look GRAINY and unprofessional. A small picture might look okay as you are designing it because it is not full screen; however, if you zoom in on just the scale . . . you get something that will not look professional.

CheckUp! Checklist to remedy errors in Prezi

Using a checklist to audit your Prezi presentation during the preparation phase of crafting your speech is a great way to remove those hurdles to the success of the speech. The activity section of this chapter provides a checklist that you may photocopy for each speech in which you plan to use Prezi.

▌*PowerPoint versus Prezi: The Choice*

Regardless of which software you choose, a speaker must commit time and energy to continuously practice presentation skills for a winning presentation.

Both software platforms have their place but whichever tool you select, take the time to master the tool to create engaging and useful rather than dull and listless presentations. Be mindful that if your presentation without the presentational aids is poor or ill prepared; PowerPoint and Prezi will only heighten that feature. Similarly, if your presentation is engaging and well crafted, PowerPoint and Prezi will add value in conveying your message to the audience. The power of the presentation comes from the effective preparation and delivery of the speech, not from PowerPoint or Prezi. A final axiom to consider, a BORING and listless format/content yields a BORING presentation no matter which platform you use!

▌ Overall Delivery with Multimedia Presentations

There are three essential delivery strategies for multimedia presentations to avoid multimedia overload.

Method ONE: 10-20-30 rule credited to Guy Kawasaki has a three pronged philosophy that some have dubbed as "PowerPoint Math."

Philosophy: Only 10 slides should be used by a presenter for a speaking period of 20 minutes and the font should be no less than 30 point font.

Ten slides is optimal and ensures that your PowerPoint presentation will be brief and not languish on into 50, 70, or 100 plus slides, which robs the audience of their attentiveness for your presentation. Generally speaking, the audience wants the facts, they want the facts quickly and under no circumstances does the audience want to strain or squint to read the content on the slides. As a matter of fact, please remember that a slide is not a canvas for your research paper meaning that you attempt to cram every detail on the slide in 10 point font! Further, remember that your audience ingests a massive amount of information daily and they really want to avoid wading through 100 plus slides to really digest the 4–10 slides with the key content. So, make the PowerPoint presentation short, sweet, and big!

Method TWO: 6 × 6 rule

Philosophy: Limit your slide to 6 words per line and 6 lines of text per slide.

We have all witnessed presenters reading from a two-paragraph slide to the audience, which makes the entire experience painful and boring to watch. Remember this, your audience does not want a slide-reader, they want a presenter. This is a fantastic method to remain organized and not overwhelm the audience—or yourself! Other presenters will argue for the 7 × 7 or reference an 8 × 8 rule, which provides you with one to two more lines of text and one to two more words per line. However, the goal is to reduce wordiness and make it easy for your audience to mentally process the meaning of your message in that 5–7 second window of time when they are initially exposed to the slide.

Method THREE: One concept per slide

Philosophy: Remember to keep your audience in mind, so it is often best to feature one concept per slide, if possible while focusing on key words and phrases. Another payoff with this method is the focus on editing for brevity (use nouns and verbs, eliminate unnecessary verbiage).

General technical tips that can impact the power of your multimedia presentation

Tip 1: Avoid being the font-a-holic syndrome. Keep in mind that your PowerPoint presentations will substitute fonts that you used to match those fonts installed on the machine displaying the PowerPoint presentation when your font and the fonts available on the machine do not match! You are strongly encouraged to use the widely installed fonts: Times New Roman, Verdana, Arial, and Tahoma.

Tip 2: Avoid using grainy or poor images. It is important to prepare early to select graphics that have a high resolution and project clarity.

Tip 3: Avoid the random slide phenomenon. Create a slide master which will maintain your slide background color, fonts, and bul-

lets used in a consistent fashion. Audiences love consistency. As an added bonus, if you load your presentation on a machine without the font you used, you can quickly change the font in the master for an almost flawless update.

Tip 4: Avoid understating what is important when using charts. Explode a pie slice or change the pie chart color scheme to emphasize the data to be highlighted. Strongly highlighting data helps listeners who to best grasp the important points.

Tip 5: Avoid inconsistency in resolution. Varying resolutions for photos you employ in presentations that you plan to use in different ways will lead to presentation disaster. Keep in mind this quick reference tip: 150 dpi (dots per square inch) for projected images, 96 dpi for PowerPoints that will be e-mailed, and 220 dpi or higher if you intend to print the slides.

Posters

In as much as posters are used in high school and were highly accepted, as a presentational support to be used in your career, posters fail miserably. Very few people are skilled at creating a professional poster. Alternatively, even those few skilled persons choose not to take the inordinate amount of time needed to create a professional poster given the vast array of mediums available. Additionally, posters provide a limited means for the speaker to make corrections, are difficult to transport to the presentation site, and pose challenges if the speaker's handwriting is less than legible. In fact, most of what can be done to a poster to make it a presentational support just doesn't match up to the other alternatives.

Transparencies

Transparencies are inexpensive ways to provide presentational supports for the audience.

A transparency is a thin, acetate film that when used with an overhead projector magnifies the image to three or five times the original size. Transparencies prevent you from spending countless hours creating a presentational support. To create a transparency, simply use your word processing software on your computer. Create the transparency using a large enough font size and type to be read and use graphics that are easily seen and reproduced in a black and white format. Speakers who photocopy charts, graphs, tables, etc., from textbooks for use on a transparency will be disappointed. These direct photocopies will rarely be sufficient for use on a transparency without significant enlargement efforts. The best alternative is to recreate the chart on the computer. Note that transparencies can be reproduced in color, but the cost significantly rises in comparisons to black and white reproductions.

As flexible as transparencies are, this flexibility can be a downfall. You will want to take care with your transparencies as the print may remove easily with scratches and bends to the film. Use a folder or notebook to keep the transparencies flat. Additionally, you will want to check the spelling on your transparency before the day of the presentation. If errors are found, you will need to create a new transparency.

Charts and Graphs

Charts and graphs are great ways for you to display large amounts of information for the audience. Charts are excellent for displaying categories or steps in a process. Audience members can easily follow the flow of the presentation when charts are used to supplement your presentation.

Graphs are good to help you clarify statistical information. For many students, statistical information is difficult to comprehend. For this reason, you will want to make any statistical portions of your presentation as concrete as possible by using charts or graphs. This helps the audience avoid mental aerobics or a tug of war to comprehend your presentation content. Graphs can also show comparisons or trends in your presentation content. Many computer software packages make creating graphs an easy task.

Handouts, Video, and Audio

All three of these presentational supports require some practiced techniques to integrate into your presentation smoothly and effectively. These presentational supports will require leading the audience into the presentational support you will use and debriefing the audience once you have finished with the presentational support. For instance, a stu-

dent preparing for a demonstration presentation on the process of manufacturing homemade clay may decide to use a handout to detail each step of the process. This speaker will want to hold the handout until the end of the presentation to maintain the interest of the audience. Speakers using the handout in this way are providing information to aid in the retention of the information.

Handouts

Handouts are wonderful retention tools for your audience. Many handouts that you will use should provide a summary of information for your audience to take with them following the presentation. Handouts lose their effectiveness if distributed during a presentation or before the presentation because they serve as a distraction for your audience. Usually, if there is information you'd like your audience to work with during your presentation, transparencies or multimedia presentational software works best at meeting both your needs and the needs of the audience. You can prepare the audience for the presentational support by saying, "Now that we have walked through the process together, I have a handout for each of you to take with you that will enable you to repeat this process at home."

Video/DVD

Videos are great tools in your presentational support "toolkit" as well; however, poorly edited videos can be your downfall during a presentation. You will want to practice, practice, practice, with the video each time to ensure your comfort level in its use. Always preview for the audience what they will see in the video clip and debrief them on what they've seen once the clip has ended. This will assist the audience in following your message.

Audio

You may also do a presentation that lends itself well to using sound in the introduction or during the first main point. You should preview the audience by saying, "Before we get into the essentials of meditation and relaxation, I would like you to sit in your seats and close your eyes. As you listen, pay close attention to what you hear and how you feel." Always have your audio and videotapes cued to the place you would like them to begin. Otherwise, you consume too much time searching for your video segments.

MP3 players like iPods now make it easy to cue the audio content to the exact place you wish to begin.

Multimedia Presentations and Slideshows

Multimedia is a coupling of media and content that combines different media formats. Multimedia can include combining such media as: text, audio, photographs, video, interactive websites, broadcasts, etc., via computerized electronic media processing devices (i.e. media players, etc.). Multimedia presentations animate and automate several presentational supports for the audience. These can be used to integrate color, slides, videos, sound, graphs, and even charts into well coordinated presentational supports. These types of presentations can also be used to integrate Web page content into your presentation. While this is a fantastic way to grab your audience's attention, this too can detract from your message. Multimedia presentations are usually easily converted into transparencies, charts, etc., should the speaker encounter a mishap at the presentation site that renders the multimedia presentation inaccessible.

For today's fast-paced world, presentational software has replaced the formerly used slide projectors to provide an inexpensive way of producing animated presentations. These types of presentations prepare you for those types of presentations you will give during your career-related work. Please note that in reference to your career-related work, there are high expectations of demonstrating competency when using presentational software. To be successful using this medium, practice is both necessary and

Image © Alexander A. Kataytsev, 2009. Used under license from Shutterstock, Inc.

critical. Additionally, it is key that that a backup plan be ready and available for speakers using this medium. The best way to achieve this backup plan presentational support is to take each of the components (video, photos, etc.) and prepare them as individual presentational supports to ensure that you have access to each if the technology fails on-site. A poorly prepared multimedia presentation could be fatal to the credibility of the speaker. While technological mishaps occur, you, the speaker must be prepared to move forward in your presentation despite the mishaps while not drawing attention to the error. While there are standards and guidelines that apply to any presentational support, multimedia presentations are especially scrutinized. Elaborating on the shortcomings of a particular presentational software product would be unsuitable as the software rapidly changes to address shortcomings and add new features. Speakers are always best served to become familiar with the software available and test drive sample presentational support to discover problem areas. You may also want to consider how you might deliver your presentational support if power was unavailable.

For those of you who enjoy using presentational software, be wary that too many different fonts, pictures, animations, colors, etc., can be distracting. Understand that your audience will stop listening to you and choose to watch your presentational supports only. The same holds true with videotapes. If you decide to use a brief selection from a videotape, you will want to preview for the audience what they are about to see and then debrief what was shown.

Slideshows are not as popular today as they once were. Today, slides are more expensive to produce, and the equipment to operate the slides is not as readily available. Multimedia presentations have quickly replaced these types of presentational supports and provide pictures that are crisp and clear and that can be arranged and rearranged at will. A multimedia presentation provide much more flexibility than its slide show predecessor.

Guidelines for Presentational Support

As you prepare your presentational supports, keep your audience in mind. You can think of being in the audience for a presentation where you struggled to see or understand the presentational support being used. Likewise, you can also think of situations where you sat and listened to a presentation without presentational supports. When you craft your presentation, you want your use of presentational supports to fall between these two extremes to help you illustrate the key points of your presentation. Effective speakers will use the following guidelines in preparing presentational supports:

1. Establish why you want to use the presentational support. Think about the purposes of a presentational support.

2. Keep it simple. Presentational supports should be simple and free form complications and clutter. Will the audience have an "Ah Ha!" moment or a "Huh?" moment?

3. Use color and sizes effectively . . . don't overdo it. Two or three colors are enough to maintain emphasis and allow the audience to keep track of your point during your presentation. Using more than three colors or sizes will result in confusion for your audience. Choose softer colors for text and bolder colors for titles and words to be emphasized.

4. Use font carefully and effectively. Fonts have two categories: serif and sans-serif. Serif fonts have appendix generally referred to as "feet" and typically are used in publications where space is limited (i.e., newspapers and magazines). Examples of serif fonts are Times New Roman, Garamond, and Book Antiqua. Sans-serif fonts are fonts that are clean letter form and generally can be displayed properly on different operating systems, unlike their serif counterparts. Examples of sans-serif font are Arial, Helvetica, Verdana, and Tahoma. Cute, elaborate, or ornate serif fonts are great for invitations but horrible for presentational support use. Stick to fonts like Times New Roman and Arial which are typically found on most operating systems. These are easy to see, regardless of font size.

5. Use one font size for the titles and another font size for the text. Most text should be at least 32-point font to be seen, and a 38-point font should be used for titles. Remember that your presentational supports must be seen from any seat in the room. Using presentational supports that are too small or difficult to read is a huge disappointment for you audience.

6. Proofread . . . proofread . . . proofread. Look for errors. Have a friend double check your presentational supports for errors to avoid embarrassing situations.

7. Use no more than six lines of text down and six words across on any presentational support. You want to maintain a frame around your presentational support that can be seen clearly from any point in the room. Creating presentational supports outside the aforementioned guideline increases the likelihood that the words will run off the surface of your presentational support (screen, poster board, etc.) or cause the audience to struggle to see the text. Text on your presentational supports should be in key word format, not full sentences, to curb your tendency to read from the presentational support and minimize a cluttered appearance.

8. Pictures chosen must be larger enough to be seen from the back of the room. Effective speakers keep their audience in mind at every stage of the presentation creation process. You will want to consider how the room is arranged and how difficult it might be to see from any seat in the room. Start with pictures that are at least $8 \frac{1}{2} \times 11$ in size. This is the smallest size you will be permitted to use.

9. Minimize the use of animation as it consumes a great deal of data space and has the tendency to be unreliable on presentation day. Most animation is a huge distraction and does not help your presentation.

10. Most Internet video websites cannot be advanced to the point which you would like to display. Attempt to find a site that arrives at the display point otherwise the audience has to sit through lengthy unintended footage.

11. Consider the aesthetic aspect to your presentational supports. You will want to make sure that you carry the visual "theme" throughout for the benefit of the audience.

Image © Diego Cervo, 2009. Used under license from Shutterstock, Inc.

12. Continuity is important to your presentational supports. You can continue an icon, logo, black border, sidebar, background color, text color, etc., throughout.

13. Be sure to check your grammar and spelling on your presentational supports. Nothing is as embarrassing as having "too" on a presentational support where you meant "two." Spell-check will not catch that misspelling because it is spelled correctly.

14. Make sure your visual can be seen by the entire audience as well as from the back of the room.

Seven Keys to Effective Practice with Your Presentational Supports

Practice is critical for effective use of your presentational supports in your presentation.

1. Practice with the presentational support in the same way you plan to use the presentational support during the presentation.

2. Never display the presentational support until you are ready to use it. Allow the presentational support to remain concealed from the audience until you are ready to use it and remove the presentational support once you are finished. Otherwise it could be distracting.

3. Plan on what you will say while the video clip is being played, while you are walking over to the presentational support, etc.

4. Always prepare to give the presentation without the presentational support in the event that the presentational support malfunctions, there is equipment failure, or the equipment is unavailable for use.

5. Always have a backup plan.

6. Decide how you will best arrange the space where you will be delivering your presentation. Make sure you, the podium, and other presentational supports are not blocking each other.

7. Always visit the location where you will be giving the presentation prior to the presentation to forecast any needs you will have and to assist in planning a effective presentation.

Tips for Using Presentational Supports in Your Presentation

1. Never block your presentational supports with your body or another presentational support.

2. Always have a "lead-in" statement or preview statement in reference to a presentational support.

3. Always share the significance of the presentational support with the audience. Explain the presentational supports . . . don't leave the audience to wonder why you are using it.

4. Place speaking cues in your speaking outline to remind you when to display the visual and when to remove it.

5. Make sure your presentational supports are in the order you will use them to avoid experiencing confusion at the podium.

6. If you are using your body as a presentational support, make sure that when demonstrating you can be easily seen throughout the room.

7. It is acceptable to point toward a screen, but avoid blocking your audience's view.

8. Preparing your presentational supports early will provide an opportunity to check for grammatical errors.

9. Practice with your presentational supports to avoid choppy integration into your presentation.

10. Always include a citation at the bottom of your presentational supports. Using presentational supports without citing the source is unethical and is equivalent to plagiarism.

Chapter Summary

The selection and strategic use of the best presentational support can aid in the audience's comprehension, retention, and interest regarding your topic. Presentational support can take on many forms (visual, audio, etc.) and come in a variety of types ranging from charts to multimedia presentations. In short, the more complicated the presentational support, the higher the expectation from the audience for the speaker to demonstrate his/her competency. Employing the content from this chapter will benefit the student beyond the classroom into their chosen career path leading to presentation confidence and competency.

Web Resources

PowerPoint© Tutorials

■ Function X PowerPoint© Tutorial *www.funcationx.com/powerpoint*

■ PowerPoint 2000© Tutorial *http://www.bcschools.net/staff/PowerPointHelp.htm*

■ PowerPoint© Tutorial for Windows and Mac *http://www.quasar.ualberta.ca/edit202/tutorial/PowerPoint/PowerPoint.htm*

PowerPoint© Tips & Tricks

■ PowerPoint Tips and Tricks *www.bitbetter.com/powertips.htm*

■ Awesome Backgrounds *http://www.awesomebackgrounds.com/powerpointtips.htm*

■ Awesome pictures on PowerPoint© *http://www.awesomebackgrounds.com/powerpointgraphics.htm*

Powering Your Presentation with Presentational Support

Starting from Scratch: Creating Vibrant Presentational Supports

Student Textbook Instructions: Get into groups of 4 or 5 and review the presentation topics in the table below. For each presentation topic listed in the table, brainstorm three presentational supports that could be used for each presentation and some brief rationale regarding the effectiveness of this presentational support choice.

Presentation Topic	Presentational Support 1 & Rationale for Use	Presentational Support 2 & Rationale for Use	Presentational Support 3 & Rationale for Use
"The Three Basic CPR Techniques"			
"The Three Basic Steps in Applying for Graduate School"			
"The Basics of Creating a Resume"			
"The Three Basic Parts of a Winning Essay"			
"The Three Parts of a Crisis Plan for a Tornado"			
"The Life of Ice Skater Michelle Kwan"			
"Handwriting Should Be Taught in High School"			
"Identity Theft Criminals Should Get Life Sentences"			
"U.S. Citizens Earning Less than $45,000 Per Year Should Be Exempt from Paying Taxes"			

Rogue Presentational Supports

Rogue presentational supports are those presentational supports used inappropriately in a presentation. Completing this activity will assist you in using presentational supports effectively as well as giving constructive feedback to your classmates. In groups, review the scenarios listed below, identify the rogue presentational support, and make suggestions for better presentational support use.

Presentation 1

Susan was all set to give her first presentation on "creating origami animals." She began with a great introduction, gave a preview of her presentation and then proceeded to hand out a sheet of colorful paper to everyone in the audience. She explained that the audience could participate as she was giving her presentation. Susan then returned to the podium, placed the piece of paper on the podium, and began to fold the paper several times without pausing. Susan's audience seemed confused because they couldn't see the paper being folded. Once Susan was done she exclaimed, "Now there! The steps are few, the process is quick and easy, and now everyone can now do origami!" The class was then given an opportunity to give Susan feedback.

Identify the rogue presentational support(s): (What did Susan do wrong?)

Suggestion for better presentational support use:

Presentation 2

Adam had just gotten a new suit and he wanted to make sure that he looked nice for his upcoming demonstration presentation on "How to plaster a damaged wall." Adam chose to use a large bucket he filled with plaster, a plastering tool, and a piece of plastered wall with a hole in it. Adam had done this several times when he worked for his dad, but he didn't practice his presentation. As Adam was demonstrating how to apply the plaster, some of the plaster fell onto Adam's new suit and also on his shoes. Adam ignored the accident and continued delivering the presentation. After the presentation concluded the class was given the opportunity to give Adam feedback.

Identify the rogue presentational support(s): (What did Adam do wrong?)

Suggestion for better presentational support use:

Presentational Support Buddy Check

For this activity, your instructor has asked you to bring in your presentation and your presentational supports. Choose a classmate and exchange presentations and presentational supports. Now, using what you've learned in the textbook, evaluate your classmate's use of presentational supports for their upcoming presentation. Be tactful but honest in your appraisal of their "draft" version of this presentation and the potential effectiveness of their presentational supports. Space has been provided under each checkpoint for your comments.

Buddy Name: _____

Topic Chosen: _____

- Font size is large enough to be seen from the back of the room

- Appropriate number of colors have been used to emphasize key points but minimize distractions

- Text on presentational support is in key word format

- Pictures are large enough to be seen

- Free from spelling or typographical errors

- No more than six lines of text down and six words across the presentational support

- Free from clutter

- Presentational support is appropriate for the topic chosen

- Other suggestions for improvement

PowerPoint CheckUp

Make a copy of this sheet for each presentation in which you plan to use PowerPoint. Next to the PowerPoint issue, make a note of whether your PowerPoint commits this offense and make a note of what needs to be done to address the offense or place a checkmark to denote that your PowerPoint presentation is free of this issue. Include this sheet with your preparation outline to demonstrate to your instructor that you have audited your PowerPoint to increase the likelihood of a successful presentation.

PowerPoint Offense	If yes, describe your strategy to Address Offense	No, offense free
Did you use PowerPoint to mask your unpreparedness?		
When you practice your speech with the PowerPoint, are you standing in a location that would block the audience's view of your PowerPoint?		
When you practice your speech with the PowerPoint, are you reading to the audience?		
Does your PowerPoint use text that is too small or has font/typeface that is illegible for the entire audience?		
Does your PowerPoint provide images/graphics that are blurry or difficult to see by the entire audience?		
Does your PowerPoint provide at the bottom of the slide the citations of the images/graphics and/or content that are not your own original work?		

PowerPoint Offense	If yes, describe your strategy to Address Offense	No, offense free
Does your PowerPoint provide too much text on any of the slides in your presentation?		
Does your PowerPoint provide a blank slide at the beginning and end of your presentation to avoid returning to the computer view?		
Does your PowerPoint provide slides that have grammatical or spelling errors?		
Does your PowerPoint provide irrelevant or unconnected information to the topic which could confuse your audience?		
Does your PowerPoint include a background color that makes the text color you have chosen difficult to see or read?		
Does your PowerPoint include poorly constructed graphs, charts, or other matter that would reflect poorly on the speaker?		
Does your PowerPoint provide excessive animation?		
Does your PowerPoint have automation settings or automatic timing applied?		

PowerPoint Offense	If yes, describe your strategy to Address Offense	No, offense free
Does your PowerPoint provide inconsistencies in color and fonts on each slide?		
Does your PowerPoint provide statistical information for which the speaker has not addressed or explained in the speech content?		
Does the speaker have a backup plan should the power or the equipment fail rendering the PowerPoint useless during the speech?		
Has the PowerPoint been test driven in the location that you plan to use it to ensure that videos/movies open appropriately, audio clips open, YouTube clips open, and there are no other issues with media added to the presentation?		
If using YouTube or another media file online or offline, has the speaker taken care to ensure the starting point begins precisely at the starting point of the section that will be used if the entire file is not essential?		
Does the PowerPoint have too many slides?		

Name: _____ Date: _____

Prezi CheckUp

Make a copy of this sheet for each presentation in which you plan to use Prezi. Next to the Prezi issue, make a note of whether your Prezi commits this offense and make a note of what needs to be done to address the offense or place a checkmark to denote that your Prezi presentation is free of this issue. Include this sheet with your preparation outline to demonstrate to your instructor that you have audited your Prezi to increase the likelihood of a successful presentation.

Prezi Offense	If yes, describe your strategy to Address Offense	No, offense free
Did you use Prezi to mask your unpreparedness?		
When you practice your speech with the Prezi, are you standing in a location that would block the audience's view of your Prezi?		
When you practice your speech with the Prezi, are you reading to the audience?		
Does your Prezi use text that is too small or has font/typeface that is illegible for the entire audience?		
Does your Prezi provide images/graphics that are blurry or difficult to see by the entire audience?		
Does your Prezi provide at the bottom of the slide the citations of the images/graphics and/or content that are not your own original work?		

Prezi Offense	If yes, describe your strategy to Address Offense	No, offense free
Does your Prezi provide too much text on any of the slides in your presentation?		
Does your Prezi provide a blank slide at the beginning and end of your presentation to avoid returning to the canvas view?		
Does your Prezi provide slides that have grammatical or spelling errors?		
Does your Prezi provide irrelevant or unconnected information to the topic which could confuse your audience?		
Does your Prezi include a background color that makes the text color you have chosen difficult to see or read?		
Does your Prezi include poorly constructed graphs, charts, or other matter that would reflect poorly on the speaker?		
Does your Prezi provide excessive zooming and twisting?		
For your Prezi, have you made an effort to slow down the zooming and twisting to avoid the "motion sickness effect" for the audience?		

Does your Prezi provide inconsistencies in color and fonts on each slide?

Does your Prezi provide statistical information for which the speaker has not addressed or explained in the speech content?

Does the speaker have a backup plan should the power or the equipment fail, intermittent Internet connectivity, or absence of the Internet connection rendering the Prezi useless during the speech?

If using YouTube or another media file online or offline, has the speaker taken care to ensure the starting point begins precisely at the starting point of the section that will be used if the entire file is not essential?

Has the Prezi been test driven in the location that you plan to use it to ensure that videos/movies open appropriately, YouTube clips open, and there are no other issues with media added to the presentation?

Does the Prezi have too many slides?

8 Delivery: It's Not Only What You Say but How You Say It

Crystal Rae Coel Coleman, M.A., J.D.

CHAPTER OBJECTIVES

At the end of this chapter, you will be able to:

- Describe the four ways to deliver presentations
- Explain the importance of clear language
- Demonstrate the devices for making the language of a speech more vivid
- Explain how words can be perceived differently
- Use of rhythmic devices to enhance delivery
- Demonstrate the seven vocal qualities that are necessary to vary for message impact
- Identify the key areas of nonverbal communication
- Demonstrate a four-step method for impromptu speaking
- List tips for delivery in mediated communication settings

D r. Martin Luther King, Jr., Adolph Hitler, Elizabeth Dole, Barbara Jordan, Ghandi, Saddam Hussein: their messages were different – The emotional impact on their listeners was just as strong.

It is about *what* you say; but it's also about *how* you say it. It's not nice to call a friend *stupid*, but it's unlikely he/she will be upset if you're laughing as you say it. However, if you call that friend *stupid*, while raising the volume of your voice and while creating an angry expression on your face, it's very possible that an altercation will take place. The words we choose to use and the way we choose to use them will impact the listener's perception of us as speakers. The words we use and how we use them will make or break friendships, romances, and business relationships.

When it comes to presentations, the content and coherency of a message is necessary if you want to make a lasting impression. However, absent a dynamic delivery, the effect will be minimal. Think about school. All of the classes are important, but usually, the classes that have the most impact on us are the ones in which instructors had interesting, unique, or dynamic delivery styles. Therefore, all speeches should be written and delivered for maximum impact or what's the use of doing them? IF YOU DON'T HAVE ANYTHING TO SAY, AND YOU DON'T KNOW HOW TO SAY ANYTHING WELL – WHY SAY ANYTHING?

This chapter focuses on four key areas: the four ways to deliver a presentation, verbal delivery, visual delivery and a four-step process for any public presentation in or out of the classroom. There are also some tips for techniques in mediated communication settings. The written text in this chapter is minimal because the verbal and nonverbal exercises should be heavily implemented after a basic understanding of each principle is explored.

READ, LISTEN, LEARN, WRITE, AND DELIVER!

Four Ways to Deliver Your Presentation

Reading Your Manuscript

Anyone can write something and read it word for word. Reading is ONLY necessary when complicated material is being presented. Financial reports, reports on healthcare, press conference information (where the attorney has approved the information) are examples of presentations that warrant reading. If you have complicated statistics or scientific data, reading that information is acceptable so that you won't misquote something or present incorrect data. However, you still should not have to read the entire presentation from start to finish; you should only have to read the sections with the complicated information.

Reading direct quotations is always acceptable. For-profit and non-profit environments foster activity that require presentations with direct quotations from various sources. Quotations often involve complicated information that must be articulated accurately. Therefore, reading that specific information would be prudent.

Memorizing Your Manuscript

Memorizing a presentation looks impressive if done properly. However, novice speakers should avoid this style of delivery because nervousness and inexperience can cause memory loss, and long pauses will make you look unprepared. This would be a detrimental error, especially if you really were prepared. You must have your speaking outline to allow for possible stumbles and lost thoughts.

Image © Andresr, 2009. Used under license from Shutterstock, Inc.

Many organizations have celebrations that have keynote speakers. If you are asked to be the keynote speaker, you should always memorize ALL of the elements of your introduction and conclusion. You should create initial excitement and poignant memories. The use of the delivery outline is great but all introductions and conclusions for any presentations should be totally memorized.

In addition, when attending any formal or informal gathering, whether it's a meeting or a banquet, announcements that reference people in the room like employee recognitions should be memorized. If you are paying tribute to someone, you should not be reading with your head down! Look that person directly in the eyes and scan your audience to hopefully reflect sincerity and trust. Just remember that some circumstances during a campus or off-campus gathering will require you to memorize your comments. Make the comments brief, accurate, and organized.

Impromptu Speaking

Impromptu speaking is probably used more often than most of us wish it were used. You may be called to "say a few words" at a fraternity function, company banquet, wedding, church gathering, etc.

Speaking without any notice is expected when you act as a moderator or as a master or mistress of ceremonies. With these roles, impromptu rather than extemporaneous speaking is encouraged. You are expected to be able to monitor the flow of the events taking place. Therefore, you need to be ready for anything! Audience members could ask questions, technical difficulties could occur, etc. so being able to speak without any notes is paramount! Most corporate and non-profit organizations have end-of-the-year or holiday celebrations where you will be asked to "say a few words" or serve as a host. Also, meetings may serve as impromptu situations due to the uncertainty of what an employer or co-worker may have to share. Their contributions may trigger a need for an impromptu comment or presentation.

Impromptu speaking is not difficult if you always remember that any gathering within the workplace or organizational setting could precipitate an impromptu moment. Try to have a quotation memorized that can fit any situation so that if you are called upon to speak, you are able to recite the quote and immediately apply it. This will allow you time to think of two main points to attach to the significance of the quotation and the theme of your impromptu presentation. Always make sure that your facial expressions do not reflect the agitation you may feel for being asked to speak without prior notice. Behave graciously and use some humor to release the primary tension you may feel at that moment.

If called to do so, the following steps, if implemented, should help you to create a speech quickly and with little apprehension.

Step 1. *Create an introduction.*

The easiest way to begin is by acknowledging what you were asked to do.

I was asked to say a few words about Sara.

You could also use one of the types of introductions discussed in chapter 5. Quotation introductions are a great resource if you memorize a few quotations that could be used in many situations, and for many types of speeches. When you're asked to speak, one will immediately come to mind. This can trigger your creativity and give you time to think of your main points.

My father always said that you can't change anyone but yourself. The wonderful thing about Sara is that she never tries to change anyone but herself. She's the person in this company who constantly strives to not only be a better co-worker but also a better citizen. She deserves this company award.

Step 2. *Think of two to three main points.*

Since you don't have a lot of time to think, and an impromptu speech is meant to be short, two to three main points are all you need to get your message across to your audience.

Two things that exemplify her dedication to humankind inside and outside of the office are her involvement in our new daycare center and her work in the city at the local Needline.

Step 3. *Support your main points with examples, statistics and testimony.*

It's hard to walk around with accurate statistics in your head, but if you remember some that would aid your speech, then use them. Otherwise, examples to support your main points are more likely to be used. If you have apersonal testimony or know of someone's true thoughts about your subject, feel free to share that information.

Be careful of quoting other people unless you are positive your quote is accurate or you may have problems later.

About ten years ago, this company resisted the idea of a daycare center fearing rejection from clients. Sara fought our former CEO and the forces that be. She almost lost her job, but, thankfully, we got a new boss, a new vision and a new daycare center. Only a few have the fortitude to fight for mothers and all family members who benefit from these centers. But Sara is not only passionate about work, she also supports all of humankind through the giving of her time at the Need line. So many need our help but only a few take the time to dedicate hours to helping someone we may never know.

Step 4. *Summarize and conclude creatively.*

Summarize the two to three main points and try to conclude with a creative statement.

So as we can see, Sara supports men, women, and children. She's a champion of human rights. So when dad stated: "Be a part of the solution and not a part of the problem," he may not have been speaking of our Sara Douglass at that time, but he certainly, unknowingly, was speaking of Sara's contributions to the betterment of all of our lives. At our company and even in society, she has always been a great part of the solution.

Extemporaneous Speaking

Preparing an entire presentation, condensing it to a one-two typed page *delivery outline*, and then presenting your thoughts to your audience is the most recommended way to deliver any presentation. You need to know more than the main points. You should write an entire presentation so your thoughts are visible. When you see your thoughts on paper, you may realize that they won't make sense to an audience of strangers. If you write down your thoughts instead of just "keeping them in your head," you will be able to make more coherent statements and you won't appear as if you threw your presentation together.

Extemporaneous speaking is the most common style of delivery. It's a combination of the three other styles. There is some glancing down at your delivery outline, some memorization of the introduction and conclusion, and some impromptu words or phrases. When training to be a competent presenter, extemporaneous speaking best serves the novice student in a classroom or in a boardroom. You never want to appear robotic and detached from your audience. Many argue that you can "over-rehearse." That is ridiculous. However, it's true that your performance can "appear" stiff and robotic. This is not due to "over-rehearsing." This is due to an inability to speak with a conversational tone and with varied facial expressions. You always want to create a complete full-sentence preparation outline. You want to make sure that you have a solid structured presentation that is well-rehearsed so that you appear professional, organized and competent. You will then deliver your presentation using the brief (key word), delivery outline.

East Tennesse University Adjunct Professor Dr. Luke Ryan Finck knows the power of delivery. His experience coaching college students for the competitive circuit has influenced his style of teaching and mentoring introductory level speech students. In the following section, he shares his knowledge of the importance of delivery especially in the business environment.

You are one of approximately 450,000 college students enrolled in a public speaking course this year.[1] Whether or not you realize it, at some point during your career you will be asked to present to a group of your colleagues. Ancient orator Quintilian noted that delivery itself had an extraordinarily powerful influence on oral arguments.[2] Delivery is essentially the emotive language of your body. Your gestures, tone, eye contact, fluency, eloquence, energy, and pathos are elements of speech delivery. A significant portion of the effectiveness of your message is not just what you say, but how you say it. Aristotle stated, delivery "is a matter of how the voice should be in expressing each emotion."[3]

When presenting to any group, particularly within the business environment, delivery is key to engaging your audience. Depending on the goal of your speech, your delivery has the ability to transition your audience from apathy to sympathy, support to neutrality, or boredom to enthusiasm. In addition to having great eye contact and controlled body movements when you present information in an organizational setting, also consider the following:

■ **Sell it.**
If you are not interested in your topic, your audience won't be either. We all know how dull meetings or presentations can be, especially if the speaker doesn't seem thrilled to be there. This is especially true when you present a new concept or program in the corporate setting. Once you have a career and you want employees to get involved in fundraising efforts or volunteer programs, you'll want to relay your excitement through your delivery. Keep in mind that passion and energy are only effective in appropriate environments. You wouldn't want to be too hyped up over presenting a new wave of lay-offs, or the elimination of healthcare benefits.

Conversely, you would not want to convey complacency during an important sales meeting presentation. Understand your message and environment when utilizing passion and energy.

■ **Your voice reflects your attitude.**
If you are not convinced that the new sales strategy will work but you are asked to present the logistics to your colleagues; your audience will hear your lack of support in your tone of voice. Also, turn up the volume! Employers or potential clients don't want to struggle to hear someone speak. If you are in a presentation of a small group, your volume will not need to be as loud as a presentation to a boardroom of ten or more and vice-a-versa.

■ **Your appearance plays a huge role in the corporate environment.**
Your overall appearance is as important as your presentation material and delivery. The way that you choose to present yourself communicates your credibility and confidence. If you dress sloppy, people will not focus on what you have to say, just how you look. Unpolished shoes, unkempt hair, overuse of cosmetics, and large distracting accessories convey ignorance or a lack of preparation. Depending on your work environment you may not necessarily need to wear a formal business suit when presenting to your immediate colleagues. However, when presenting to individuals that are outside of your work unit, you should elevate your level of dress. This is of particular importance when you are presenting to outside constituents. Your appearance should communicate to your target audiences that you have the knowledge and say to conduct business in a professional way.

■ **Nervousness is natural.**
Your nerves speak to how much you care about delivering an effective speech. In the business environment, your nerves can help to fuel your preparation and delivery. Sometimes, when we get nervous, our bodies react. You may play with your hair or sway back and forth. This speaks to the need for you to practice prior to your speech, preferably in front of a mirror, so that you can eliminate some of these negative nervous habits.

With practice, your nerves will enhance your passion rather than inhibit your delivery.

Citations

1. Pearson, J.C., Child, J.T., & Kahl, D.H. (2006). Preparation meeting opportunity: How do college students prepare for public speeches? *Communication Quarterly, 54*(3), 351-366.

2. Johnstone, C.L. (2001). Communicating in classical contexts: The centrality of delivery. *Quarterly Journal of Speech, 87*(2), 121-143.

3. Fredal, J. (2001). The language of delivery and the presentation of character: Rhetorical action in demosthenes' against meidias. *Rhetoric Review, 20*(3), 251-267.

Verbal Delivery

Verbal delivery includes the language we create and the vocal qualities we use. It could include the tone in our voices, the pitch of our voices, our choice of language and even our volume.

Language

The key to language is: keep it simple and make it memorable!

Language should be used clearly, correctly, and vividly, with a sense of gender and culture differences and with an awareness of the connotative and denotative meanings of words.

Language Should Be Clear

Everyone is unique, so the words we use could be perceived differently by different people. Therefore, words that can be interpreted the same way by the majority of people are the best words to use. Words like **a lot, many,** and **always,** are dangerous because they can have multiple meanings. These words are abstract and have ethical considerations because their usage categorize, information that may not be statistically true. **A lot** could mean 20 or 2,000 depending on who hears the message. You don't want your message to be confusing if your listeners discuss your presentation afterwards. Using *specific* names and numerical references are better than generic titles.

Some tennis players are outstanding role models does not present as clear a meaning as Venus and Serena Williams are outstanding role models in the field of professional tennis.

Language Should Be Used Correctly or Not at All

There is nothing worse than mispronouncing a word or mispronouncing someone's name during a presentation. When in doubt, look it up or ask! Make sure all names of people you don't know are double-checked for correct pronunciation. People are often offended when their names are pronounced wrong because it gives the perception that you didn't care enough to make sure they were identified correctly.

All non-standard words should also be used in the correct context. Speaker credibility is extremely affected when a word is used incorrectly in a sentence. Some words often misused are: *amiable, compel, ascertain, ramification, rectify, implore, patronize,* etc.

Vivid Language Will Enhance a Message

Metaphors, similes, personification and hyperbole can create imagery. You don't want to be overdramatic, but you do want to create mental pictures of your message so that the audience has a clearer understanding of your main points. People are often visual, so showing something or creating images in our minds will make a lasting impression.

The following devices should be used but sparingly. Too many imagery techniques can make you appear insincere. Make sure you have some of these in all of your speeches but don't use them in excess.

Metaphor: A metaphor is text that creates an image that shows the similarity between two things that are different.

The forgiveness of God is an ocean of love.

Simile: A simile is text that creates an image that shows the similarity between two things that are different and the words *like* or *as* are always used.

*The forgiveness of God is **like** an ocean of love.*

Personification: Personification is attributing human qualities to inanimate objects.

Forgiveness is an ocean.

Hyperbole: Hyperbole's are extreme exaggerations.

I've forgiven my friends a million times.

Ronald has received tons of standing ovations.

Language Can Reflect One's Gender/Culture without Being Offensive to Others

There's nothing wrong with being happy with yourself as a person, but be aware of gender differences. The simplest word can be perceived as sexist or exclusive to your audience.

- Don't use words that are masculine when referring to both men and women: *he, chairman*

- Don't label genders based on professions that are traditionally male or female because there are men and women in all job categories. *I'm sure **he** was a nice policeman. I think the nurse will be here soon. I hope **she's** nice.*

- Be sensitive to other cultures and subcultures. Investigate the usage of words that you know could be offensive. Stay away from regional and local slang. *Anyways* is not a word, and *ya'll* is not proper English. Know your audience and adjust your language.

- Be careful of profanity. If a presentation contained profanity and you were in the audience, would it bother you? Perhaps it would depend on what the profanity was or how it was used and by whom. Nevertheless, it's best not to use it unless you are positive that it has some important significance for your message and you're sure your audience will embrace it. REMEMBER: Professionalism and credibility!

Be Aware of the Denotative and Connotative Meanings of Words

An awareness of denotative and connotative meanings can help a speaker to choose words that the masses will understand and embrace.

The **denotative** meaning of a word is the dictionary definition of a word. The words *American flag* will have the same dictionary definition meaning for the majority of people. The American flag is a symbol. It's cloth. It has red and white stripes. It has stars.

The **connotative** meaning of a word is figurative, variable and emotional. So, the American flag also has a connotative meaning for those who listen to a speech about it. You have to be aware of the uniqueness of life experiences. Some words will create strong emotions in some and no emotion in others. The American flag will trigger thoughts of freedom, war, peace, etc., depending on who is listening.

Rhythm Enhances Message Retention

Beginning and advanced speakers should use methods for creating rhythm from language that produces emotion and memorable words. Using alliteration, antithesis, repetition, parallelism, and onomatopoeia can enhance the rhythm of a speech.

Alliteration: Alliteration is the repeating of the initial consonant sound in a sentence.

Final exams cause some students to cram, cringe, cry, and call home for support.

Antithesis: The use of antithesis is excellent to show opposite ideas in the same sentence.

It's not about how we can get the most out of this world; it's really about how this world can get the most out of us.

Repetition: Repetition is the repeating of words, sounds or phrases. The most famous speech that exemplifies repetition is Martin Luther King's "I Have a Dream" Speech. The following is an example of repetition.

I'm not going to talk about war, I'm going to tell you about peace. I'm going to speak about the things that will inspire and motivate you to be more productive. I'm not going to talk about war. There are enough negative and destructive speeches heard in the classrooms and in the boardrooms. I'm not going to talk about war. We need to concentrate on what will enhance our lives and not cripple our minds. Today, I refuse to talk about war.

Parallelism: The construction of parallel wording helps your listeners to remember your ideas. Putting your sentences and phrases in a similar pattern will create memorable rhythms.

College students are often overlooked during presidential campaigns; and they are perceived as immature.

But let's talk about who the real college students are.

These students are intelligent.

These students are aware.

These students are involved.

These students are informed.

And these students are concerned.

These are the real college students.

Onomatopoeia: This device involves using words that sound just like the objects they are signifying.

The train whistle blew Woo Woo! and we jumped off the tracks and ran away as fast as we could.

Effective Delivery Requires Seven Vocal Qualities

1. The **volume** is the loudness of your voice. It must be varied throughout the presentation. Increase and decrease your volume when you want to emphasize certain points. Different emotions can be conveyed with a loud or soft voice depending on what message you wish to convey. Practice the different levels on a tape recorder and practice in front of a mirror.

2. The **rate** of your voice refers to how fast or slow you speak. The rate of a speaker's voice needs to vary according to the emotional level of the presentation.

3. The **pitch** is the highness or lowness of your voice. Raising and lowering the pitch of the voice will impact the final impression a speaker leaves with an audience.

4. The **pronunciation** of words should be clear and correct! Pronunciation is the accepted sound of words.

5. **Articulation** has to do with the clarity of speech sounds. Consonants are often left off words and cause articulation problems. The use of *axe* instead of *asked* is a major mistake. Articulation during a presentation is important for speaker credibility. The end of each word should be clear. The speech sounds you make will affect whether you appear intelligent or lazy. When a speaker says I fell on the *flow* instead of *floor,* an otherwise intelligent person will be perceived as unintelligent. This may be unfair but unfortunately it's true.

   In addition, **dialects** need to be controlled. If you grew up in a region of the country where people say I'm going to *warsh a load of clothes* instead of I'm going to *wash* a load of clothes, you must be aware of the sub-cultural bias that could affect the perception of your message in a traditional corporate workplace.

6. **Enunciation** *is the preciseness of speech sounds.* You must be able to *speak* distinctly and not blend your sounds together. *Howya doin* is a clear error of enunciation. *How are you doing?* is appropriate.

7. **Effective pauses** are essential for signaling the important main points or subpoints. Pauses are planned and free from fillers like **"um," "ah," "you know," and throat clearing** Pausing is especially effective during the last sentence of any conclusion. The slight pause in the middle of that last sentence, followed by a full glance at the entire audience, will help signal the end of your presentation. At other times, pauses are great when you want to get an audience's

full attention for a point you are making. When the room is quiet, people will focus directly on you.

Visual Delivery

Visual delivery includes the speaker's appearance, body movements and facial expressions. It will impact whether an audience sees you as a credible speaker or as a nervous presenter.

Appearance

A speaker's appearance should reflect competence, character, and credibility. If you look sloppy, chances are your mood and delivery will be sloppy. Unless you intentionally dress to emphasize a point like the tragedy of homelessness, an unkempt appearance will likely affect the strength of your message. You should be neat for classroom speeches and professional business presentations.

Eye Contact and Facial Expressions

A speaker must have *constant* eye contact with his or her audience and use facial expressions that reflect the emotion of the language. If you read your presentation or ignore looking at certain areas of a room, the people you don't connect with will be the people who don't listen to what you have to say.

If you want to emphasize certain points within your presentation, your expressions need to reflect the exact emotions you are trying to convey. Using a monotone voice for a sales presentation will not convince us to buy a product from you. An absence

Image © Dmitriy Shironosov, 2009. Used under license from Shutterstock, Inc.

of a smile when you are speaking about a loved one will not convince us that you truly love that person. Let your face reflect your words.

Body Language and Gestures

Body movement should be poised and controlled, and planned gestures are necessary for making a speaker appear vibrant and not rigid. (There should be an absence of swaying, touching hair, throat clearing, hands banging on the podium, hands constantly moving, etc.)

Although your body movement should be controlled, planned gestures to emphasize points or to create a visual image in the minds of audience members are strongly encouraged. When saying: "*I live in a big house,*" stretching your arms out wide to your sides is a good way to gesture and show that your house is large. This would be planned and noted in the margin of your speaking outline so you remember when to gesture.

April Rene Payne Rives, ABD was a state and national award-winning speech and debate champion when she was an undergraduate student. However, it took years to perfect her presentation skills. Now, she teaches the techniques she learned. As she completes her doctoral program in communication studies, she shares her insight about the transition from being a speech student to a speech teacher in hopes of letting you know that delivering a great presentation is possible with desire and practice. In keeping with the proper structure of a presentation, she offers the following:

The art of public speaking is like the wind. Like wind, the "art" is something we cannot see. We know it is there. We feel it. But suddenly and without warning, it can be gone. All is still.

Essentially, the wind represents the flexible nature of life; and that which was certain can suddenly be fleeting. The certainty you feel in your life before enrolling in public speaking and the nervousness you feel as that confidence blows away is normal. Relax. You are in the majority.

After speaking in public for over six years and instructing students for a year, I consider myself fortunate to have a duality of perspective. I have been where most of you are sitting right now, full of anxiety, apprehension, and doubt. Thankfully, I have learned how to harness those fears into positive energy to fuel excellent presentations. After winning several awards at both the state and national level, I accepted a Graduate Teaching Assistantship at Murray State University. I have had the privilege of literally watching students grow into great speakers. Today, I am going to share with you several guidelines for success that have helped me personally when delivering speeches. Additionally, we will examine a few unconventional tips that have aided students in the public speaking process.

Success in a presentation course involves control and practice. The main thing that I always do is ask myself a simple question: "What is the worst thing that could happen?" The answer usually is something like "I could fall" or "I could forget my speech" or "What if they don't care about what I am saying?" Then I take a breath and realize that I can control all of these things. I can control walking poised, calm, and confident to the podium. If I forget part of my speech, how is the audience going to know?

They don't have a copy of my delivery outline. I can control what I say and how I say it. And I can control making them care. If I stand up in front of my audience with an apathetic attitude, read to them off of my outline, and speak robotically without inflection in my voice then yes, they will zone out. But if I am charismatic, direct with my eye contact, and passionate, then they will listen. I can control that. I can make them at least hear what I am saying. The apprehension that I felt prior to giving my speech melts away because I realize that I am in control. So are you.

Now that we have looked at this simple lesson of control, let's take a look at another important step for success in delivering your presentation — practice.

I know, everyone always explains how important practicing your speech is. But how many of us actually do it? I admit I am guilty of "winging" speeches sometimes, but the truth of the matter is that the more rehearsed you are, the better you will be. Before different speaking engagements, I recommend arriving an hour or so early in order to use to the room. Practice your introduction and conclusion to make sure the acoustics of the room are compatible with your voice. Make sure your visual aid is set up appropriately. Also practice walking up to the podium. Don't just practice the words, practice the process.

Realizing that you are in control and that you know the information that you are discussing are vital to successful presentations. Yet, they are very conventional ideas that many public speakers employ. The following tips I am going to share with you are a little more unconventional in nature. Several of them were utilized when I was president of the Murray State University Speech and Debate Union. They helped me dramatically, and I am confident that they will help you as well. Many of my current and former students can attest to their strength.

- **To calm your nerves, I recommend playing music.**
  Bring your iPod with you to class. Prior to delivering your speech, ask your instructor if you can take a minute and step out in the hallway. Listen to about 30 seconds of soothing music. If you feel like your energy levels are low, listen to more upbeat and positive music to get your blood flowing. It may sound silly — but trust me. It works.

- **Dress professionally.**
  The purpose of dressing professionally is to enhance your credibility. However, few people recognize that it is almost like you are putting on

Continued

your "uniform." Whenever I am dressed up, I personally feel better and more confident about myself. This helps me with delivering my presentation in a more poised manner.

■ **Be creative.**
I don't care how boring the topic is that you are speaking on, you can make it interesting and fun. The goal of any presentation is to both inform and captivate the audience while you do it. It is a delicate balance of content and delivery. You need to have substance to your topic, but also realize that the audience will not retain anything if you aren't charismatic and excited

about the topic yourself. How you speak determines what kind of audience members you will have. Creative and enthusiastic presentations breed dynamic and engaged audiences and vice-versa.

Today I have shared with you a couple of guidelines for success that I employ when speaking. I have also provided a few unconventional tips that you can use when giving a presentation. Public speaking is something that should not be feared. If you learn how to harness your energy, you too can become a great orator. Just like the wind, this class will come and go. However, the effects of it can be felt through your impassioned words forever.

Delivery in Mediated Communication Settings

Delivering presentations in mediated communication settings can be different. Microphones, cameras, and constant audience feedback can make a speaking situation more stressful. There is more uncertainty about your audience, and more delivery techniques are required to be successful when speaking in a mass communication setting.

Microphones

Speaking with a microphone requires an awareness of sound. Too often, people speak too closely or too far away from a microphone. If you are not accustomed to using a microphone and one is provided, you must test the sound before beginning your presentation. You should arrive early and practice using the microphone. Ask someone to stand in the back of the room while you talk. They should provide feedback as to whether they can hear you clearly or not. If the microphone squeaks, hold it further down from your mouth or stand farther away from the podium. If you can't be heard, speak louder and more clearly. You must know how to handle a microphone or your message can be disturbing to your audience, despite its worthwhile content.

Cameras

It's been said by the television industry that cameras add 10 pounds. Be aware that your appearance on camera may look different. In addition to the extra weight, camera lighting may distort your appearance. White shirts without any color are often discouraged, and absent the proper lighting, all black could make you look washed out. Avoid colors that are too dramatic, and stripes are not the best for camera appearances. Neutral colors and conservative clothing are best. Hair, jewelry, and make-up should look neat and not distracting.

Public Forums

Question and answer sessions can be stressful due to the uncertainty of audience questions. You must be poised and prepared for these forums. Be ready to tell short stories for some of your answers and be ready to just answer with a "yes" or "no." Stand still and don't fidget or you will look nervous and possibly dishonest. Try to use people's names as much as possible. Make direct eye contact. If possible, try to move away from the podium and stand closer to the audience. You want to appear friendly and willing to answer their questions. If you don't know an answer, don't try to fake it. Just tell the person that you will find out and get back to him or her later.

REMEMBER

■ You get one chance to present your message!

■ Use the four-step process for verbal and visual delivery!

■ Practice with a tape recorder and listen for vocal flaws!

■ Practice in front of a mirror and correct nervous movements!

■ Know the setting!!!

■ Know the audience size!!!

■ Know if you have a microphone!!!

■ Know if you have a podium!!!

■ Know yourself and practice, practice, practice!!!

Ethics

You must make sure that your delivery and language are ethically sound. The tone of your voice and the words that you use should be emotionally charged but they should not incite reckless or dangerous behaviors from your listeners. You should not promote violence, destruction or intentional emotional distress. Your role as a speaker is to inform, persuade or entertain. The information doesn't always have to be serious but *you* should be serious about your role as a positive communicator. Don't be abusive, biased or offensive. Watch *what* you say and *how* you say it!

ACTIVITIES

Delivery: It's Not Only What You Say but How You Say It

I've Got Rhythm

Read one of the famous speeches by Martin Luther King, Jr. (Ask your instructor for titles). Write down as many words or sentences that reflect repetition, alliteration, antithesis, onomatopoeia, parallelism, metaphors, and similes. Share your results with the class. This can be done individually or in groups.

Poetry in Motion

Read the following poem with emotion. Raise and lower your volume and pitch. Speak slowly and then speak quickly. Notice what sounds good and what doesn't. Make a point to vary your voice as much as possible. Practice it over and over out loud and do it differently each time. This will help you to get comfortable with vocal variety and facial expressions. **This exercise is most effective if done in front of a mirror and with a tape recorder.**

I am my poem.

Wrapped around a rhythm and a rhyme and a reason.

Full of meaning, and life and energy and anger and joy and love.

I am my poem.

Read the lines, read between the lines, the lines are lined with me.

It's all about me and how it's never about me but about you.

I am my poem.

For those who wish to read it, I'll never stop writing.

Will you stop reading . . . did you ever start?

Stop.

Poem courtesy of Dr. Crystal Rae Coleman.

Nonverbally Speaking

Get into groups of **3-6** people and create a **30** second television commercial using an object in your room. You cannot speak. You must get your message across without talking. Use body language and facial expressions to relay your group's message. Each person in the group must participate in some way. Take 20 minutes to prepare. Perform the commercials for your classmates and discuss the various *visual delivery* techniques that were used.

Two By Two

Practice building confidence and enhancing your delivery by working with at least two other people in creating messages two words at a time. Just start your story with two words: "My friend . . ." The next person adds two words: ". . . is amazing . . ." Each person adds two words until the story is complete. This helps one practice being confident, flexible, and articulate in uncomfortable speaking situations.

Team Presentations

Tina A. Coffelt

CHAPTER OBJECTIVES:

At the end of this chapter, you will be able to:

- Understand the importance of team presentations in modern organizations.
- Modify presentations appropriately for team presentations.
- Give a team presentation implementing criteria for seamless team presentations.

The importance of accomplishing organizational tasks in modern organizations with teams or groups cannot be overstated. At least 78% of U.S. organizations use self-managing teams (Lawler, 1999). Organizations are likely to assign employees to work in teams or groups. For example, committees form to deliberate organizational strategies. Departments hold intermittent meetings to report on work and discuss opportunities for synergy. Sales, marketing, or advertising teams work together to create product and service solutions for clients. The applications of group and teamwork in organizations are endless. Groups or teams frequently present their ideas, progress, or results to customers, clients, prospects, or managers. These team presentations, when compared to individual presentations, require additional considerations. This chapter will elaborate on the use of groups and teams in organizations and discuss the unique aspects of giving a group presentation.

▪ Groups and Teams in Organizations

The shift from individual work to team work presents challenges for many students and employees in the United States. In a culture that values individual effort and achievement, the dependence and reliance on others to complete an assignment can result in a dislike for group work. Employees in U.S. organizations resist working in teams for a variety of reasons including fairness, equity, accountability, trust, and individual ability or confidence (Kirkman, Jones, & Shapiro, 2000). However, modern organizations have adopted team or group work as a common way to achieve organizational objectives. For example, Microsoft used to rely on two to three computer programmers to build a new product. Over time, team size has expanded to up to 12 programmers who collaborate to develop new products (Cusumano, 1997). As a result of the shift from individual to team work, employers expect college

graduates to adapt to this form of communication. Universities show their commitment to prepare students for team or group work through required courses such as Small Group Communication and/or group assignments in a plethora of courses. Groups provide opportunities to share ideas and information. Collaboration often results in well thought out decisions and high performance levels. Multiple considerations are made and aspects of a project do not get overlooked when several people contribute their thoughts and ideas. **Synergy,** when the group is able to achieve more than the sum of each member's efforts, is created (Kirkman & Rosen, 2000). For example, consider several musicians who are playing individual selections on their respective instruments at the same time. If a stranger walked into the room, he or she would hear many loud noises without coherence. Now, think about those musicians again. This time, suppose each musician had the sheet music to the same song. Each performer is playing a designated part, but the coordination and cooperation among the performers results in a beautiful masterpiece of sounds and rhythms. That is synergy.

The terms *team* and *group* are often used interchangeably. However, each term represents a specific form of communication among a small number of individuals. A **group** "consists of three to fifteen people who share a common purpose, who feel a sense of belonging to the group, and who exert influence on one another" (Beebe, Beebe, & Ivy, 2009, p. 3). A **team** is "a coordinated group of people organized to work together to achieve a specific, common goal" (Beebe et al., 2009, p. 5). Note that the major distinction between a group and a team is their objective. A group has a common purpose or shared reason for coming together, while a team has a specific goal or objective. An example of a group would be managers who come together for the common purpose of sharing best practices. The group members may come from various departments within an organization and meet regularly to share ideas about managing employees. The group itself has no objective goal they are striving

Image © Yuri Arcurs, 2009. Used under license from Shutterstock, Inc.

to achieve. Rather, they come together to support each other's development as effective managers. By contrast, a team consists of members with a clear goal. Team members have specific assignments based on their unique expertise or position in the organization. For example, a process improvement team in a manufacturing facility would come together with the goal of improving productivity on a line. Team members may include one or two representatives from management, engineering, line workers, quality, and perhaps an outside member of the organization. The team members work together until the goal is achieved. Then, the team disbands. This chapter will use both *group* and *team* because either form has the potential to deliver an oral presentation.

Within organizations, effective teams are also **empowered** teams (Kirkman & Rosen, 2000). Kirkman and Rosen (2000) found that empowered teams exhibit potency, meaningfulness, autonomy, and impact. First, **potency** means that group members collectively have confidence in their abilities. These team members have been observed sitting close to each other during team meetings, and they make frequent eye contact with each other. Teams that exhibit **meaningfulness** have a sense of commitment. Team members are intrinsically motivated to do well. **Autonomy** refers to a sense of freedom groups believe they have over their work. Selecting group members is one way to experience autonomy in a college course, even though team assignments are often made by managers in organizations. Teams also exhibit autonomy by setting their own times to meet, selecting the topic they want to talk about, as well as making other group decisions. A sense of **impact** is achieved when others outside the group comment on work done by the group. In organizations, a sense of

impact would be accomplished when a team can see its ideas implemented by management. In a college course, a sense of impact would be achieved when classmates tell the team how much they learned.

As teams interact to achieve their goals and objectives, it is highly likely that an oral presentation will be required. With some teams, their primary objective may be to give oral presentations, such as with a sales team. Regardless of the type of team, team presentations require additional considerations beyond those already covered for individual presentations.

Team Presentations

A **team presentation** is a "well-coordinated presentation by a cohesive group of speakers who are trying to inform or influence an audience of key decision makers" (Engleberg & Raimes, 2004). Examples of team presentations are found in sales, healthcare, auditing, research teams, or product design teams, among many others. Specifically, organizations may send a team of three or four sales representatives to present their product or service to prospective clients. Or, a small group of health care providers who want to construct a new facility and start their own practice could present a business plan to financial institutions in search of a loan. In another example, community members might select a few residents to present a proposal to potential donors for a community center for neighborhood youth. Regardless of major or industry, employees and organizational members are likely to encounter situations in which they will be called upon to give a presentation with other colleagues.

There are at least three advantages to presenting as a team. First, many minds and bodies decrease the amount of work that would otherwise be given to one person. Second, more minds generate more ideas, thereby increasing the quality of the presentation. Third, the audience will benefit from hearing multiple voices and perspectives when they hear the presentation. There are disadvantages to team presentations, as well. First, working with others requires coordination and puts pressure on individuals' schedules. Second, team presentations are likely to take more time to prepare than an individual presentation because of the dialogue about the presentation. See Table 9.1 for suggestions on overcoming some of the challenges of working as a team.

TABLE 9.1 Problem Solving

Teams or groups may encounter problems as they work on their project. Below are a few problems you may encounter followed by possible solutions. Look to these issues as opportunities to practice new communication skills. Talk with your instructor and ask for guidance to facilitate discussions among team members. Perhaps your instructor has guidelines on consequences for team members who do not seem to carry their weight.

Problem	Solution
You may not know your team members very well. In an organizational setting, you have a greater opportunity to get to know colleagues because of the longer commitment employees have to organizations as opposed to a one-semester college course.	Upon first forming a team in your public speaking course, spend time introducing each other and talking with each other about the class, other commitments, likes, and dislikes. These relationship-building conversations may contradict your need for efficiency and staying on task, but the rewards of having a cohesive team will shine when your group makes its final presentation.
You are busy and don't have time to meet with team members. In college, you have multiple classes with various assignments. Plus, you have a part-time job and are involved in assorted student organizations. You have relationships you want to build and maintain. Coordinating with three to four other people who are equally busy seems to be a daunting task.	You are not alone. Your team members have similarly busy schedules. You have an opportunity to practice coordination, planning, and problem solving. When you work for an organization, you will also have multiple assignments to juggle with competing deadlines. Your ability to master this complex task now will make you valuable to an employer in the future. Be patient with each other.
Team members have different levels of motivation. You are highly motivated and want an A on this project. Or, you may be the team member who is unmotivated by group work, doesn't like the teacher, and just wants to get a grade and get the class over with.	Early in your team meetings, discuss your individual expectations with team members. Then, lead your team members toward setting a goal as a group. Is your goal to get an A? Perhaps your goal is to wow the professor with the best team presentation he or she has ever seen. Or, perhaps your goal is to spend as little time as possible on the assignment so you can just get it done. Regardless of the specific goal, negotiate as a group what you hope to accomplish. As time goes by and team members struggle with competing priorities, remind each other of the team goal and what each person needs to do to fulfill the goal.
You don't want part of your grade to be based on someone else's work. Your fears are reasonable. It is difficult to trust other people we do not know with rewards that are individually based. Someone else's work may influence *your* grade. In organizational settings, employees seem to be motivated by the task, the job, or the fear of getting fired. Doing a team presentation in college does not seem to carry the same weight as team work in organizations.	Accept the assignment for its merit. Team work may be a new experience for you and this is your opportunity to learn or improve on your ability to trust others. A team assignment simulates experiences you will encounter in the future. Show your adaptability now when the stakes are not as high as they will be in your career.
Your team members pester you about being late and missing meetings. You see no reason to have so many meetings and think your group members should just relax.	Show up and be on time. Your colleagues have made this project a priority. Your team talked about and agreed upon meeting times. Failure to show up or failure to arrive on time sends a message of disrespect to your team members. Work is delayed. Each member of the team is valuable, important, and needed. Respect each other and commit to strong ethics.

TABLE 9.1 Continued

One or two team members arrive late or they don't show up. They don't even bother to call, e-mail, or text to tell you they are late or can't make it to the meeting.	Make sure the team has discussed expectations for attendance at team meetings. Ask the team member what keeps him or her from coming to meetings on time or showing up at all. Relax and remember that others cannot be controlled. Work with the team members who do show up and talk with your instructor about the slacker in the team.

A polished, savvy team presentation is seamless in every way. "A team presentation is not a collection of individual speeches; it is a team product" (Engleberg & Raimes, 2004, p. 186). Highly effective team presentations leave the audience mesmerized by the flow of content and ease of transition between speakers. A team presentation flows as if spoken by one person. Disruptions from speaker transitions or multiple speakers are eliminated. Such unity is achieved through group cohesion, preparation, and practice. The tendency for team is to prepare a broad outline, then assign individual members to cover a portion. Team members scatter to prepare individual parts, and then show up on the day of the presentation to speak. This approach, while efficient, lacks in cohesion among group members. Failure to consult each other during the planning and preparation process results in a presentation that is disjointed and difficult for the audience to follow. Team members must be accountable to each other by sharing ideas for individual parts as well as discussing overarching themes. For example, is there a key quote given in the introduction that other speakers could connect with later in the presentation? Does a speaker, early in the presentation, make several key points that will be expanded upon by a later speaker? Each speaker must be knowledgeable about other speakers' parts and contribute to the development of the presentation. Specific aspects of the team presentation that contribute to a seamless delivery include the introduction of team members, speaking order, and transitions between speakers. Additionally, team presentations must attend to dress, presentational aids, practicing, and fielding questions. Each of these points as they relate to team presentations will be covered in the following sections. The information that follows adds to the other aspects of oral presentations that have been covered in this textbook.

Introduction of Team Members

Having multiple members of a presentation requires introductions of your team members to the audience. Introductions may be handled by someone not in the team or by the team directly. If introductions are made by a non-group member, this person may introduce the group as a whole, such as "Representatives from the Murray Company have joined us today to tell us about a new opportunity." When this type of introduction is given, plan to introduce individual team members to the audience during the introduction of the presentation. Alternatively, the team may be introduced by team and individual names. If the audience is unclear about which person is attached to which name, the team will want to reintroduce themselves to the audience. However, if the audience is clear about the name that is attached to each team member, there is no need for the group to restate this information.

When introducing the team members, plan to do this in the introduction of the presentation. Recall that one of the functions of an introduction is to establish credibility. Plan to introduce each team member and establish his/her credibility at the same time. Consider stating each person's name and their job title or function on the team. For example, "Quisha Smith is the Director of Recruitment." Continue to describe Quisha's experiences with recruitment that are relevant to the presentation. Also, consider who will make the introductions. If one manager and three employees are presenting, the manager may introduce him/herself and each employee. By comparison, if team members are of equal status within the organization, consider having each team member introduce him/herself. Regardless of the approach, the goal is for the audience to be clear about the identity and credibility of each team member. For shorter presentations, make all the introductions near the beginning of the presentation. For longer presentations or workshops, it may be

Image © Dean Mitchell , 2009. Used under license from Shutterstock, Inc.

necessary to reintroduce the respective team member and remind the audience of his/her role and credibility.

Speaking Order

Decisions about speaking order and speaking parts are also important to a seamless delivery. The introduction and conclusion, two critical components of your presentation, should be made by one speaker. This speaker should be one of the stronger speakers on the team who is capable of gaining attention and providing closure. While each team member should speak during the presentation itself, each person may also have more than one speaking part. Avoid the temptation to have each speaker take one part of the presentation and go in a set sequence, unless the organization of the presentation and expertise of the speakers justifies this approach. If the team has organized the presentation in a way that makes the most sense for the audience, then assign speaking parts based on the expertise of respective group members. Be open to

the possibility of having each team member speak more than once. Also consider if there are meaningful ways team members can interact. For example, if your presentation is organized with a problem-solution pattern, perhaps one team member could present the problems, and other group members could present possible solutions. (See Table 9.2) Organizing, outlining, and selecting speakers should be an iterative process. In other words, the team should prepare drafts of the outline, discuss it as a group, talk about who will speak, revise the outline again reflecting new points brought up by team members, discuss it, and so on and so forth. Do not limit yourself to making the outline and then assigning members to take a specific part of the outline. While this approach may be the decision that is ultimately made, discuss other alternatives that will give your presentation high impact and audience appeal.

Transitions

Transitions are key to a seamless team presentation. Recall the use of transitions from Chapter 5. Group members should use these same devices to transition from one speaker to another. Allow the content to guide the transitions. Avoid statements such as, "And now, Bethany will talk about the first step in the process." Such statements underscore the speaker, rather than the content. Further, these simple statements direct the audience away from the content and flow of information. A carefully planned and skillfully executed transition statement enhances the continuity of your presentation. Consider writing out the transition sentences and memorizing these pivotal lines. Also, become

TABLE 9.2 Sample Outline

In the body of a speech with a problem-solution organizational pattern, consider the following speaking order:
    a. Problem A. (Speaker: Tracy)
        i. Solution for A. (Speaker: Scott)
    b. Problem B. (Speaker: Tracy)
        i. Solution for B. (Speaker: Jorge)
    c. Problem C. (Speaker: Tracy)
        i. Solution for C. (Speaker: Leticia)

TABLE 9.3 Examples of Transition Statements

An average approach to making a transition in a team presentation:
    And now, Kristen will talk about the next step in the process.

A seamless presentation will have transitions like this:
    Derek: You've just heard about the first step in the process. The next step in the process is...Kristen: During this part of the process...

    Notice the flow of information. The speech itself was not interrupted when a transition was made from one speaker to another.

familiar with the transition statement for the speaker who comes before you and after you so that each group member is knowledgeable of the speaking order and confident about the flow of the presentation. (See Table 9.3)

While focusing on the presentation itself, it is reasonable to overlook the nonspeaking members of the group. Multiple speakers make team presentations unique because there will be individuals who are not speaking during the presentation. The focus of these nonspeaking speakers is frequently neglected when preparing a presentation. However, the audience will see all members of a group and evaluate the team as a unit, rather than individual speakers. Therefore, planning what nonspeaking speakers do necessitates attention.

The room setup and length of the presentation each control some aspects of the group positioning. First, for short presentations, all team members should remain standing for the duration of the presentation. When a person speaks, he or she should step forward. For lengthier presentations or workshops, it is appropriate for nonspeaking team members to sit. Your team should discuss the audience and what they consider a long or short presentation to be. Speakers with physical disabilities that limit or restrict their ability to stand will make appropriate accommodations according to their specific disability.

Second, the room in which you are speaking may mandate where nonspeakers sit or stand. In rooms with limited capacity, nonspeaking members may need to sit with the audience in the front row. Larger auditoriums or conference rooms may have chairs available that should be placed to the right or left of the staging area. Alternatively, your team might divide the team so that members alternate speaking from the right or left side of the room, or enter from the right or left side and speak at the center of the staging area. There are numerous combinations of placement positions when there are multiple speakers. Your team should discuss the placement that makes the strongest impact on the audience. You could even have team members scattered among the audience and on a given cue, simultaneously emerge and walk to the front of the room. Consider adding music for higher impact. The opportunities are endless!

Dress

Team members must also attend to their physical appearance and attire. The most important consideration is for team members to be dressed with the same level of formality. One member in a suit and one in a pair of jeans would be inappropriate. Therefore, discuss if you will all wear suits, dress in business casual, or wear khakis. Jeans are acceptable for professional presentations in very specific industries. Some organizations have uniforms or articles of clothing with a company logo that are appropriate. For a college class, you might consider matching colors that coordinate with the topic of your presentation or your presentational aids. For example, if you

Image © iophoto, 2009. Used under license from Shutterstock, Inc.

are giving a team presentation persuading the audience to be more environmentally friendly, each group member could wear one article of green clothing. Focus on ways your group will make the strongest impact on your audience and present yourselves as a cohesive unit.

Presentational Aids

There are several unique aspects of presentational aids for team presentations. First, designate one team member to operate presentational aids. The physical transition between team members flows better without clickers or remote devices being passed off. Track and field relay teams devote considerable time practicing the passing of the baton. If your team is limited on time, don't pass the device. However, if you elect to do so, make sure the passage is practiced. If your team is using more than one medium to deliver your presentational aids, assign one team member to each medium. For example, if you will show a video clip using a TV/DVD combination and use a PowerPoint presentation, have two different team members operate each set of equipment.

Refrain from looking at or speaking to the group member who is operating the equipment. Recall the importance of eye contact from Chapter 8. Maintaining eye contact with the audience takes more practice in group presentations because team members may want to communicate with each other. However, with proper planning and practice, the operator will know what each speaker is expected to say and when it is time to launch the appropriate presentational aid. Saying "next slide please" or nodding the head to communicate with the operator distracts the audience members and disrupts the flow of the presentation. Recall that your objective is to have a seamless presentation.

In addition to content, presentational aids should also be seamless. Formatting guidelines, colors, fonts, themes, etc., should demonstrate consistency. When multiple members contribute small components to presentational aids, oversight will be needed to ensure a unified final product. For example, if team members each prepare a few slides to put into a larger PowerPoint file, the final presentation should have the same color scheme, same font style and size, and similar quality of photographs, clip art, charts, or graphs. Attending to these details enhances the professionalism of your presentation. In class, the results of your efforts could be a high grade and an impressed audience. In the workplace, the results could be making a sale, convincing a group, or getting a promotion.

Practice

Practicing a presentation is just as important with team members as it is for an individual presentation. In fact, team presentations often require both. You will want to practice your individual speaking parts *and* meet with team members. During practice sessions, team members can practice making transitions, decide where to sit and stand, and coordinate presentational aids. Each speaker should already be familiar with his or her speaking part so that team practice sessions can be devoted to the essential elements of presenting as a team. Practicing as a team will ensure that you have a seamless presentation with a strong connection to the audience. Practice also reduces the need for team members to communicate with each other during the actual presentation. Talking to each other during the presentation reduces the quality and professionalism of your presentation. By practicing together, the need to talk to each other in front of the audience is eliminated.

Fielding Questions

After the presentation, audience members may ask questions. Team members should be prepared for this aspect of the presentation, as well. Some audience members may ask a specific speaker a question. In that case, the specific member should answer the question. Other audience members may want to hear information from each speaker. Reply accordingly and be brief in your answers. Audience members will lose interest if each speaker gives a lengthy, detailed answer. Other audience members will ask a question and leave it up to the team members to decide who should answer. **The team should have a protocol for answering questions.** For example, the person with the highest organizational status (i.e., the manager) could answer all questions. Or, team members could decide to answer only those questions unique to their expertise. For example, if the team members include a sales manager, a sales representative, a computer programmer, and a customer service associate, each team member has a clear area of expertise. Thus, if an audience member has a concern about the product interfacing with their existing software, the computer programmer would field the question. Similarly, if an audience member has a question about service after the sale, the customer service associate would be the appropriate person to answer the question. Avoid the situation where every group member answers every question because the audience is likely to become restless and bored with information overload.

Chapter Review

Team and group work are important and oft-used ways for organizations to achieve their goals and objectives. Teams and groups are required to give presentations for various reasons. Giving polished, savvy team presentations is one more way to exhibit competitive advantage within an organization. You can demonstrate high-quality team presentation skills by contributing your ideas to the group, preparing your individual part, practicing individually and with the group, and making the group presentation seamless in every way. Groups and teams have many options for presenting as a

team. It is imperative that the team discuss, plan, and practice every aspect of the presentation.

Thought/Application Questions

1. Do you think your presentation for class places you in a group or team? Why?

2. Think about a job or career you would like to have. What situations do you think would be appropriate for a team presentation?

3. What aspects of group work do you like? Dislike?

4. Who do you know that has given a team presentation at their job? What was the presentation about?

5. Search "group presentations" on YouTube and view the clip. Critique the team presentation skills. What did the group do well? What would you recommend they do to improve their impact?

References

1. Beebe, S. A., Beebe, S. J., & Ivy, D. K. (2009). *Communication principles for a lifetime: Communicating in groups and teams*. Boston: Pearson.

2. Cusumano, M. A. (1997). How Microsoft makes large teams work like small teams. *Sloan Management Review, 39*, 9-20.

3. Engleberg, I., & Raimes, A. (2004). *Pocket keys for speakers*. Boston: Houghton Mifflin Company.

4. Kirkman, B. L., Jones, R. G., & Shapiro, D. L. (2000). Why do employees resist teams? Examining the "resistance barrier" to work team effectiveness. *The International Journal of Conflict Management, 11*, 74-92.

5. Kirkman, B. L., & Rosen, B. (2000). Powering up teams. *Organizational Dynamics, 28*, 48-66.

6. Lawler, E. E. (1999). Employee involvement makes a difference. *Journal for Quality and Participation, 22*, 18-20.

10 Persuasive Presentations

Patty S. Parish

CHAPTER OBJECTIVES

At the end of this chapter, you will be able to:

- Explain why the persuasive presentation is the most demanding type of presentation
- Define persuasion
- Define attitudes, belief, and values and know the importance of each to persuasive speaking
- Understand the importance of audience analysis and the three areas of audience analysis: attitudinal, demographic and situational
- Explain the importance of credibility and the factors that create credibility for the audience
- Define inductive, deductive, analogical, and causal reasoning
- Explain the importance of emotional appeals in persuasive presentations
- Define cognitive dissonance and explain how persuaders use it to motivate their audience
- List the five steps of Monroe's Motivated Sequence and use it in a persuasive presentation
- Define ethics
- Explain how persuasive presentations involve ethical decisions

Persuasion is a vital part of life. If you think carefully, you use persuasion almost every day. If you have ever asked a friend for a few dollars, convinced your professor to give you an extension on an assignment, or been on a job interview, you were involved in the art of persuasion. You are constantly selling yourself and your ideas to others. The important question is, how effective are you? President Eisenhower once said, "Persuasion is the art of getting people to do what you want them to do, and to like it" (Bergdahl, 2006). Your ability to effectively persuade your friends, colleagues, and customers and earn their cooperation is key to being a success in life. How well you achieve your goals, both personally and professionally, depend on how well you speak and write persuasively.

We are social creatures and the nature of our lives demands that we work closely with other people to accomplish our goals and the goals of the workplace. Gone are the days when leaders and managers were able to demand performance from their employees and expect results. When you think of persuasion in the workforce, you may believe that it is limited to selling and negotiation. However, the majority of persuasion that occurs in the workplace today is leading people to work as a team and accomplish the goals of the company. The face of today's business is rapidly changing, and the old style of command and change is gone. The most effective leaders and managers are the ones who can effectively persuade people to work together well. According to Erin White (2008), writing in *The Wall Street Journal*:

"Managers say they increasingly must influence rather than command others in order to get their own jobs done. The trend is the result of leaner corporate hierarchies and the erosion of division walls. Managers now work more often with peers where lines of authority aren't clear or don't exist . . . . It is a skill needed more and more today."

Clearly, much of your future success as a leader and manager will often depend on how well you are able to persuade those you work with closely.

Also, as a part of your company, you will often be asked to present your ideas and information to others. You must effectively convince them that your ideas and plans are the best choice. Your success depends on how persuasively you develop and present your ideas. If you are going to be a successful persuader, you will need to understand the challenges of persuasive presentations.

■ The Challenge of the Persuasive Presentation

Up to this point, you have studied the guidelines to effective informative presentations. Many of those rules will apply to your persuasive presentation. Having good research, a strong audience analysis, logical organization, effective introductions and conclusions, and good verbal supportive material still apply to the persuasive presentation. However, the persuasive presentation makes greater demands on the speaker than any other type of presentation. In an informative presentation, you are providing knowledge to the audience. It is your listener's choice how to process that information. In the persuasive presentation, not only you are providing information to your audience but you are also issuing a challenge to the audience about what to do with that information. In the persuasive presentation, you are asking your audience for CHANGE. You are asking the audience not only to accept your information but to act in a way that is consistent with your purposes and goals. For the persuasive presentation, the demands are greater on every level! To be an effective and successful persuasive presenter, you must convince your audience you are an expert on your topic and create solid credibility. Your knowledge and research must be

Image © Kzenon, 2009. Used under license from Shutterstock, Inc.

thorough! A simple audience analysis will not accomplish your goals. You must know the knowledge level of your audience as well as their specific attitudes and beliefs toward your topic. To be persuasive, you cannot simply present information, but you must construct arguments that are logical, well developed, and realistic. Then, you must emotionally involve your audience with that information and know what will motivate them to act in the way you desire.

Persuasive presentations are a great challenge. It is a process where you lead the audience to accept and ultimately act on your ideas. To rise to that challenge, you will need to understand and apply the concepts in this chapter. Let's start by asking the question, "What is persuasion?"

What Is Persuasion?

Persuasion is a psychological process in which a presenter is asking the audience for a change. You may be asking your audience to change their thoughts about a particular subject, to make a commitment to a group on campus, or give their time to a cause. When you are making a persuasive presentation, you are giving a call for a specific action. Ultimately, **persuasive speaking** is the creation of oral messages that will increase commitment, alter beliefs, attitudes or values, and ultimately ask for a change in the audience's actions.

Persuasive speaking makes demands upon the audience that goes beyond informative speaking. You are attempting to influence the audience to act or to think a specific way according to your predetermined goals. You may be trying to convince a group to donate time to help out your favorite cause. You may be trying to get your employees to work together to accomplish an important project with a looming deadline. You may be presenting your company to a group of potential investors. As a presenter, your goal is to move your audience from the point where they are to where you want them to be.

Knowing Your Goals: What Do I Want of My Audience?

A persuasive presentation often fails long before it ever reaches the ears of an audience. Why? So many times, the presenter never stops to ask the important question: "What are my goals for my audience? What is the end result that I want to accomplish? What specifically do I want my audience *to do* at the end of my presentation?" If you are not clear about your goals and do not communicate those goals clearly, how will your audience know what you want them to think or do?

The goal for your audience depends on the particular persuasive goal you have in mind. In Chapter 4, you learned there are three types of people in your audience: the confused, the skeptical, and the apathetic. You have to make your audience believe, understand, and care. To reach your goal, you must move the confused audience to understanding, the skeptical to believing, and the apathetic to caring. These are not three separate goals, but one overall goal for your persuasive presentation. Before you can get anyone to act, you must first make them understand your message, believe your message, and care enough to become involved. The more specific you make your goal, the better you can arrange your arguments, your emotional appeals, and your call to action.

How to Identify Your Persuasive Goals

At this point, you have selected your topic, done your research, and gathered your verbal supportive material. The next step is to identify your general goal and specific goal. Your general goal of course is to persuade. Your specific goal comes from the questions: What do I want the audience to KNOW, to FEEL, and to DO? If you are persuading your audience to regularly donate blood, what do you want them to know, feel, and do? Here's an example:

What do I want my audience to **KNOW?**
    The importance of regularly donating blood
    How low the normal daily supplies are
    There isn't a sufficient supply in case of emergencies
    There is a greater demand for certain blood types
    There may not be a supply of blood if a loved one is in need

What do I want my audience to **FEEL?**
    A sense of urgency about donating blood
    Concern about the supplies
    Fear about the lack of supplies for their loved ones

What do I want my audience to **DO?**
    Know where the local donation centers are located
    Know their own blood type.
    Donate time to their local blood drive
    Give blood on a monthly basis.
    Encourage their friends and family also to regularly donate blood.

Now you have laid the foundation for your presentation. You have just specifically answered, "What do I want my audience to know, feel, and do?" The more specific you are, the better you can tailor your persuasive presentation. The answers to these questions will also help you later when you organize your speech in Monroe's Motivated Sequence. Also, it has provided a base for determining what you need to know about your audience's attitudes, beliefs, and values.

Attitudes, Values, and Beliefs

What is the difference between attitudes, beliefs, and values? It is important to understand the difference between the three, because it will affect the way that you approach your persuasive presentation. An **attitude** is a learned predisposition to respond either favorably (like) or unfavorably (dislike) to an object, person, etc. An attitude is something that you have learned over time from others, or from your own experience (Frymeir & Nadler, 2007). You may not like broccoli because one of your friends told you it was terrible, or you may not like it because you tried it and it tasted horrible! No matter how you have learned that attitude, it is a predictor of how you are going to act. If you do not like broccoli (a negative attitude), then it is very likely that you will not eat broccoli unless someone persuades you to try it. An attitude is a predisposition that indicates how you or your audience will act. When you persuade your audience to change an attitude about something or someone, you will also influence them to change their actions toward that thing or person.

A **belief** is the way that you look at the world or the way that you structure your reality. A belief helps you to understand and organize the world around you. It helps you to determine what is true or false, fact or fiction, in the world. Beliefs tend to be stronger and more enduring than attitudes. When giving a persuasive presentation, you must be aware that it is more difficult to change beliefs than attitudes. The challenge to persuade your audience becomes greater, and you must adapt your presentation to reflect this challenge. With beliefs, your logical arguments and motivational appeals must also be stronger.

Even stronger than beliefs are **values**. Values are core beliefs about how much "worth," "impor-

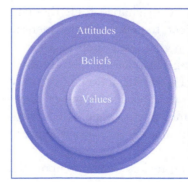

The closer to the center, the more persuasive you will have to be. Values are harder to change than beliefs and beliefs are more difficult to change than attitudes!

tance," "preciousness," or "sacredness" something or someone has. These values (e.g., "I think diamonds are precious jewels.") then guide your thoughts and actions (e.g., "I will give my precious girlfriend a diamond ring!"). Your collections of beliefs and values are enduring beliefs at the core of the person, which help the person determine right or wrong (i.e., his/her ethics). According to Frymeir and Nader (2007, p. 29), values are closely linked to one's identity and sense of self. Because they are so closely linked to who you are, your values are extremely difficult to change. Also, your values are often directly linked to your behavior. If you believe it is wrong to lie, you will not lie. If you value your democratic rights, you will vote.

By understanding the differences between your audience's attitudes, beliefs, and values, you can determine the purpose of your persuasive presentation and write your outcome statement. An **outcome statement** is a sentence that summarizes what you ultimately want your audience to do. It should be specific and have a measurable, observable action for the audience to perform. Here are some examples:

- The audience will *donate* one day of their time to help build the city's new park.

- The audience will *make a donation* to the United Way to help adult literacy.

- The audience will *call* their national representatives to urge the passing of the New Clean Water Act.

Each of these purpose statements has a specific call to action for the audience.

Now that you have determined the overall goal of your presentation, you can analyze your audience and develop your arguments tailored to their specific attitudes, beliefs, and values. By analyzing your audience, you will be able to assess how they will respond and adjust your presentation to make it as clear and convincing as possible.

Analyzing Your Audience and Adapting Your Goals

If you want to effectively persuade your audience, you must realize that every audience is different and needs a different approach. What is successful with one audience may not work with another audience. As a teenager, you automatically knew that if you wanted to borrow a car and $25 dollars on Friday night, you did not approach your father the same way you approached your mother. You instinctively knew that you had to adapt your persuasion if you wanted to be successful! You used different arguments with Mom than you did with Dad. For Mom, it was important to know who you were with, where you were going, and when you would be home. For Dad, you probably had to promise to be careful, not scratch the car and put gas in the tank before you came home. You understood what motivated each parent and used the right persuasive arguments to borrow the car on Friday night. Persuasive presentations are no different. Just like you did with Mom and Dad, when you give a persuasive presentation, you must tailor your presentation to the needs, desires, and predispositions of your audience. The best way to do that is to conduct an audience analysis. The audience analysis helps you to understand three things: (1) who is in your audience, (2) what external factors are influencing your audience, and (3) what moves or motivates your audience.

Audience Analysis—The Key to Persuasion!

When people first meet, they begin asking each other questions and telling about themselves to help reduce the initial uncertainty of the situation (Berger & Calabrese, 1975). Similarly, the audience analysis allows you to size-up your audience so you will have some idea about who they are, what they are like, what behaviors/habits they practice, and how they will respond to your persuasive message. This information will make you not only a more confident presenter, the audience analysis is the only way to discover what may or may not persuade your audience! Remember, people resist change! They don't want to be told what to do! However, the purpose of persuasion is to influence people to adopt new thoughts and behaviors. By thoroughly analyzing your audience member's attitudes/feelings about a topic, habits/behaviors related to that topic, and their level of knowledge/beliefs about the topic, only then can you craft a persuasive presentation that may change their thoughts and actions.

▌ *Three Areas of Audience Analysis*

As introduced in Chapter 4, an audience analysis includes (1) a demographic analysis, (2) a situational analysis, and (3) an attitudinal analysis. Let's start with the goals of the demographic analysis.

Demographic Analysis

A demographic analysis is a descriptive summary of the audience's objective characteristics or traits. Descriptive characteristics you may need to measure include the age, income level, rank, race, gender, and educational level of your audience members. For example, delivering a persuasive presentation to a room of 20-year-old men is very different than presenting to a room full of 60-year-old women. While we cannot say all men or women thing the same way, evaluate your examples, facts and illustrations in a way that will appeal to both genders. Similarly, you need to present a more sophisticated and well-supported argument to a highly educated audience (e.g., lawyers). However, you would need to use less sophisticated language and arguments with a minimally educated audience (e.g., 6th graders). If you were trying to persuade your audience to change Medicare benefits, you need to know how many Republicans, how many Democrats, and how many medical professionals are in your audience. Other topics may have more relevance to audience members' religious backgrounds, ethnic or racial heritage, marital status, job/work background, and a number of other traits/characteristics.

Combined, these demographics can help you select the most appropriate persuasive facts, arguments, and appeals based on the audience's similarities and differences. By identifying and measuring these important demographic traits, you can begin to understand the types of people you will be addressing and which strategies will be most persuasive with your unique audience. Here are some of the most common demographics that may have relevance to planning your persuasive presentation:

- Gender—what is the percentage of men and women in my audience?
- Age—what age groups are in my audience?
- Education—how educated is my audience?
- Affiliations—what social, religious, political, or professional groups are in my audience?

Situational Analysis

Always carefully consider the situation, occasion, and setting which you will be presenting. Consider the situational variables of presenting at a large church on Sunday morning. This situation would call for a different delivery style and content than presenting at the Monday morning departmental meeting at work. Likewise, the occasion of a funeral is very different than the occasion of a birthday party; each requires very different approaches to persuading others to appreciate and celebrate a person's life. Here are some key situational variables you should consider and adapt to when delivering a persuasive presentation:

- Occasion (purpose of this event, other recent events, other speakers they heard, etc.)
- Mood/tone (serious, celebratory, formal, informal, etc.)
- Time (time of day, amount of time given to speak, order of presentation, etc.)
- Location (indoors or outdoors, seating, lighting, size of space/room, stage, etc.)

Attitudinal Analysis

An attitudinal analysis is the most important step in analyzing your audience. An attitudinal analysis is an assessment of your audience's general disposition (attitudes, beliefs, and values) and knowledge level about your topic. While it is important to understand your audience's demographic characteristics

All three elements are necessary to persuade your audience. Ignore or fail to develop one of the elements and your persuasive presentation will fail to move your audience.

(e.g., age and gender) and the situation in which you will be presenting, your most important insights come from analyzing your audience's attitudes, behaviors, and knowledge level. Understanding what your audience likes, values, beliefs, and desires will give you a better chance of persuading your audience. Knowing whether the audience agrees with your topic or will react negatively will determine how you will adapt your topic and your persuasive strategies. Knowing if your audience is apathetic toward your topic or if they will react strongly will help you determine which emotional and motivation appeals will be appropriate. By effectively adapting your content to their lives, needs, hopes, habits, etc., you have the best chance of delivering a clear, credible, and persuasive presentation. Here are some of the key issues you'll want to examine in your attitudinal analysis:

- The audience's desires, likes, dislikes, motivations, and needs related to the topic?

- The audience's habits/behaviors related to the topic?

- The audience's knowledge of and beliefs about the topic?

- The audience's values related to the topic?

- The audience's sense of right/wrong (i.e., ethics) related to the topic?

▌ Where Do I Get Demographic, Situational, and Attitudinal Information?

Now that you understand the type of information you want to gather in an audience analysis, the next issue is finding the demographic, situational, and attitudinal information you need. But, where do you look? Audience analysis information can be gathered through several different sources.

1. *Ask the person who invited or gave you permission to present.* He/she will be familiar with the situation, the demographic composition, and some of the attitudes, beliefs, etc., of your audience.

2. *Ask someone who has presented to this audience in the past.* Past presenters can give you insights into the type of audience members you will be addressing, the situation, and how they reacted to previous presentations.

3. *Talk to individuals who will be members of your audience.* When possible, talk to individuals who are members of your future audience. They can give you firsthand information about the setting, the audience members, and their dispositions. These individuals can give you great insights into the wants, needs, and knowledge levels represented in your audience.

4. *Read published information about your audience.* Suppose you were presenting at a manufacturing tradeshow or the annual meeting of a national organization. Newspaper articles, Internet websites, and company/organizational publications are often valuable sources for information about the type of individuals who are members of these organizations or work in these industries.

5. *Survey members of your audience.* A written survey is the best method for gathering demographic and attitudinal information from your audience. It allows you to ask specific questions about your audience's behaviors, dispositions, beliefs, and knowledge. While this is a common practice in the classroom, having the opportunity to distribute a survey to the employees of an organization or members of a community group is rarely possible. Typically, you would not have a chance to do such before a sales presentation, business meeting, or presentation to a local organization.

▌ Advice for Creating Audience Analysis Surveys

If you do have the opportunity to develop and administer a written survey of your audience's demographic and attitudinal data, there are three types of questions you can use to gather information: (1) **closed-ended questions**, (2) scale **questions**, and (3) **open-ended questions**. First, **closed-ended** (or fixed-alternative) questions provide respondents with options from which they can select the appropriate answer. Examples of closed-ended questions include true/false, agree/disagree, or multiple-choice questions (e.g., Circle one: Male or Female or Check one: Democrat___, Republican___, Independent___). Second, **scale questions** measure the respondents' impressions or reactions to a question or statement. If you wanted to measure the audience's feelings about current economic conditions, you could propose a statement (e.g., "The economy will be stronger one year from today") and have respondents rate their reactions (strongly disagree – 1 – 2 – 3 – 4 – 5 – strongly agree). Finally, open-ended questions do not provide options from which respondents select answers. **Open-ended questions** allow respondents to freely answer questions in their own words. Open-ended questions can provide great insight into the dispositions, beliefs, and actions of the audience (e.g., "If you did vote in the last presidential election, explain the most important factors influencing your voting decision." "What qualities are you looking for in our next US President?" "If you did not vote in the last presidential election, please explain why you did not.").

Clearly, these three types of questions produce different types of useful data. The key is to select the best combination of these questions to reveal the most important information about your audience's demographic and attitudinal traits. Here are some helpful guidelines to keep in mind when creating an audience analysis survey.

1. *Keep them brief.* The survey should be brief enough that an audience member can complete it in 5–10 minutes. Remember that closed-ended questions take the least amount of time and open-ended questions take the most time to answer.

2. *Ask clear, unambiguous questions.* Vague questions produce vague answers. Specific questions will provide more helpful information. For example, "How should society punish criminals?" is too vague. Providing questions about specific crimes will elicit clearer insight into respondents' beliefs about "appropriate punishment for criminals."

3. *Carefully plan and pretest to ensure your survey will elicit the desired information.* It is a great idea to ask a few friends to complete the survey before you distribute it to audience members. Based on their feedback, you can determine if questions need to be revised, added, or deleted, and if the survey questionnaire is an appropriate length.

Now that you have successfully analyzed your audience and understand their viewpoint, you are ready to craft arguments that will successfully persuade your audience. Again, it is not enough to simply give your audience information. You must create an argument that is convincing. An **argument** is a set of statements or reasons given that persuade an audience that your goal is the right or best one. Your arguments are what "lead" your audience to their final decision. Creating the most persuasive argument involves (1) building your credibility with your audience, (2) creating a logical argument that your audience can follow, and (3) using appeals that will motivate or emotionally move your audience. In the following section, we will discuss how to tailor your persuasive presentation using these three critical elements.

Creating Your Arguments— Using Credibility, Logical Reasoning, and Emotional Appeals

Your Credibility (Ethos)

Aristotle held that persuasion was made up of three main elements: ethos, logos, and pathos. **Ethos** is the credibility and character of the presenter. Aristotle broke ethos down into three dimensions, which are good character, good will, and intelligence. Today, we would think of **credibility** more as the audience's perception of the expertise, trustworthiness, and dynamism of the presenter (Frymeir & Nadler, 2007). Your **expertise** is how skilled and knowledgeable you are about your topic. Trustworthiness is how you demonstrate your honesty, sincerity, and ethical concern for the audience. Finally, **dynamism** is the power and energy in your delivery. In all presentations, it is important to build one's credibility, but it becomes critical in the persuasive presentation. Because you are asking your audience to change their beliefs or behave in a new way, your audience is going to question your motives, knowledge, and sincerity. The higher your credibility with the audience, the more likely your persuasive presentation will be a success. So how do you build your credibility with your audience? By becoming a presenter who is seen as competent, trustworthy, and dynamic! You will be more persuasive to your audience if you demonstrate your expertise about your topic. A persuasive presentation demands a greater depth of knowledge and research than the informative presentation. You must provide your audience with the information that they need to make an informed decision. By providing ample supportive material, citing your sources, being aware of other positions on your topic, and presenting your material in an organized way, your audience will see you as a credible presenter. Do not forget that part of your expertise is including your experience, recognitions, and positions that you hold in relation to your topic. If you are not given an introduction prior to presenting, explain your qualifications at the beginning of your presentation! Including your experience along with your research and knowledge in your introduction will build your audience's respect for you as a speaker.

You will also be seen as a credible presenter if your audience believes that you are **trustworthy**, or sincere and honest, in your presentation. By understanding your audience's position and showing a concern for their opinions, you gain the trust of your audience. Persuasion is a process of leading your audience to your position. Do not alienate your audience by saying that your ideas or beliefs are superior! Instead, create a persuasive argument that demonstrates the benefits of your position and the disadvantages of their position. Your audience will also trust you if you handle your information and statistics in an honest manner. If your audience suspects that you have put a "spin" on the information that you are presenting, or are manipulating statistics, you will quickly lose your credibility!

Dynamism is important throughout your presentation. People typically feel that a presenter is more credible if the presentation is delivered in an energetic and polished manner. A presentation that is delivered with good movement, strong eye contact, appropriate gestures, and enthusiastic vocal inflection will gain the audience's respect and attention. An audience feels more connection and concern with a speaker who smiles at them and makes good eye contact. Have you ever smiled at a stranger? What happens? They normally smile back at you. Smiling and making good eye contact with your audience makes them smile and look back at you. You gain their respect and attention immediately. Also, relaxed movement and gestures communicates to the audience that you are confident about what you are saying. If you display confidence in what you are saying, the audience will also feel confident in your information. Enthusiastic vocal

inflection will help to hold your audience's attention. How often have you fallen asleep in a presentation when the speaker read in a monotone voice? By varying your volume, tone, and pitch, you can set the mood of the audience. Speaking softly and slowly will relax your audience. Raising the volume and pitch can bring excitement to your point.

The best way to develop a confident and polished presentation is through practice! A speech is not really a speech until it is spoken out loud. Rehearsing your presentation out loud will help you discover problems in your speech before you are in front of an audience. Also, practice will increase your confidence in your ability to give a dynamic presentation!

Your Logic and Arguments (Logos)

The second element in persuasion is *logos*, or the logical appeals incorporated in the presenter's arguments. You will be a more effective persuader if you can provide your audience with logical, well-constructed arguments that are effectively supported with evidence. Again, you should start with your audience in mind when constructing your arguments and gathering your **support material**. What will your audience need or demand from your arguments? Is the audience receptive, neutral, or skeptical? A skeptical audience will demand more evidence and reasons to support your position. What types of evidence will they need to accept your arguments and be moved to action? If you are asking the audience to invest in your business, you will likely need statistical information and charts, information on past performance, market trends, and future projections. If you are giving a presentation on a community issue, you may need expert testimony, cost projections, past information on the issue, and information on competing issues. By carefully considering your audience and topic, you can determine the arguments and evidence that will best persuade your listeners.

Developing Your Arguments

Developing your arguments is the same as presenting your audience with reasons that they should accept your position. Careful research and taking the time to think about the topic should identify a list of reasons that your audience should do what you suggest. If your outcome statement is: "I want the audience to begin a 30-minute exercise program three times a week," your reasons might be:

1. Americans are living an unhealthy lifestyle.

2. Americans are heavier than they have ever been.

3. Most health problems Americans face are related to inactivity.

4. The health costs to inactive Americans are incredibly high.

5. Americans can avoid many health problems through moderate exercise.

6. Americans can live longer, healthier lives with a moderate exercise program.

Now that you have developed a good list of arguments, select three or four that will be the best arguments. Your criteria for selecting your arguments should be the ones that best prove your main point, can be supported through reliable evidence, and will have the most impact on your audience. Once you have developed your reasons, you need to find evidence to support that evidence. Ask questions like: Who does my audience think is an expert? Where is the best place to find my information? What is my audience reading? These questions will help you determine where to locate the most credible information. Remember, your audience will be evaluating your support, so be sure to find the most up-to-date information from the best available sources. If you are asking your audience to begin a moderate exercise program stating, "According to the latest Surgeon General's report, people who are usually inactive can improve their health and well-being by becoming even moderately active on a regular basis" can serve as an expert opinion. For each argument, provide enough evidence that will support your point. Use a variety of supportive material to make your point stronger. You can start with a story, followed by a statistic, provide an explanation, and finally relate a testimony. Remember the amount of support depends on what you are asking your audience to do. Values are harder to change than beliefs and attitudes. Your support must reflect this challenge. The better job that you do at providing support for your arguments, the better chance you have of persuading your audience to do what you ask.

Pointers for Developing Your Arguments

- *Organize your arguments* – start with your strongest arguments first and move to weaker arguments or from weakest to strongest. Your organization will help your audience follow your reasoning.

- *Use ample supportive material* – don't be afraid to use several different types of supportive material. A story followed by a statistic supported by expert testimony can motivate your audience to listen to your arguments. Including novel evidence will also encourage your audience to pay attention to your arguments.

- *Know the opposing position* – knowledge of the opposition's position can give you strength in developing your arguments.

- *Know your audience's objections* – every audience will have objections to your proposal. Thoughtfully and respectfully answering those objections can move a skeptical audience.

- *Avoid arousing hostility* – don't directly attack the opposition. Your audience may develop an "underdog" mentality and support the opposing position.

- *Address negative attitudes indirectly* – just as you don't want to directly attack the opposition, don't directly attack the audience. Approach the topic indirectly or present your position positively.

Using Logical Reasoning

Now that you have developed your arguments and found your supportive material, you are ready to arrange your arguments logically. By incorporating logical reasoning into your presentation, you can help your audience draw the proper conclusions from your arguments. You use **logical reasoning** every day to move you from one thought to another. You might say, "If I don't study for this test, then I will probably fail the test. If I fail the test, then I may do poorly in the class. If I do poorly in the class, then my GPA will suffer." You have just walked through a logical procession from failing a test to having a poor GPA. Your audience is also looking for logical connections in your presentation. It is your responsibility in your persuasive presentation to make those connections for the audience clear and compelling. There are four main types of reasoning that you can use in your presentation: inductive reasoning, deductive reasoning, analogical reasoning, and causal reasoning.

Inductive reasoning is reasoning which moves from a specific instance to a general conclusion. You are presenting a specific example and making a claim that the general conclusion is also valid. If you were persuading an audience that raising taxes on businesses is a bad idea, you could use inductive reasoning:

Specific Instance: In Baymont, Minnesota, when the Town Council raised the taxes on local businesses, many of the town's main businesses were forced to move or close their doors.

Furthermore, business taxes across the state of Minnesota have made many businesses close their doors or find states with lower tax rates.

This situation has been repeated in many states that have raised their taxes on businesses.

General Conclusion: Raising the taxes on business in the United States would cause many businesses to close and move their operations overseas.

By including evidence that supports your points, you have given your audience a powerful reason to agree with your argument.

Deductive reasoning is applying a generally accepted idea to a more specific instance. The difference between deductive reasoning and inductive reasoning is that deductive reasoning usually has a second premise. With deductive reasoning, if the generally accepted premise is valid, then the specific conclusion will also be true (Gronbeck, McKerrow, Ehninger, & Monroe, 1994). For example:

General Premise: All plants are alive.
Secondary Premise: Pansies are plants.
Conclusion: Pansies are alive.

This is a simplistic example, but shows the relationship between the general premise, secondary premise, and the conclusion. Since all plants are alive (generally accepted concept) and the supporting premise "pansies are plants" is also true, then it is logical to assume the conclusion will also true. You can incorporate this into your persuasive presentation. Suppose you are trying to persuade your audience to approve funding for your local school district. One of your arguments would be that if funding were approved, students would benefit from expanded programs. Deductive reasoning would state:

General Instance: Students benefit from expanded school programs.
Secondary Premise: Music and art are beneficial programs for students.

Conclusion: Students would benefit from expanded music and art programs in school curricula.

When using deductive reasoning, the conclusion is certain. With supportive material that supports your claims, your arguments are strengthened and your audience is moved to your desired conclusion.

A third type of reasoning is analogical reasoning. Analogical reasoning compares a concept, situation, or object that may be unfamiliar to the audience with a familiar concept, situation, or object. In analogical reasoning, you are helping your audience to make connections. If you are arguing the point that stricter DUI laws are needed in your state, you can compare it to the stricter laws that were enacted in a nearby state. Another example of analogical reasoning is: In New York City crime has dropped dramatically after the streets were physically cleaned. Our city should clean up the streets to reduce the number of crimes. By showing the audience a similar situation, you can make the argument that similar results can be expected. With analogical reasoning, it is important to make sure that the comparisons that you make are relevant and between similar concepts or objects. If the audience does not agree that the comparisons are similar, then your arguments will be rejected.

Causal reasoning is reasoning where you demonstrate that one event is related or caused by another event or situation. You can state that because the literacy rate in schools has improved, graduates are finding better jobs. You are linking literacy to better jobs. Causal reasoning can be a powerful type of reasoning, but you must make sure that there is a true relationship between the two events. You must provide ample support to demonstrate that there is a factual relationship between the two events that you are comparing. You could state that because of the limited parking, students are consistently late to 8:00 a.m. classes. The argument could sound good, but is that always the reason that students are late to 8:00 a.m. classes? If you do not provide a strong enough connection between the events, then your audience will not be persuaded by your arguments. When using causal reasoning, be aware that it is a powerful type of reasoning, but it also can be simplistic. Often there is more than one contributing cause for an event. You could use causal reasoning to persuade your audience that carbon emissions from cars are causing global warming. Is that the only reason for global warming? Probably not. Global warming can be caused by a variety of factors. When using causal reasoning, your support must make a strong link between the two factors and should be well supported.

Your Emotional Appeals (Pathos)

Once you have developed the logical arguments in your presentation, you must think about your emotional and motivational appeals. Aristotle said that there are three elements in effective persuasion: the ethos, logos, and pathos. Without all three, your persuasion will not move your audience. Your pathos, or emotional appeals, are just as important as the logical arguments. People will often say that they are persuaded by the logical arguments of a presentation, but in reality most people will not commit until they "feel" something in your presentation. Think of how many times you have heard the statistics about how many children go to bed hungry. The statistics are terrible, but you are not moved until you see the face of the hungry child and "feel" upset about the child's condition. Just giving information will not move your audience to believe or act. They must be motivated through your appeals. There are three ways to motivate your audience to action: through emotional appeals, motivational appeals, and cognitive dissonance.

Emotional appeals are messages directed at heightening one or more of the basic human emotions. Some of the most commonly used emotions in persuasion are:

- Fear
- Guilt
- Sorrow
- Happiness
- Joy
- Love
- Pride
- Satisfaction
- Greed

Your presentation and your audience will determine which emotional appeals will work best. The early question "What do I want my audience to feel?" will help you determine the best emotional appeal. Fear appeals are commonly used in many persuasive presentations because they work! We are highly motivated to avoid negative consequences. Fear appeals when directed toward the audience or toward a close friend or family member are extremely effective at getting the audience to change their beliefs or behavior. Fear appeals are normally presented as "if – then statements": "If you use drugs you could destroy your future." "If you don't give blood, it may not be there when someone you love needs it." The most effective fear appeals are the ones where the audience feels the power to take action. Strong, realistic fear appeals are the most effective at moving the audience if you are able to support that there is a threat to the audience (Beebe, Beebe, & Ivy, 2009).

Other emotions are also effective at motivating your audience. In Ronald Reagan's address to the nation after the 1986 Challenger tragedy, he used hope and pride to challenge the nation to continue the space program:

> I've always had great faith in and respect for our space program. And what happened today does nothing to diminish it. We don't hide our space program. We don't keep secrets and cover things up. We do it all up front and in public. That's the way freedom is, and we wouldn't change it for a minute. We'll continue our quest in space. There will be more shuttle flights and more shuttle crews and, yes, more volunteers, more civilians, more teachers in space. Nothing ends here; our hopes and our journeys continue. (American Rhetoric)

Through the Challenger address, Reagan used emotional appeals to convince the American people that the Space program was an important part of America's future.

Emotional appeals are powerful and are often more effective at moving the audience to action than logical appeals. The more you incorporate emotional appeals into your presentation, the more involved your audience will become and the more persuasive your presentation will be.

Motivations and Emotions

Another way to persuade your audience is to use **motivational appeals** to stir the audience's deeply felt emotional desires and motives. Motivational appeals are messages that are linked to the values and beliefs of the audience. Motivational messages highlight the audience's internal drives or needs. Everyone is driven by internal desires. You may want to be successful. You may value personal achievement. You enjoy being appreciated for your work. Your personal motivations are powerful and determine many of your actions. How do you use motivational appeals? First, knowing the values and beliefs of your audience is important in deciding which motivational appeal will be the most effective. Some general motivational values that you can use in your persuasive presentation are:

- Security
- Comfort
- Excitement
- Adventure
- Personal achievement
- Tradition or family values
- Acceptance/Belonging
- Recognition
- Personal improvement
- Power
- Success

This is only a short list. If you think about it, you can probably quickly add several more. However, these are some motivational needs that your audience commonly feels. The simple line, "We can achieve these results together!" can tap into several

Image © Yuri Arcurs, 2009. Used under license from Shutterstock, Inc.

motivational values: success, personal achievement, and belonging. The well-known Army slogan "Be all that you can be" uses personal improvement and personal success as motivators.

Your choice of which motivational appeal to use will depend greatly on the purpose of your persuasive presentation and the general demographics of your audience. If your persuasive presentation is asking for group action, an appeal to acceptance or belonging may be appropriate. For example, John is trying to persuade his audience to participate in community service. In his speech, he motivates the audience by appealing to personal improvement and belonging.

Together, we can make our community a better place. By giving a few hours of your time, you can teach a child to read, help an elderly person with their errands, or make our neighborhood a safer place to walk. We can work together. We can build our community together. We can become better citizens and better people with a few short hours of our time.

If you want individual action, a motivational appeal to personal success, personal improvement, or personal security may be more appropriate.

As you can see, motivational appeals are important. Think of motivational appeals as triggers that are preset in your audience, ready, and waiting to be activated. By pressing the appropriate trigger, your audience is motivated to act or believe in a desired way.

Using Cognitive Dissonance to Motivate Your Audience

Another way to motivate your audience to action is through **cognitive dissonance**. Cognitive dissonance occurs when you realize that your beliefs (thoughts), emotions (feelings), and actions (behaviors) are inconsistent with one another. These inconsistencies create psychological discomfort and you are motivated to relieve that discomfort by changing your either your beliefs, emotions, or actions. For example: If you believe it is important to put aside a portion of every paycheck into savings, but at the end of the month, you have spent your whole paycheck, then you will feel bad (cognitive dissonance) about not saving your money. If that uncomfortable feeling is great enough, you will either change your belief, or you will begin to put money into savings. Effective persuaders know that creating cognitive dissonance in the listener can motivate the listener to change their beliefs or be compelled to act. The easiest way to create dissonance in your audience is to point out that their beliefs do not match their behaviors. The advertisement by the AdCouncil that says "Friends don't let friends drive drunk" is a good example of using cognitive dissonance to persuade people not to let others drive after they have been drinking. If you are a good friend (and who isn't?), you will not let your friend drive drunk. If you do let your friend drive, then evidently you are not a "good" friend. The uncomfortable feeling that you have causes you to take your friend's keys and drive them home.

When using cognitive dissonance, your audience has several choices in how to eliminate the uncomfortable feeling. They can deny that a problem exists. Your logical arguments should be strong enough to prevent their denial. Your audience can discredit you as a speaker. However, if you have taken time to build your credibility, it will be difficult for your audience to do. Your audience can stop listening, but you should have enough verbal supportive material to hold their attention. Or your audience can change their attitudes, values, or behaviors. If you have given your audience a suitable solution to the problem and your audience is able to comply with your request, they will be motivated to act in the way you suggest.

Monroe's Motivated Sequence

Now that you have constructed your arguments and developed your appeals for your presentation, it is time to organize it into an approach that will motivate your audience. Your final organization is the approach that targets your audience and directs them to your ultimate goal. If you have ever been awake late at night, found yourself mesmerized by an infomercial, and felt the need for the product just advertised – you have experienced the power of Monroe's Motivated Sequence. Monroe's Motivated Sequence is a psychological process which moves the listener to immediate action through five steps: Attention, Need, Satisfaction, Visualization, and Action. Developed by Allen Monroe in the 1920s, this organizational pattern taps in the personal needs and goals of the audience and motivates the audience to immediate change in belief or action. Monroe's Motivated Sequence is effective because it is readily adaptable to a variety of topics and can be personalized to an audience's unique needs and desires. It guides your listener through an organized series of psychological steps that develops a sense of need or want. After establishing the need or want, Monroe's Motivated Sequence provides your listener a way to satisfy that need. By painting a compelling picture of the future, your audience is motivated to act to produce that future.

Attention	• Effectively gain attention and create desire to listen
Need	• Clearly state the need. Your audience must be convinced that the need is important
Satisfaction	• Offer your solution to the need
Visualization	• Tell your audience how this will benefit them
Action	• Give a clear and compelling call to action or change

■ Step 1—Attention

The first step in Monroe's Motivated Sequence is to gain your audience's attention. In Chapter 6, you learned effective ways to gain the audience's attention through stories, dramatic statements, novel questions or humor. The best planned presentations will be wasted if you cannot immediately win your audience's attention. Within the first minutes of your introduction involve your audience with your topic so they want to know more. Beware of beginning any presentation with "Today I want to tell you . . ." or "My presentation is about . . . ," especially a persuasive presentation. Tap into your audience's sense of curiosity and interest. Novel stories and illustrations are effective in gaining and holding the audience's attention and work well with Monroe's Motivated Sequence. In the sample speech at the end of the chapter, Debbie begins her presentation with a compelling story:

He has big brown eyes and a bright, beautiful smile. He is an amazing little boy. To see him today you might not suspect his difficult beginning in life. His birth mother, for reasons known only to her, decided she couldn't keep her baby boy. So, at four weeks of age she left him with a Guatemalan lawyer and disappeared forever. The little boy was sent to live in an orphanage. Sadly, this is the case for many children around the world.

This story effectively grabs the audience's attention and piques their interest in what is coming next. At this point you can begin to establish why your topic is important to your audience.

■ Step 2—Need

Once you have gained your audience's attention, you must establish why the topic is important and why they should be concerned. You must clearly make the point that the topic is personally relevant to their interests. In developing your presentation, create a clear and compelling statement that demonstrates the need.

The problem of orphaned children throughout the world has reached epidemic proportions.

One you have given a clear need statement, you should support your statement. Your verbal supportive material should be relevant, up-to-date, and clearly impress upon your audience that a problem exists. Facts, statistics, and expert testimony can help your audience understand the scope and seriousness of the problem. If you are not able to convince your audience that a problem or need exists, you will not be able to move them to action in the final step.

Continue to stress the importance of the need by presenting the ramifications of the topic (Gronbeck, et al., 1994). What will happen if this problem is not addressed? What will be the consequences? Add the arguments you created earlier until you have sufficiently demonstrated to the audience that there is a clear compelling need.

The U.S. State Department website, taken on June, 10, 2004, states that the number of immigrant visas issued to orphans coming to the U.S. for adoption increased from about 7,000 in 1990 to 18,000 in the year 2000. Of course, these numbers only reflect orphans able to be adopted because they are from countries that have adoption procedures. Many countries have no established procedures for international adoption or simply don't allow it.

Finally, directly tie the problem to the audience's situation. How will the audience be affected if the problem is not solved? Tie the problem directly to their personal happiness, security, physical health, or self-esteem. Here Debbie ties the need of adopting children to the future of our society:

Every child deserves a family. The problem of orphaned children affects all of us because a society that cannot or will not care for its most helpless, children, is a society in grave danger.

By impressing the audience with the seriousness of the problem and making it personal, you will hold your audience's attention and they will be open to consider your solution in the Satisfaction step.

■ Step 3—Satisfaction

Now that you have convinced your audience that there is a clear and compelling need that must be addressed, your audience will be automatically searching for a solution. Provide your audience with an acceptable solution that satisfies the problem that you introduced in the Need step. Make sure that your solution to the problem is realistic. If your solution is unrealistic or your audience does not feel capable of performing, they will reject your solution. Support the validity of your solution by using more verbal supportive material. Offering illustrations, expert testimony, facts, explanations, and statistics demonstrates to the audience that your solution is the best choice.

> *While the issues that create the situations that cause children to be in crisis are complex, there is one solution that works in many cases, adoption.*

Also in your Satisfaction step, show how your solution satisfies all the issues that you have introduced in the Need step. For each issue, illustrate how your solution adequately addresses that problem. This will further persuade the audience that your solution is the best choice.

Another way to demonstrate that your solution is the best choice is to answer any objections that the audience may have to the solution. If you are addressing a skeptical audience, they may be questioning your solution. Questions like: "What are the problems with my solution?" and "Why would this solution not work?" will help you to test the validity of your solution and uncover objections to your solution. Debbie does this by addressing the audience's concerns by stating

> You might be thinking, "But I have heard that families who have adopted children are having lots of problems with those children."

and

> "However, you might also argue that adoption is way too expensive."

Debbie answers two major objections that her audience may have about adoption. She further supports her statements with statistics and examples that answer her audience's specific concerns about problems with adopted children and prohibitive costs. By thoughtfully considering and addressing the objections, you strengthen your Satisfaction step and create a foundation for the Visualization step.

■ Step 4—Visualization

The Visualization step is where you allow the audience to "see" how their life would be better if they accept your solution. This step helps intensify the want or desire that the audience has and makes them more willing to believe, feel, or act upon your call to action. It is during this step where you can paint a vivid picture of how much better their lives would be: happier, healthier, more secure, more fulfilled. It is important in the Visualization step to use vivid language and imagery. You are painting a picture of the future for your audience. Use thick, descriptive language. Analogy is an excellent way to add imagery to your presentation. An analogy is a comparison based on the similarity between the objects. You can say that the "leaves blew across the sidewalk" and your audience will get the idea. However, you can use an analogy and paint of vivid picture of action by saying "the leaves skipped and danced across the sidewalk like happy children." Using metaphors can also illustrate an idea. Instead of saying that it is a heavy rain, you can say that the "rain is coming down in sheets." You have involved your audience's imagination through your description.

Further involve your audience by using words such as "us," "we," and "our." By using inclusive language, you lessen the risk of alienating your audience. In Barack Obama's 2009 inaugural address, he used inclusive language throughout his address to gain the support of the American people. A brief excerpt from his speech illustrates this:

> For everywhere we look, there is work to be done. The state of the economy calls for action, bold and swift, and we will act – not only to create new jobs, but to lay a new foundation for growth. We will build the roads and bridges, the electric grids and digital lines that feed our commerce and bind us together. (NPR)

By using inclusive language you incorporate your audience into your solution.

Along with using vivid imagery and inclusive language, it is important to link back to the Need step where you presented the problems. For every problem that you described in the Need step, you have the opportunity to show the audience the positive way life will be if they immediately act. Systematically go through each problem and give the audience a picture of the future where this need is satisfied by your solution.

To further strengthen your Visualization step, you can also present the negative outcomes if the audience does not choose to act. Vividly describe how bleak their life and future will be if your solution is not accepted.

You can use either the positive method or negative method of describing the future or a combination of both. Your persuasive presentation will determine which approach is best. If you are speaking to a receptive audience, a positive approach may be best. If you are presenting to a skeptical or unreceptive audience, a combination of the positive and negative approach may be more effective at moving the audience to action.

Debbie effectively paints the picture in the Visualization step by sharing her story. She speaks about how adoption has changed her life for the better.

How do I know adoption works? Let me show you how I know . . . . . I'd like to introduce my son . . . . Brandon. Remember the little boy in the story? This is him! Our family is now complete, thanks to adoption.

Debbie actually used her son to create the Visualization step. She could have also described the wonderful changes that have occurred to her family, or told about what they could have missed by not adopting. She could also personalize it and show her audience how their lives would be richer by adopting a child, or what they would miss by not adopting.

When developing your Visualization step, be sure to make it realistic. Describe the outcomes in a believable manner that your audience can accept. Don't overinflate either the positives or the negatives. If the audience perceives that the outcomes are personally relevant and realistic, they are more likely to adopt your solution and behave accordingly.

■ Step 5—Action

The Action step is the summation of your presentation. This is the point to which you have been building. The action step is the **clear**, **direct**, and **specific** call to your audience to think, believe, or act in a particular way. You must make your call to action clear to your audience. They must know exactly what you want them to think, believe, or do. For the speech on adoption, you can ask your audience to research adoption, to talk to friends about the experience of adoption, and to locate local adoption agencies. If your request is too general, your audience may be confused about what action they should take.

It is important to adapt this step to your audience. Every audience is unique and you must offer a solution your audience is capable of doing. Your audience must feel that they have the ability to perform the action. It is also important to make it as easy as possible to comply with what you are asking the audience to do. If you are asking your audience to take action on government legislation, provide them with the addresses or websites of their representatives or members of Congress. If you are encouraging your employees to do community service, bring in people from those organizations and reserve time to connect with the organizations after the presentation. The easier it is for your audience to do what you ask, the more likely they will do what you ask.

Remember, your Action step is your conclusion. In your Action step, do not be afraid to clearly ask your audience to believe or act in a way that you desire. Your goal is to move your audience to action. It is not persuasion until it becomes action! It is important that at the conclusion you do not give your audience an "out" by saying "Please think about what I have said . . ." or "You don't have to agree with me, but . . .." If you offer your audience a way out of making a change, they will happily accept it. If you have effectively held their attention, sufficiently established a need, offered a realistic solution, and demonstrated how their lives will be improved, your audience will be ready for your call to commitment. Make your call to action clear and compelling!

■ Ethical Considerations of Persuasive Speaking

All communication has an effect. Every communication encounter creates a change in the participants. You may walk away with new information or a new perspective or a casual conversation with a friend may make you feel better on a bad day. No matter how imperceptible, you have been changed by your communication. It is important to realize that your communication has consequences. Because persuasive speaking involves intentionally changing a person's attitudes, values, beliefs, or actions, there are greater ethical demands on you as a presenter and persuader. **Ethics** are the principles or guidelines that one uses to determine what is right or wrong in a situation. Often the term "ethics" is used interchangeably with **morals** (Frymeir & Nadler, 2007). Professional communicators face ethical decisions throughout the presentation process. You should think about the goals and motives of your presentation. Would you want your audience to know your true motives? Also, an ethical presenter will deliver the best information available. That requires thorough and careful research, not something you may have pulled off the Internet the night before! As you develop your persuasive presentation, you must respectfully consider your audience's positions. You will earn the respect of your audience if you can demonstrate that you understand their position, even if you are trying to persuade them to adopt yours.

As you present your information, you must consider the ethical implications of your emotional appeals. As you have learned, an emotional appeal can be very powerful and is a vital key to persuading your audience. Using good emotional and motivational appeals are not unethical. However, you must ask the question: "Are my emotional appeals and language honest and reasonable?" Have you provided enough information that the audience can make a rational decision or are you simply trying to sway the audience emotionally? You should never ask your audience to feel an emotion without asking them to rationally think about the topic and the possible outcomes.

Finally, as an ethical presenter and communicator, you must ask yourself what the results will be if the audience is persuaded. Have you asked the audience to do something that will be harmful or unethical? Unethical behavior is always wrong. For an ethical persuader, the ends do not justify the means. What will be the consequences for your audience if they follow through on your suggestions? If you can foresee that something negative or harmful would happen to your audience, then you should not request that action. Even though you are trying to persuade your audience to do something, you should always keep your audience's best interests in mind. If you cannot do that while persuading your audience, then you need to check your motives or your call to action. Your persuasion should always produce beneficial results for your audience, both immediately and in the long-term.

Chapter Review

The persuasive presentation is the most challenging presentation that you can deliver. You are overtly

Ethical Questions to Ask Yourself

- What are my audience's expectations? Am I violating their ethical expectations?
- Have I examined my goals and motives to make sure they are ethically sound?
- Do I demonstrate good character, sincerity, and honesty?
- Did I consider the positions of my audience and treat them with respect?
- Have I used confidential information or potentially dangerous information?
- Have I presented my material in a fair and reasonable way?
  - Did I give my audience enough information to make an informed decision?
  - Did I "slant" or misrepresent my information?
  - Did I use my statistics in an accurate way?
- Have I quoted my sources properly and given credit – even in my visual aids?
- Have I used my emotional appeals ethically?
- What will be the consequences for my audience if they do what I ask? Will they be doing something unethical or eventually harmful?
- Does my persuasion benefit just me or does it benefit my audience?

asking your audience to make a change in their attitudes, beliefs, and actions. Clearly understand and state what you want your audience to believe and do. Once you have clearly defined your objectives, you are ready to target your audience's attitudes and beliefs. Knowing what your audience thinks and believes is important in deciding how you will create your arguments.

With the persuasive presentation, it is important that you build credibility with your audience. Your knowledge and experience on the topic will give your audience a reason to listen to your presentation. You build your credibility by thoroughly researching your topic, showing a concern for your audience's opinion, and presenting your material in a professional and dynamic manner.

To be persuasive, you must also build strong, realistic arguments that are well supported. Developing your reasons and supporting those arguments with a variety of verbal supportive material is vital. Your audience will determine the amount and type of supportive material that you will need. A skeptical audience will demand more and better evidence to support your position than a receptive audience. However, all persuasive presentations demand a greater amount of evidence and supportive material than an informative presentation.

After you have gathered your arguments and supportive material, you have a choice in how to arrange those arguments. Four types of logical reasoning can be used to arrange your points: inductive reasoning, deductive reasoning, analogical reasoning, and causal reasoning. Choosing the appropriate type of reasoning to develop your arguments allows you to lead your audience to the proper conclusions about your topic.

It is not enough to simply provide logical arguments when trying to persuade your audience. No one is persuaded until they "feel" moved to action. You can move your audience to action by using emotional and motivational appeals. Heightening the appropriate emotions, appealing to the audience's internal drives and beliefs, and using cognitive dissonance are effective ways of triggering action in your audience. When your audience understands the problem and feels the urgency to act, they will be persuaded to accept your claims.

To strengthen your persuasive appeal, you can utilize Monroe's Motivated Sequence. Monroe's Motivated Sequence is a psychological process which automatically leads the listener to action. Monroe's Motivated Sequence is organized into five steps. The first step is to gain the audience's attention in the *Attention* step. Once you have effectively gained their attention, you present the *Need* step, or why your topic is important. The third step, or *Satisfaction* step, is where you give your solution to the problem. It is important to give your audience a vivid picture of how the future will be better in the *Visualization* step. Finally, clearly and confidently ask your audience for change in the *Action* step.

Finally, because persuasion is communication that asks the audience for change, it is important that you speak ethically. Your goal is to give a persuasive presentation that not only meets your goals but also keeps the audience's bests interests at heart!

Persuasive Presentations

Investigating Demographic Variables

A demographic analysis allows you to gather information about the descriptive traits and objective characteristics of your audience (age, gender, cultural background, etc.).

As a class, develop a demographic survey to determine the characteristics represented by all your classmates. Look back at the section on demographic analysis to determine what demographic traits could be measured in the classroom. Generate as many as possible demographic questions listing them on the board or on a flip-chart. Have one member record the answers for the entire class and display the statistical results of the survey (e.g., total students = 25; males 10 (40%), females 15 (60%) . . . etc.). Have the entire class share their opinions about the following questions:

- ■ What generalizations can be made about how the audience would think or act?

- ■ What presentation topics do you think would be well received by this audience?

- ■ What topics would be most difficult or challenging to relate to this audience?

Answering below, explain how should you adapt your next speech topic to fit the audience's demographic traits and characteristics.

_____

_____

_____

_____

_____

_____

_____

_____

_____

_____

_____

_____

_____

_____

Developing Scale Questions

The "attitudinal analysis" helps you determine the audience's dispositions, beliefs, and values related to your topic. One way of measuring the intensity of those dispositions, beliefs, and values is through the use of scale questions (e.g., scales ranging from "strongly agree" to "strongly disagree," "very likely" to "very unlikely," "very important" to "very unimportant" etc.). For each of the following purpose statements, formulate **two related scale questions** that would provide you unique and valuable insight into the audience's attitude, beliefs, values, etc.

- ■ To inform my audience about the four steps to protecting themselves against identity theft.
- ■ To inform my audience about the process of sewage treatment.
- ■ To persuade my audience to become parents through adopting children.
- ■ To persuade my audience to stop drinking carbonated soft-drinks.
- ■ To persuade my audience to subscribe to the *Wall Street Journal.*

Developing Open-Ended Questions

Open-ended questions allow audience members to provide answers to questions in their own words. Effectively phrased, open-ended questions can give you the most insight into their feelings, wishes, behaviors, and thoughts. Returning to the same topics in question #3, develop **two open-ended questions** for each of the following specific purpose statements. Keep in mind that you need to develop questions that go beyond information already provided in closed-ended or scale questions.

- ■ To inform my audience about the four steps to protecting themselves against identity theft.
- ■ To inform my audience about the process of sewage treatment.
- ■ To persuade my audience to become parents through adopting children.
- ■ To persuade my audience to stop drinking carbonated soft-drinks.
- ■ To persuade my audience to subscribe to the *Wall Street Journal.*

Name: _____ Date: _____

Audience Analysis Surveys

The following audience analysis surveys have several mistakes or weaknesses. Identify what is wrong with each and suggest corrections.

Exercise and Health

1. How do you feel about your current health and amount of daily exercise?

2. What type of health problems do you associate with a lack of exercise?

3. How important is it to you to live a long life?

   a. Very Important

   b. Important

   c. 50/50

   d. Little Importance

   e. Not Important

4. In your opinion, list the main reasons that people do not exercise daily.

Retirement

1. What is your name?

2. What is your age?

3. What is your ideal job?

4. How much money do you expect to be earning 5 years after graduation?
   $20-30,000_____ $30-40,000_____ $40-50,000_____ $50,000+_____

5. At what age do you plan on retiring?

6. How much money do you save each year towards retirement?

7. Rate how you feel about the following:

Home	"Very Important" 1 – 2 – 3 – 4 – 5 – 6	"Very Unimportant"
Children	"Very Important" 1 – 2 – 3 – 4 – 5 – 6	"Very Unimportant"
Success	"Very Important" 1 – 2 – 3 – 4 – 5 – 6	"Very Unimportant"
Family	"Very Important" 1 – 2 – 3 – 4 – 5 – 6	"Very Unimportant"
Community	"Very Important" 1 – 2 – 3 – 4 – 5 – 6	"Very Unimportant"
Recreation	"Very Important" 1 – 2 – 3 – 4 – 5 – 6	"Very Unimportant"
Friends	"Very Important" 1 – 2 – 3 – 4 – 5 – 6	"Very Unimportant"

Example Outline: Monroe's Motivated Sequence

Name: Walter Haney
General Purpose: To Persuade
Outcome Statement: At the end of my presentation, my audience will understand Complex Regional Pain Syndrome and mail a letter to their state representatives urging them to take action in raising awareness of Complex Regional Pain Syndrome.
Thesis: We should, along with health-care professionals, take an active role in raising awareness in Complex Regional Pain Syndrome so that our friends and family never have to worry about being denied treatment.

Attention

I. Trust. The number one thing that all patients have with their physicians, especially right before they are about to cut you open for a "painless and simple" surgery. For a 20-year-old boy, this simple surgery turned into an unbearable, excruciating recovery where the pain didn't stop. No blood, no cool scar. All he had was just deep pain, powerful enough to cause a grown man to go to the floor in tears if a loved one hugged him too hard. Months and months passed, along with the doctor's appointments. People calling him crazy along the way, until he found out the pain had a name. Complex Regional Pain Syndrome (CRPS) or what was once known as Reflex Sympathetic Dystrophy (RSD) had stricken this boy. CRPS is a dreadful disease that has no cure, and for many little hope.

Need

I. Education and awareness of CRPS for health-care professionals in hospitals, doctor offices, as well as educating the general population, is a must in promoting awareness for this disease.

II. According to the Reflex Sympathetic Dystrophy Association website, between 200,000 and 1.2 million Americans have RSD.

   A. This is due to the lack of diagnosis by doctors around the country.

   B. Some doctors are not even aware of the disease or its existence.

   C. The National Institute of Health website describes CRPS as a chronic pain condition that is a dysfunction in the central or sympathetic nervous system.

   D. It can be caused by the slightest trauma or occur without any obvious cause.

   E. It causes severe burning pain, swelling, and extreme sensitivity to touch.

   F. It can spread without rhyme or reason leaving you debilitated.

III. Many of you or your loved ones may suffer a small injury, sprain an ankle, or have to undergo a minor surgery one day. What if your loved one complains of these symptoms?

   A. According to the RSDA, the average CRPS patient sees five doctors before receiving a correct diagnosis.

   B. Do you want your loved one to get caught up in the uneducated world of doctors?

Satisfaction

I. With all this being said it is impediment that legislation gets passed that makes the doctors more educated on this dreadful disease. In turn, this will educate Americans along the way.

II. According to Dr. Edward Carden's, one of the few "experts" in CRPS, webpage he says the earlier the diagnoses the more likely it is to enter remission.

    A. If all doctors are aware, they can provide the proper medication.

    B. Physical therapy is vital to keeping the muscles from crumpling.

    C. Nerve blocks are available, if done correctly can help facilitate some of the pain.

    D. IV Ketamine infusions are available to help with the horrible burning pain.

    E. More treatments can become researched through experience with the disease.

III. Dr. Carden treats patients with all methods and has seen remission with these steps.

IV. Kill the objections

    A. Why does the RSDA say most patients see five doctors before receiving a CRPS diagnosis? Because people and doctors will say the pain does not exist. Pain is measured on a subjective scale, and if a doctor cannot see it sometimes they will not accept it.

    B. Others claim a person with CRPS just has a low pain tolerance. Doctors think that the patient is seeking drugs. They believe that the person can live with a little "back" pain.

        1. According to the McGill Pain Index, this compiles all types of chronic pain anywhere from cancer to a toothache, CRPS ranks the highest.

        2. If the doctor just listens that there is pain, it could put the patient into remission.

        3. With that being said, it shows you how ugly this beast of a disease could be to your mom or dad.

Visualization

I. If we continue to look past this crippling disease we are continuing to leave a little bit of hope behind for 1 million Americans who are trying to find a doctor to listen to their pain plea.

II. This is a pain plea that at times you wish death would come and wraps its arms around you. How do I know this? I stand before you as that 20-year-old boy. I found Dr. Carden in California. He said if I would of Waited a month longer I could have been untreatable and the disease could have started to spread.

III. Hope is what is needed for those 1 million people. Hope is what is needed for me. Hope is what is needed for you or your loved ones if they are ever struck with this horrid disease.

Action

I. Imagine knowing that there is a way to help, not only others, but yourself. Think of your family, friends, even yourself. If this disease strikes any of them, it will take legislation to make things different in hospitals and doctors office.

II. I am not asking you to move any mountains. Don't let the times grow old with you. No excuses! I am asking that you don't sit back and let hope slip through the fingers of everyone fighting CRPS. Do your research on this disease. Know the facts. Go to the websites I have provided to get more information.

III. Most importantly, I want you to write your elected official. I have provided all required materials. This includes a complete prewritten letter encouraging your Kentucky state representatives to pass the current bill that is currently in debate on requiring physicians to undergo an educational training in what CRPS/RSD is and how to properly treat this horrid disease.

IV. All you have to do is sign the letter, address the prepaid envelope provided, and drop it in the mail box. Time is of the essence! Remember, once this fire starts, you can't put it out.

References

1. About CRPS. (2010). *Reflex sympathetic dystrophy syndrome association.* Retrieved from *http://www.rsds.org/2/what_is_rsd_crps/index.html*

2. Beebe, S., Beebe, S., & Ivy, D. (2009). *Communication principles for a lifetime: Presentation speaking* (vol. 4, p. 145). Boston: MA: Pearson Education, Inc.

3. Bergdahl, M. (2006). The ten rules of sam walton. Hoboken, NJ: John Wiley & Sons, Inc., p. 44.

4. Berger, C., & Calabrese, R. (1975). Some explorations in initial interaction and beyond: Toward a developmental theory of interpersonal communication. *Human Communication Research*, 1, 99–112.

5. Dr. Edward Carden, a pioneer in the field of complex regional pain syndrome (CRPS)/reflex sympathetic dystrophy (RSD). (January 14, 2010). Retrieved from *http://www.forgrace.org/documents/carden-non-physician.pdf*

6. Drunk Driving Prevention Campaign. (1983–Present). Retrieved from *http://www.adcouncil.org* retrieved March 19, 2009 from *http://www.adcouncil.org*

7. Frymeir, A.B., & Nadler, M.K. (2007). *Persuasion: Integrating theory, research, and practice.* Dubuque, IA: Kendall/Hunt.

8.. Gronbeck, B., McKerrow, R., Ehninger, D., & Monroe, A. (1994). *Principles and types of speech communication* (12th ed., p. 452). New York, NY: Harper Collins College Publishers.

9. NINDS complex regional pain syndrome information page. (January 13, 2011). *National Institute of Neurological Disorders and Stroke.* Retrieved from *http://www.ninds.nih.gov/disorders/reflex_sympathetic_dystrophy/reflex_sympathetic_dystrophy.htm*

10. Obama, B. (2009, January 20) Inaugural address [transcript]. Washington, D.C.: National Public Radio. Retrieved from *http://www.npr.org/templates/story/story.php?storyId=99590481*

11. Randall chronic pain scale. (2011). *American RDS hope.* Retrieved from *http://www.rsdhope.org/ShowPage.asp?page_id=116*

12. Reagan, R. (1986, January 28).The space shuttle Challenger tragedy address [transcript].

13. Washington, D.C.: American Rhetoric. Retrieved from *http://www.americanrhetoric.com/speeches/ronaldreaganchallenger.htm*

14. White, E. (2008, May 19). Art of persuasion becomes key: Managers sharpen their skills as lines of authority blur. *The Wall Street Journal.* Retrieved from *http://online.wsj.com/article/SB121115784262002373.html?mod=2_1357_leftbox*

11 Your Career: Communicating, Listening and Leading

Stephen A. Cox

CHAPTER OBJECTIVES:

At the end of this chapter, you will be able to:

- Justify the career significance and application of strong presentation skills.

- Explain why all workplace communication requires ethos, logos, and pathos.

- Explain why leadership and followership require effective communication.

- Explain how an effective presentation leads individuals and organizations to change.

- Explain how effective communication leads individuals and organizations to succeed.

- Explain why great leaders communicate with purpose, personality, passion, power, and pleasure.

- Defend the importance of listening as a leadership skill.

- Apply the 10 listening habits of effective leaders.

- Defend leadership as a process of communicating and listening well.

- Justify why everyone has the potential and obligation to provide leadership.

■ "And Now Presenting . . . Your Career!"

When you enrolled in college, family and friends were quick to ask, "So, what do you want to do with your life? What's your major?" Those are big decisions! Our career paths and the work we do become major sources of personal identity. Once you have graduated, "What do you do for a living?" soon becomes the most commonly asked question when meeting someone new. While some of us may declare a "major" that sounds like a lifetime career (e.g., nursing or elementary education), sources state that the typical U.S. worker will change careers 3 to 7 times during their lifetime, and U.S. workers currently change employers an average of every 2.2 years between ages 18 and 42 (see the Bureau of Labor Statistics, *www.bls.gov/NLS/nlsfaqs.htm#anch41*; Career Change Now, *www.coolercareers.com*; and Job Seeker Glossary, *http://www.quintcareers.com/jobseeker_glossary.html*). Each of these transitions requires you to "sell yourself" to get the next job and "sell your ideas" to stay employed. While you may not have thought about it this way, your presentation skills help you become employed, take on greater responsibility at work, and make significant contributions to the workplace.

Let's review 20 reasons why your career will benefit from the presentation skills you developed this semester:

1. You will be a more confident, purposeful, engaging, and credible communicator.

2. You will balance persuasion, information, and entertainment to meet your goals.

3. You will have more relevant, interesting, and reliable facts, examples, stories, etc.

4. You will have clearer logic and more compelling information.

5. You will use words that are more vivid, accurate, and concise.

6. You will adapt your message and style to fit each audience, setting, and occasion.

7. You will be very organized, concise, prepared, and well-rehearsed.

8. You will make it easy for others to follow and remember your ideas.

9. You will start strong by grabbing people's attention and building rapport.

10. You will finish strong by reinforcing your ideas and purpose in a memorable way.

11. You will design and use multimedia aids wisely, effectively, and sparingly.

12. You will speak to others in a conversational, extemporaneous style.

13. You will minimize the use of notes and maximize eye contact with listeners.

14. You will use facial expressions and body movements to reinforce your message.

15. You will vary your vocal rate, tone, rhythm, and volume to enrich your message.

16. You will share information, extend knowledge, and resolve misunderstandings.

17. You will engage your listeners' "hearts" by appealing to their emotional needs.

18. You will use logic and emotion to persuade others to take action.

19. You will design and deliver effective team presentations with your coworkers.

Image © Aaron Amat, 2009. Used under license from Shutterstock, Inc.

20. You will be a far more effective and discerning listener when others present their ideas and attempt to persuade you.

The presentation skills you have practiced are a vital part of your professional development and future career. Every career field agrees that communication competence is vital! Education, engineering, health care, architecture, public service, non-profit administration, ministry, chemistry, geology, entertainment, banking, finance, tourism, law enforcement, social work, insurance, construction, journalism, advertising, counseling, computer science, hospitality, transportation, manufacturing, retail, wholesale, agriculture, law and every other career field seeks professionals who are knowledgeable, confident, and articulate communicators.

College helps you develop specialized skills and knowledge that employers want, but your future compensation and promotions will depend upon how well you apply these to lead the organization. What good is it if you have advanced knowledge and new ideas if others do not hear about them? This is why all workplace communication, ranging from formal presentations to less formal conversations, is so important. Strong communication skills allow you to share knowledge and generate new ideas so both your career and the entire organization will thrive. This is why you are "required" to develop effective presentation skills.

Ethos, Pathos, and Logos at Work

Consider these diverse forms of workplace communication:

- Persuading
- Informing
- Selling
- Negotiating
- Advising
- Requesting
- Thanking
- Discussing
- Inquiring
- Training
- Teaching
- Counseling
- Correcting
- Questioning
- Debating
- Collaborating
- Congratulating
- Consoling
- Introducing
- Orienting
- Explaining
- Coaching
- Celebrating
- Disciplining
- Announcing
- Delegating
- Directing
- Defending
- Complementing
- Interviewing
- Storytelling
- Encouraging
- Empathizing
- Joking

- Listening
- Leading

How are these related to presentation skills? Each of these communicative acts requires some degree of **ethos**, **logos**, and **pathos** – they all need to be communicated with credibility, logic, and sincerity/conviction; otherwise, people will ignore us and our ideas. This illustrates why workplace communication is more diverse than, yet entirely consistent with, the presentation skills you developed this semester. From selling to customers to collaborating with coworkers to interviewing job candidates to defending your ideas at a meeting, we have to be reliable, knowledgeable, genuine, organized, and engaging communicators.

Follow the Leader

Paraphrasing Maxwell's (1998) idea from his book, *"The 21 Irrefutable Laws of Leadership,"*

> **If you think you are a leader and no one is following you, then you are just out for a walk.**

Being a leader means that you have followers. However, many leaders try to lead but are shocked when no one follows them. The only way to lead is to influence others to follow you and your ideas (Maxwell, 1998). This is why "Selling Yourself and Your Ideas" is the title of this book and the key to being a leader.

Do you recall being a very young child and playing "Follow the Leader"? The game depended upon everyone agreeing to stand behind the leader, hold hands, and follow wherever the leader went. If every child followed the leader, the children could stay together and make progress as a group. The challenge was to see how far and fast the group could go until someone took a wrong turn, fell down, or let go of his/her partner's hand. And when it did happen, the entire group stopped, laughed with delight, helped one another up, changed leaders, rejoined hands and took off once more to face the unknown. This childhood game teaches very important lessons that we all need to remember:

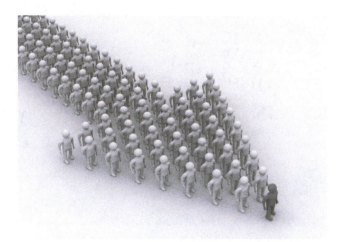

Image © Ilin Sergey, 2009. Used under license from Shutterstock, Inc.

1. Leaders provide vision and direction for the group.

2. Leaders are leaders only because others agreed to follow.

3. Leaders go fast enough to keep it exciting but not so fast that the group falls apart.

4. Followers lead other followers in the right direction.

5. Followers hold onto and help one another.

6. Groups must share leadership.

7. Groups must find a way to laugh and learn from mistakes, but keep going.

While the roles of leaders and followers are much the same in the game, adult life is far more complicated. "Leaders" should still provide clear vision and direction, while "followers" should work with others to help them make progress towards the goal. Unlike the "Follow the Leader" game of childhood, providing direction and vision is far more challenging in today's competitive, global economy! Organizations of every type (e.g., corporations, non-profits, schools, families, and even nations) seem to be struggling to make progress. The only way to make progress is for every follower and leader to openly discuss the objectives, successes, failures, challenges, and opportunities that lay ahead.

Without open communication among all members of an organization, the organization cannot go in the right direction. When people do not understand what obstacles and opportunities the organization faces, they cannot contribute to its success. In the broadest sense, a "leader" is anyone who contributes to the ongoing dialogue to help others understand and commit to moving the organization forward towards a better tomorrow. Jack Welch, former CEO of GE, summarized it this way:

> Leaders share information so everyone understands the vision and contributes to its success. That's what communication is all about. And it's at the heart of managing the modern corporation (Shaffer, 2000, p. 187).

Therefore, the roles of "leaders" and "followers" are constantly evolving, shared among every member of an organization who has the courage to speak up. Regardless of your title, your communication has the potential to provide leadership to others.

■ Communication Creates Change (... Or What's the Point?)

> "The problem with communication is the illusion that it has been accomplished."
>
> ✍George Bernard Shaw

To effectively communicate (e.g., to make common, to commune, to have community) with others is difficult work. Although preparing and delivering a presentation is challenging, communicating "with" others so shared meaning is created and change occurs proves far more difficult. We have all spoken up at work or given advice to our friends, but then observed that nothing changed. Most of the presentations you listened to this semester were quickly forgotten. Often it seems that our ideas "fall on deaf ears" because people do not think about or act upon our words. We then say, "I told them but they did not listen to me!"

Actions really do speak louder than words! People's reactions to our presentations help confirm if others understood what we were saying and if our words influenced their thinking and actions. Otherwise, what's the point in communicating?

In any setting, a presentation should trigger a communication chain-of-events that creates change in our listeners and in our organizations:

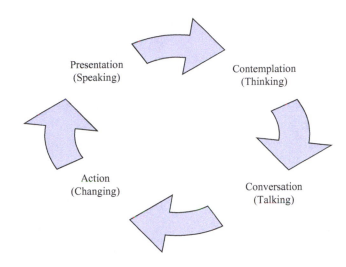

1. **Presentation – Speaking is formal.** Did you prepare? Did you adapt to the audience, setting, and occasion? Did you hold their attention? Were you credible and were your facts reliable? Were you logical, organized, and informative? Did you speak with purpose, passion, and personality?

2. **Contemplation – Thinking is intrapersonal.** Were your ideas memorable? Did they stick and become part of your listeners' long-term thinking/knowledge? Were your ideas thought provoking? Did you spark new questions and new ideas in the listeners' minds? Did your ideas continue to stir their emotions as well as inform their logic?

3. **Conversation – Talking is interpersonal.** Did listeners talk to you about your presentation? Did listeners tell others what they heard? Did listeners talk to others to interpret your ideas? Did your ideas inform and spark new conversations, debates, and/or agreements among people?

4. **Action – Changing is cognitive and behavioral.** Did your ideas eventually cause change to occur in and among people? Were actions taken? Were attitudes or beliefs changed or strengthened? Did your ideas help generate new commitments, experiments, procedures, decisions, innovations, etc.?

To summarize, an effective presentation causes listeners to think, informs/stimulates conversation, and generates change/action (cognitive or behavioral). Learning to present well has equipped you to create positive change in your personal life, work life, and your public/civic life. When you effectively *adjust ideas to people and people to ideas* (see Chapter 1), you influence others to think and act with greater clarity and purpose. Maxwell (1998) writes, "Leadership is influence – nothing more, nothing less" (p. 13). When your words influence others to change their thoughts and actions in new or better ways, this is leadership. Think about the influence your words have on others:

- Did you gain someone's trust and commitment?

- Did you delight someone who needed a good laugh?

- Did you clear up someone's confusion?

- Did you extend someone's knowledge?

- Did you motivate someone to keep going?

- Did you revive someone who needed encouragement?

- Did you persuade someone to try something new?

Every day your employer, coworkers, family, and community all need you to be an influential leader who clearly communicates information and persuades people to change today for a better tomorrow.

Communication Drives Success

An organization's successes or failures are the outcome of communication processes. For example, think about your favorite sports team. When your team wins, is it because of the coach or the players that they won? Actually, the answer is "both." Leading and following are one interdependent process in which leaders and followers communicate to mutually shape performance. The performance level of any organization/team is an outcome of how well its members communicate to understand vital information and decide who should take which actions when and in what order to adapt to an ever changing, competitive environment. As an organization's competitors change, or change occurs within the organization, communication is needed to share this information, discuss it, and make adjustments. Communication breakdowns among leaders and followers create failure, but excellence requires

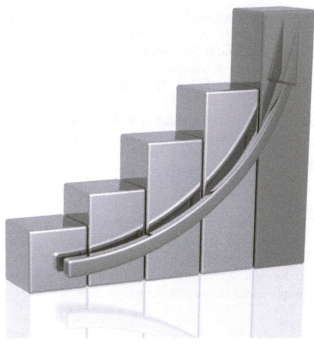

Image © suravid, 2009. Used under license from Shutterstock, Inc.

mutual understanding and collaboration so the organization and its members can adapt to and thrive in the competitive environment.

Any organization you work for shares the same goal – to be successful. A collection of people, processes, and things does not become organized and set into motion until communication allows everyone to understand who should do what, when, where, why, and how. Communication and feedback about progress, innovations, challenges, mistakes, opportunities, etc., must continue to achieve an optimal level of success. Without open, ongoing communication, the organization cannot ensure the success of everyone affected by the organization (e.g., employees, customers, shareholders, suppliers, and citizens).

Regardless if your job is to practice medicine, run a small business, pastor a congregation, teach 3rd grade students, or govern a state, you need to communicate with ethos, logos, and pathos. Communication that manifests ethos, logos, and pathos is required to spark collaboration so everyone has the opportunity to contribute and succeed. This is why your presentation skills will help you to contribute to the success of your workplace, as well as your family and your community. By sharing information, creating understanding, and motivating others to act, you will help lead others to succeed.

The 5 P's of Great Leaders

Recall the "5 P's of Effective Presentations" outlined in Chapter 2. How well did you demonstrate purpose, personality, passion, power, and pleasure in your presentations? Likewise, these five principles are defining characteristics of great leaders:

1. **Purpose** – Great leaders communicate a sense of purpose by answering two fundamental questions: "Where are we going?" (Vision) and "What are we trying to achieve?" (Mission). Great leaders communicate a compelling vision of the future and a sense of personal mission, persuading others to believe in and commit to the vision and then take action to achieve the mission.

2. **Personality** – Great leaders are authentic, believable communicators. They are "real people," not talking heads or robotic actors. Great leaders are trustworthy, respected, and admired for their personal character. When these leaders communicate, people feel drawn to and can identify with the leader forming a relationship.

3. **Passion** – Great leaders communicate with passion, conviction, and emotion, captivating the attention of others. They select vivid words and compelling stories that stir others to feel the significance and urgency of the moment. Their passion manifests in their vocal patterns, facial expressions, and body movements. Great leaders speak from "the heart" so others know what they passionately value and believe.

4. **Power** – Great leaders are powerful because followers willingly give these leaders control. A leader's power level depends upon the influence and respect shared between leaders and followers. Leaders become more powerful as they persuade followers to devote more of their energy and ideas to achieving the mission and vision. As leaders inspire followers to commit to the vision and mission, they must then empower followers to take action. As followers are empowered to act, the leader then has more influence over follower's actions. If leaders do not empower followers to act, then followers resist these leaders' influence and the leaders lose power. Effective communication = Influence = Power = Leadership

5. **Pleasure** – Great leaders experience the pleasure of a job well done. The reward of leading well comes from fulfilling the vision, achieving the mission, and meeting the expectations of key constituents (e.g., customers, shareholders, donors, etc.) through the followers. Likewise, followers who were inspired and empowered by the leader to participate in this work then experience a great sense of accomplishment and the rewards of success.

The difference between a "great leader" and a "manipulative leader" is important to note. History is full of examples of "manipulative leaders" who accomplished much by controlling followers through deception or coercive intimidation. In addition to political dictators and tyrants, think of the many recent examples of unethical corporate leaders whose deception led to great fame and even greater infamy – Enron, WorldCom, Adelphia, Tyco, and most recently Bernie Madoff's $64 billion investment fraud. Deception and coercion may exploit followers and achieve the wishes of leaders, but it does not make these leaders "great." Rather, a great leader persuades followers to do the right things for the right reasons for individual and collective benefit. This is why your presentation skills are the means by which you will provide "great" leadership to benefit your family, community, and workplace.

While "free speech" and the skill to present well are essential for the maintenance of our democracy and economy, we must carefully examine our own words and those of others to evaluate motives and weigh the consequences of those words. Did your words, either as a formal presentation or as hallway conversation, deceive and manipulate or did they help inform and persuade? These are the important questions by which you, and every other leader, will be evaluated.

Listening for Leadership

Leadership scholar and author Warren Bennis (1997) provides the closing insight into the relationship between communication skills, leadership, and your career:

> [T]he longer I study effective leaders, the more I am convinced of the under-appreciated

importance of effective followers. What makes a good follower? The single most important characteristic may well be a willingness to tell the truth....Followers who tell the truth, and leaders who listen, are an unbeatable combination. (p. 157)

If only "leaders speak" and "followers listen," then your organization will suffer. Most leadership books fail to discuss the vital leadership skill of listening well. Every leader is born with two ears and only one mouth for a good reason . . . so they can devote twice as much time to listening! "Leaders" at the top of the hierarchy and the "followers" below will always have different perspectives and information about the organization. For example, standing at the top of a mountain gives you a very different perspective than when you stand at the bottom. Listening to both perspectives provides a much fuller understanding of the "territory" ahead and confirms that everyone is looking at the same "map." But reading a "map" (the plan) is far easier than actually making progress through the "territory" (e.g., competitors, customers, and constituents). This is why the leaders and followers must continually talk and listen to one another. While Chairman of AlliedSignal, Larry Bossidy summarized it this way:

We must talk with – and listen to – each other all the time, at every opportunity, and about everything that affects the business and the experience of working here if we are to become a premier company (Shaffer, 2000).

Everyone can benefit from better listening skills, but listening is a challenging process to do consistently well. When someone has really "listened" to us, they have . . .

a. Heard sound.

b. Selected which sounds were "noise" and which were "symbols."

c. Interpreted or assigned meaning to those symbols.

d. Responded to those ideas.

e. Remembered what was said.

To be a good leader and follower, we have to hear, select, interpret, respond to, and remember what we are told, which is a very time and energy intensive process. Looking at the steps of the listening process, it is easy to see why listening fails to happen:

a. Listeners may not physically hear the message or may have poor hearing.

b. Physical noise, mental distractions, or poor enunciation inhibit listeners' ability to distinguish "noise" from symbolic codes/words.

c. Listeners may have limited vocabularies that limit understanding. Also, it is very common to misinterpret the meaning of a word (e.g., "I need this ASAP.").

d. Listeners may not respond due to timing, distance, noise, or opportunity (e.g., you heard President Obama's presentation but never had the chance to speak to the President about it).

e. Every listener has a different brain capacity for remembering what they heard. Some messages are forgettable! Information overload also prohibits remembering every idea in a message.

Obviously, these factors undermine effective listening, but there are positive listening behaviors you adopt to become better leader. Here are 10 listening habits to become a more effective leader:

1. **Listening can provide you a free education . . . so hush-up and listen-up!**

2. **Minimize physical and mental distractions and noise.** (NOTE: This is why so much "business" is conducted at the golf course . . . seriously!)

3. **Focus your mind on the person who is speaking.** You want to understand the person as well as his/her ideas. Remember, what he/she is trying to "sell" you may be a real bargain!

4. **Remain open-minded.** Minimize your prejudices and presumptions towards the person or the topic. Remember, you need to hear the truth, even when it hurts. You cannot listen to a person or an idea if you have already closed your mind!

5. **Focus your eyes and your ears on the person who is speaking.** Do not let your eyes distract your ears. (NOTE: Some cultures find direct

eye contact to be threatening or disrespectful, so adjust accordingly. But every culture appreciates an attentive ear!)

6. **Listen for the "substance" of the message.** Listen for the connections among the facts, concepts, stories, arguments, emotions, etc., being presented. This is where learning occurs!

7. **Do not let your listening be distracted by delivery style and multimedia.** Not everyone puts on a great "show," while others are "all show" and no substance. Do not let your listening be turned off nor distracted by the person's delivery or multimedia.

8. **Resist planning your counter-attack.** Wise decision-makers need to think seriously about what they hear, but save that for afterwards. Mental capacity spent thinking about a rebuttal distracts you from listening.

9. **Take notes!** Note-taking helps for two reasons: 1) notes help you record and remember the key information that was said, and 2) notes allow you to ask follow-up questions so you can get all the information you need. Great leaders know the right questions to ask to get the right information to make better decisions!

10. **Respond!** Provide feedback and ask for clarification. Paraphrase what you thought they said to confirm understanding. Acknowledging points of agreement, interest, and/or appreciation are all methods to start conversation and build relationships (with friend and foe alike). Most importantly, state what you will do next with the message – learn from it, keep thinking about it, investigate it further, share the message with others, use it to make a decision, or some other type of action you plan to take.

Effective leaders work hard to listen well and present well; to be both the sender and receiver of ethos, logos and pathos. Fortunately, we can all develop these 10 listening habits so we can maximize the synergy among all leaders and followers – it just takes time, commitment, and effort.

■ Chapter Review

Learning to make presentations is not an end in itself, nor was this class just another University Studies requirement to pass. Rather, building presentation skills is a fundamental part of your professional development and your future career. Your ability to gain employment, remain employed, and build a career will depend upon your communication skills. In any career you choose, you are paid for your knowledge, ideas, and ability to work with others, all of which require you to communicate with ethos, logos, and pathos. All of your communication, both formal and informal, must be credible, logical, and enthusiastic/passionate or people will not listen to you. If no one listens, then you cannot make a positive difference at work (as well as in your personal and civic life). Only when people listen to you can you influence their thinking and actions. This influence is leadership – effective communication = influence = leadership!

Presenting well allows you to provide leadership, and leadership creates positive change so everyone succeeds. This is why every corporation, non-profit, community, family business, school, etc., needs leaders who clearly communicate the vision, mission, and processes that solidify commitment, breed cooperation, and spur progress. Every organization and occupation is crying out for effective leaders and it is your obligation to provide that leadership, regardless of your job title. By communicating sound ideas, persuading people to take the right actions, and listening carefully to others, you will help create a better tomorrow for everyone.

References

Bennis, W.G. (1994). *An invented life: Reflections on Leadership and Change*. New York: Basic Books.

Bureau of Labor Statistics. *www.bls.gov/NLS/nlsfaqs.htm#anch41*. Accessed March 20, 2009.

Career Change Now. *www.coolercareers.com*. Accessed March 20, 2009.

Job Seeker Glossary. *http://www.quintcareers.com/jobseeker_glossary.html*. Accessed March 20, 2009.

Maxwell, J.C. (1998). *The 21 irrefutable laws of leadership: Follow them and people will follow you*. Nashville, TN: Thomas Nelson Publishers.

Shaffer, J.C. (2000). *The leadership solution*. New York: McGraw-Hill.

APPENDICES

Appendix A: Glossary

Adrenaline – a hormone secreted in response to a threat or stress which increases heart rate and prepares the body for fight or flight response.

Alliteration – the repeating of the initial consonant sound in a sentence or phrase.

Analogical reasoning – reasoning that compares a concept or object to another concept or object that the audience is familiar with.

Analogy – a comparison based on the similarity between two things

Antithesis – the use of an opposite concept in a phrase.

Apathetic (The) – members of the audience who don't care because their interest has not been stirred by the message.

Argument – a process of reasons or a set of reasons presented that lead the audience to the desired conclusion

Articulation – the clarity of speech sounds.

Attitude – a learned predisposition to respond either favorably or unfavorably to an object

Attitudinal analysis – process whereby you determine the audience's personal thoughts and expectations toward a topic which includes their attitudes, beliefs, or values

Audience analysis – the process of assessing an audience in order to provide the appropriate level of information. An audience analysis consists of three types of questions: attitudinal, situational and demographic.

Autonomy – the power of self or group direction. A sense a freedom that groups believe they have over their own work.

Belief – the way that you look at the world or the way that you structure your reality

Causal – organizational pattern where the main points are ordered to show a cause and effect relationship.

Causal reasoning – reasoning that demonstrates that one event is related or caused by another event or situation

Chronological – organizational pattern where main points are organized by time or in order of process.

Cognitive dissonance – an uncomfortable mental state when one's behavior and beliefs are not consistent

Cognitive restructuring – see reframe or reframing

Confused (The) – members of the audience who don't understand one's message because one's facts or ideas are not clear.

Credibility – the quality of being believable or trustworthy.

Deductive reasoning – reasoning that moves from a general example to a specific conclusion

Delivery outline – a shortened version of the preparation outline used for delivering the presentation which includes only key words or phrases and delivery cues to prompt the speaker.

Demographic analysis – process to determine the dimensions and dynamics of an audience which includes factors such as age, gender, ethnicity, socioeconomic level, educational level, and political affiliation

Derived credibility – the credibility that is created while giving a presentation based on the quality of sources, organization, logic and delivery style used in the presentation.

Dialect – the special variety of language related to a particular region of the country and around the world.

Dialectic – a philosophical method of questioning resembling group discussion; the art of investigating the truth of a subject by discussion.

Dynamism – the power or energy in the delivery of the presenter

Emotional appeals – messages directed at heightening one or more of the basic human emotions, such as fear, guilt, joy, happiness, sorrow, excitement, disgust rather than logical or rational factors

Emotional proof (pathos) – the ability to influence others by inspiring the passions or emotions.

Enunciation – the preciseness of speech sounds.

Ethical proof (ethos) – the credibility of the speaker due to good character.

Ethics – the principles or guidelines that one uses to determine what is right or wrong. The character and credibility of the presenter.

Ethos – the credibility and character of the speaker, the audience's perception of the trustworthiness, knowledge and sincerity of the presenter.

Expertise – the research, knowledge, and experience of the presenter

Extemporaneous delivery – a conversational manner of presenting where the speaker presents from a delivery outline, but they are not reading or reciting the material.

Fight or flight response – the response of the nervous system which prepares the body to fight or flee from a threatening situation.

General purpose – the overall purpose of a presentation. Three main types are: to inform, to persuade, and to entertain.

Group – three to fifteen people who share a common purpose, who feel a sense of belonging to the group, and who exert influence on one another.

Hyperbole – an obvious and extreme exaggeration.

Imagery (guided imagery) – a purposeful relaxation technique during which a person repeatedly visualizes successfully delivering each step of a presentation.

Impact – to have an effect upon. When others outside the group comment on the work done by the group.

Impromptu – a presentation which afford little or no time for development and organization of content.

Inductive reasoning – reasoning that moves from a specific example to a general conclusion

Initial credibility – the credibility the presenter initially brings to the presentation including the presenter's reputation, research, experience experiences and training.

Internal preview – a sentence or phrase which provides the audience with a preview of the key ideas that are coming next in the presentation.

Internal summary – a sentence or phrase which reviews what has already been discussed in the previous main point or points in order to help the audience retain the information and move on to the next step.

Logical reasoning – the proofs or arguments the speaker employs through evidence or reasoning.

Logos – the logic of the presentation, or the logical organization of words or information shared in the presentation (e.g. evidence, facts, or reasoning).

Main points – the key ideas of the presentation the audience should remember about the topic.

Meaningfulness – having significance, purpose or value. When team members have a sense of commitment and they are intrinsically motivated to do well.

Metaphor – a text that creates an image that shows the similarity between two things that are different.

Mnemonic/Gimmick – organization of main points in a way that spells out a word or another type of memory device.

Monroe's Motivated Sequence – a psychological process used in persuasive presentations that moves the person to action and consists of five steps: Attention, Need, Satisfaction, Visualization, and Action

Morals – used interchangeably with ethics, principles, or guidelines one uses to determine what is right or wrong

Motivational appeals – messages that are linked to the values and beliefs of the audience

Nonverbal transitions – the use of nonverbal gestures, vocal cues or movements to indicate that the presenter is moving from one idea in the presentation to another idea.

Onomatopoeia – the formation of words which sound like the objects they represent.

Outcome statement – a sentence which presents the specific goals of the presentation. The outcome statement should identify the topic and have specific and measurable action(s) that the audience is asked to perform

Parallelism – the construction of parallel wording in sentences or phrases which possess a distinct rhythm.

Pathos – the emotional or motivational arguments or appeals used in the presentation (e.g. appeals to love, pride or power).

Personification – attributing human qualities to an inanimate object or concept.

Persuasive speaking – the creation of oral messages which will increase commitment, alter beliefs, attitudes, or values, and ultimately ask for a change in the audience's actions

Pitch – the highness or lowness of the speaker's voice.

Potency – when group members working collectively have confidence in their abilities.

Preparation outline – the full sentence outline that comprises about 80% of the speaker's presentation.

Problem-cause-solution – organizational pattern where information is presented in three main sections: (a) the nature and significance of the problem, (b) the causes and effects of the problem, and (c) the best possible solution to the problem.

Pronunciation – the correctness or accepted sounds of the words.

Psychological unity – concluding the presentation by referring to ideas or concepts which were referred to in the introduction.

Rate of speech – the quickness or slowness of the speaker's voice related to the emotional level of the presentation.

Reframe or Reframing (cognitive restructuring) – a mental strategy used to identify negative or maladaptive thoughts or feelings and redefine them as neutral, constructive, or positive.

Repetition – the repeating of words or phrases in a presentation.

Rhetoric – the art of effective or persuasive speaking or public address.

Signposts – brief words or statements that tell and audience where to focus their attention such as "First," "Second," or "Third."

Simile – a text that creates an image that shows similarity between two concepts or objects that are different with the explicit use of connecting words (like, as, so, than, etc.).

Situational analysis – process to determine the external or environmental and technical factors which will influence the presentation such as audience size, physical location, time of day, and availability of technology.

Skeptics (The) – members of the audience who don't believe a presenter's message.

Sophists – wandering Greek teachers who taught the people for a fee; believed rhetoric was the art of persuasion by any means, sometime involving trickery and/or manipulation.

Source – the document, book, webpage, person, etc. that supplies information for the presentation.

Spatial – organizational pattern where the main points are organized by location or direction.

Support (supporting materials) – the information that effectively validates the claim or main idea in the presentation.

Synergy – when the efforts or creation of the whole is greater than the simple sum of the parts. When the group is able to achieve more together than the individuals working alone.

Team – a coordinated group of people organized to achieve a common goal.

Team presentation – a "well-coordinated" presentation by a cohesive group of speakers who are trying to inform or influence an audience of key decision makers.

Terminal credibility – the credibility created at the end of the presentation including the quality of the presenter's conclusion, as well as how the presenter responds to questions and answers.

Thesis – A declarative sentence summarizing the main or central idea of the presentation. The main or central idea of the presentation. A once sentence statement which presents the main points of the presentation.

Thesis – a declarative sentence summarizing the main or central idea of the presentation. A once sentence statement which presents the main points of a presentation.

Topical – organizational pattern where the presenter decides on the main points of the presentation.

Transition sentence – a sentence or sentences which connect one topic or idea to another in a smooth and logical manner.

Trustworthiness – the presenter's honesty, sincerity, and ethical concern for the audience

Values – core beliefs that guide your actions

Wiki – a collaborative website which allows anyone to add, modify or delete information.

Appendix B: Assignments

Presentation 1: Past, Present and Future Presentation

In this first assignment, you will begin establishing your "personality" and "credibility" (**ethos**—who you are and why we should listen to you). You will provide deeper insight into yourself as a person, as well as demonstrate a basic understanding of informative presentations. First, collect three (3) personal items, one representing your past, one representing your present, and one representing your future. Next, find an interesting container for these items/objects that represents you as a whole. These will be your visual/presentation aids. Create a brief, written outline to organize your presentation into an interesting introduction, a detailed body, and a conclusion. In describing the items you bring, explain how they relate to your past, present, and future so the audience will better understand who you are and what makes you unique.

Your three unique items should symbolize what is important to you: your values, interests, experiences, goals, concerns, etc. The best presentations will provide a clear and thoughtful description/explanation of the objects and how they illustrate who you are. Additionally, demonstrate a well-rehearsed, extemporaneous speaking style—no reading, no memorization, no "winging it". Practice out-loud many times to ensure you know your content, how you will use your three items, and to ensure you speak between 2 to 3 minutes.

Your three items (which serve as your "visual aids") are subject to approval by your instructor. Throughout the semester, items such as weapons, explosives, illegal drugs, alcohol containers, or anything related to explicit sexual acts are not allowed as visual/presentational aids. Due to audience fears and allergies, no pets or animals are allowed.

To present you will:

- Speak for 2 to 3 minutes.

- Provide an introduction and a conclusion (see Ch. 2).

- Describe/explain 3 innovative items representing your past, your present, and your future, as well as the container representing you as a whole.

- Make sure the items are large enough to be seen, not too common, and appropriate for this classroom.

- Dress appropriately.

- Use an extemporaneous delivery style.

To turn in:

- "Past, Present and Future" Critique Sheet (See Appendix B)

Presentation 2: Pet Peeve Presentation

The purpose of this assignment is to inform your audience about a specific "pet peeve" or minor issue that you find personally bothersome/frustrating/concerning. The audience should leave understanding why this "little issue" is such a "big deal" to you. This can be either a serious or a humorous topic. This presentation will help you develop your confidence, delivery skills, research skills, and organizing/outlining skills. This is a chance to express your emotions (**pathos**) about something that really bothers or irritates you. In order to seem sincere, you should use vivid language, gestures, facial expressions, and vocal variety for emphasis. Additionally, this is the first "informative" presentation that requires research. In addition to your personal opinion, you must provide supporting materials drawn from documented sources to justify, explain, and illustrate your topic (**logos**). The use of audio/visual aids may be permitted—ask your instructor about his/her expectations.

You can develop this presentation in one of two ways. You can choose one problem that really bothers you and speak about that problem only. You can choose two different, but related problems and connect them together in your presentation. Either way, craft your presentation with your **outcome statement** in mind—"At the end of my presentation, my audience will be able to . . . "

Keep the presentation appropriate by adapting to your audience. Do not pick a topic that is offensive to any person or group of people. Topics must be approved by your instructor in advance.

To present you will:

- Speak for 3 to 4 minutes.

- Provide an introduction and a conclusion (see Ch. 2).

- Identify and explain why a situation or issue is a "pet peeve".

- Use a variety of supporting materials (e.g., stories, statistics, definitions . . . see Ch. 4).

- Cite at least 2 documented sources.

- Dress appropriately.

- Use an extemporaneous delivery style.

To turn in:

- "Pet Peeve Presentation" Critique Sheet (see Appendix B)

- Preparation outline, including a list of your documented sources.

- Peer Evaluation Form—"Pet Peeve" (see Appendix C)

Presentation 3: Informative Presentation

The goal of this assignment is to deliver a well-developed, well-researched informative presentation that extends your audience's knowledge. Don't tell us what we already know! Your topic may be an interesting object, a person, a place, an event, or a concept. You must show that you are credible, knowledgeable, creative, and enthusiastic. You must use at least one audio or visual presentation aid (e.g., Powerpoint slides, physical objects, charts, photos, etc.).

Build your full-content, **preparation outline** around your **thesis** (i.e., one-sentence summary) and **outcome statement** ("At the end of my presentation, my audience will be able to . . . "; see Ch. 5). Capture the audience's attention and extend their knowledge by focusing on the most important and unique aspects of your topic. As you present, you must carefully monitor your audience's nonverbal feedback so you can adapt your content and delivery during the presentation. This is the heart of "extemporaneous" delivery—well-prepared and rehearsed ahead of time, but conversational and adapted to the audience's feedback as you present. Prepare and use a brief **delivery outline** for the actual presentation.

Remember, your mission in an informative presentation is to educate, enlighten, and transform your audience taking them to a higher level of understanding. Although your insights and experiences contribute to your overall credibility (**ethos**), thorough research to gain a wide base of information is essential for creating a logical, accurate, and well-supported presentation (**logos**). Research and develop the presentation in a creative way that will hold the audience's attention and broaden their sphere of knowledge. Also, 4 to 5 minutes goes by quickly; therefore, practice, practice, practice!

To present you will:

- Speak for 4 to 5 minutes.

- Extend the audience's knowledge by informing them about a fascinating topic.

- Provide a thorough introduction and conclusion.

- Use at least 1 audio/visual presentation aid.

- Use a wide variety of supporting materials (facts, examples, quotes, statistics, etc.).

- Cite at least 3 documented sources.

- Dress appropriately.

- Use an extemporaneous delivery style.

To turn in:

- "Informative Presentation" Critique Sheet (see Appendix B).

- Preparation outline, including a list of your documented sources.

- Peer Evaluation Form—Informative (see Appendix C).

Presentation 4: Impromptu Presentation

The goal of this assignment is to develop the ability to "speak on your feet" by using the key organizational and delivery skills you learned in earlier presentations. You will be given a topic by the instructor about which you already have some knowledge. Although "impromptu" presentations are typically "on-demand" with no advanced warning, you will be given 3–4 minutes to prepare a <u>delivery outline</u> of your presentation. This 2–4 minute impromptu presentation should have a solid introduction (reveal topic, establish credibility, preview, etc.), a body with 2–3 main points supported with illustrations/facts/examples, and a thorough conclusion.

To present you will:

- Speak for 2 to 4 minutes.

- Have a well developed introduction and conclusion.

- Effectively inform the audience about the topic.

- Use a wide variety of supporting materials (facts, examples, quotes, statistics, etc.).

- Use an impromptu delivery style, adapting your vocal variety, gestures, language, etc. to fit the topic and audience's feedback during your presentation.

To turn in:

- "Impromptu Presentation" Critique Sheet (See Appendix B)

- Peer Evaluation Form—Impromptu (see Appendix C)

Presentation 5: Team "Problem-Cause-Solution" Presentation

The team "problem-cause-solution" presentation assignment will help you develop your team presentation, collaboration, and critical thinking skills. It requires you to collaborate with others to develop and deliver a presentation as a team—one purpose, one message, one voice. Your responsibility is to get everyone in your team to collaborate, coordinate, deliver, and unite as a team and perform as one cohesive unit. This will require all team members to meet outside of class, work together to select and research a topic, write a preparation outline, create and use at least two appropriate visual aids, practice the content together, and deliver a united presentation. Because your 3-5 member team must speak in "one voice" and deliver one united message, this will take time, planning, and practice as a team so the visual aids, content, and transitions flow seamlessly. **Review Ch. 9—Team Presentations**

NOTE: *Inform your instructor of any personnel issues and emerging conflict in the team well before your speech delivery date. You will evaluate the contributions of all your team members (see Appendix C, Team Members Evaluation Form). These evaluations will be considered by the instructor when grading the assignment.* **YOU CAN BE FIRED BY YOUR TEAM! Non-contributing or under-performing members will be pulled from the team presentation at the instructor's discretion.** *If removed, an alternate "problem-cause-solution" presentation (7-8 minutes) will be required of the student but can earn no more than half credit. Failure to do the alternate presentation on the assigned day/time will result in zero credit for the assignment. If your team fires someone, the team is still responsible for the full time requirement and content.*

Too often we apply solutions to problems without fully understanding or fixing the root causes. We use a "quick fix" or convenient solution for a complex problem, thus not addressing or eliminating the real causes of the issue, then the problem gets worse! To fully create a lasting solution to a complex issue you must identify the root causes at the core of the problem. The problem-cause-solution pattern (**see Ch. 5**) is a great strategy for helping others understand the prevalence, causes, and effects of a significant, complex problem and evaluate the advantages of a proposed solution.

This problem-cause-solution presentation is more than an informative presentation—it is a thorough argument for the merits of a solution—but it is not a fully developed persuasive presentation. While you will study and practice "persuasion" in Chapter 10, think of this problem-cause-solution presentation as a mid-point between an informative presentation and a persuasive presentation that causes people to change their behaviors. Your team will be presenting an argument about a problem and how/why its causes are best addressed by one solution versus others. But you ARE NOT asking your audience to take action by personally adopting the solution (e.g., changing a habit, donating money, buying a product, etc.). The problem-cause-solution presentation, instead, provides the audience with the information needed to arrive at a desired conclusion about the merits of a proposed solution and how/why it addresses the root causes of the problem. The problem must be thoroughly reviewed and understood (i.e., its history, prevalence, and significance to the audience and others). The causes and effects of the problem must be thoroughly reviewed and explained so the underlying causes are well understood and the audience understands how/when/where these effects occur (e.g., direct/indirect, short/long-term, etc.). The solution must be clearly identified, explained, and defended as the best solution so the audience understands how and why it will solved the problem versus alternative solutions. **Review the "Team Problem-Cause-Solution Critique Sheet" in Appendix B.**

To present you will:

- 15-minute maximum per group; 3 to 5 minutes per member.

- Present as a "team"- united purpose, content, and voice.

- Use the "Problem-Cause-Solution" speech pattern.

- Use a wide variety of supporting materials to build your argument.

- Cite a minimum of 2 sources per team member.

- Use at least 2 separate visual aids. One visual aid must be PowerPoint or Prezi.

- Each member must have his/her own delivery outline.

- The team should dress appropriately, united in purpose and appearance.

- Use extemporaneous delivery style.

To turn in:

- Team Problem-Cause-Solution Critique Sheet (Appendix B).

- A single team preparation outline, including all documented sources for the entire presentation.

- Team member evaluation form (Appendix C).

Alternate Presentation 5: Team "Persuasive" Presentation

This team "persuasive" presentation will help you develop team presentation skills. Team presentations are very common in the workplace. Your responsibility is to get everyone in your team to collaborate, coordinate and deliver as a united "team"! This will require all team members to work together outside of class to conduct research, write the preparation outline, create the visual aids, practice as a team, etc. Your 3–5 member team must speak in "one voice" and deliver one united message. This takes commitment, planning and practice as a team so content flows and transitions between members are smooth. The entire team is accountable for what the team presents! Your team will persuade the audience to take some specific action about a clearly defined issue. This persuasive presentation will be a well-structured and logically sequenced presentation so all members have an equal opportunity to present content that the team prepared. The team must use Monroe's Motivated Sequence. <u>Review Ch. 9— Team Presentations</u>.

NOTE: *You will evaluate the contributions of all your group members (see Appendix C, Team Members Evaluation Form). These evaluations will be considered by the instructor when grading this assignment (see Appendix B, Team Presentation Critique Sheet). Inform your instructor of significant team issues well ahead of the scheduled presentation date. Non-contributing or under-performing members may be pulled from a team presentation at the instructor's discretion. An alternate persuasive presentation would then be required but can earn no more than half credit for this assignment. Failure to do the alternate* *presentation on the assigned day/time will result in zero credit for this assignment.*

To present you will:

- 15-minute maximum per group; 3 to 5 minutes per team member.

- Present as a "team"—united in purpose, content, and voice.

- Use Monroe's Motivated Sequence.

- Persuade the audience to take action regarding a significant issue.

- Use logical appeals and emotional appeals.

- Cite a minimum of 2 sources per team member.

- Use a wide variety of supporting materials (facts, examples, quotes, statistics, etc.).

- Use at least 2 audio/visual aids as a team.

- Each member must have his/her own delivery outline.

- All team members should dress appropriately, united in purpose and appearance.

- Use an extemporaneous delivery style.

To turn in:

- "Team Presentation" Critique Sheet (see Appendix B)

- A single preparation outline, including a list of documented sources, for the entire team presentation.

- Team Members Evaluation Form (see Appendix C)

Persuasive Presentation: Audience Analysis Survey and Report

Prior to your persuasive presentation, you must have a clear understanding of your audience members' opinions, experiences, values, etc. concerning your topic. Are they for it, against it, unaware of it, or apathetic about it? What do you need/want to know about them to be most persuasive? The audience analysis allows you to adapt your content to fit your audience. Do not make assumptions based solely on the demographics of your audience. Review Ch. 4 for information about developing an audience analysis.

1. **Audience Analysis Survey:** Based on the topic of your persuasive presentation, create an audience analysis survey to gather data about the audience's attitudes, interests, values, beliefs, experiences, etc. Observe the following guidelines:

   - Maximum: 12 "closed-ended", "scale" and "open-ended" questions.

   - 1 page; typed.

   - Your name must appear in the upper right-hand corner.

   - Surveys must be anonymous; do not ask respondents for their name.

   - Bring enough copies of your survey for the entire class and your instructor!!!

2. **Audience Analysis Report:** Based on the responses to your survey, write a 1–2 typed page "Audience Analysis Report". Explain how the analysis data helped you adapt to your audience's dispositions/values/etc. in each step of Monroe's Motivated Sequence. Attach your report to the preparation outline of your persuasive presentation. Answer the following questions:

   1. What did you learn about your audience's attitudes/values/etc. towards your topic? How did the audience's attitudes/values/etc. differ from your own? What did you find most surprising and valuable?

   2. How did you use the analysis data to help you establish your credibility and build a connection with your audience?

   3. Based on the analysis data, how did you adapt your content, voice, language, etc. to gain the audience's "attention"?

   4. How did the analysis data help you adapt your logical and emotional appeals, voice, language, etc. to establish the "need" and relate it to the audience's lives? How did you apply the analysis data in the "satisfaction" step of your presentation?

   5. Based on analysis data, how did you adapt your logical and emotional appeals in the "visualization" and "call to action" portions of your presentation? Why do you feel these appeals were persuasive to this audience?

Presentation 6: Persuasive Presentation

The purpose of this presentation is to "Sell Your Ideas" . . . to persuade your audience to "buy-in" and "take action" about a clearly defined issue. It is easy to inform people compared to the challenge of persuading others to take action (e.g., change old behaviors, donate money, protest an injustice, adopt new beliefs, tackle a new challenge, or forgive someone). This "action" will vary based on the audience's disposition towards the topic. For example, an audience that is "supportive" of your cause/issue is asked to take very different actions than an audience who is "against" your cause/issue. You must persuade your audience that the issue is significant and impacts their lives in ways they never realized. You must appeal to both their logic (**logos**) and their emotions (**pathos**) to be persuasive. You must also demonstrate your personal credibility and conviction about this topic (**ethos**). If you want them to care about your cause/issue, then you must demonstrate your passion about it. Directly address your audience's predisposition towards your topic based on your audience analysis data. You must use Monroe's Motivated Sequence.

To present you will:

- Speak for 5 to 7 minutes.

- Use Monroe's Motivated Sequence to structure your presentation.

- Persuade the audience to take action regarding a significant issue.

- Use logical appeals and emotional appeals.

- Use a wide variety of supporting materials (facts, examples, quotes, statistics, etc.).

- Cite at least 4 documented sources.

- Use at least 1 audio/visual aid.

- Dress appropriately.

- Use an extemporaneous delivery style.

To turn in:

- "Persuasive Presentation" Critique Sheet (see Appendix B)

- Preparation outline, including a list of your documented sources.

- The "Audience Analysis Report".

- Peer Evaluation Form—Persuasive (see Appendix C)

Self-Evaluation 1: Past, Present, and Future Presentation

After giving your presentation, respond to each of the following questions in a paragraph/short essay form. Your evaluation must be typed and double-spaced. Self-evaluations may be no more than two pages in length.

1. Discuss your self-confidence before your presentation; how would you characterize your attitude/expectations in preparation for this assignment? During the presentation itself, describe how you felt physically and emotionally. What steps did you take to control your anxiety? What were your feelings/thoughts immediately following your presentation?

2. Discuss the steps you took to prepare for this assignment including gathering objects, taking notes/speaking outline, rehearsing, etc.

3. Comment on your overall delivery. How do you feel your use of visual aids, appearance, movement, attire, voice, etc. affected your credibility/effectiveness?

4. Identify the specific aspects of your presentation that were especially strong.

5. What steps will you take to improve in the next assignment? What specific goals will you set in terms of organization, content, and delivery for the next presentation? ("Doing better." "Getting an A." and "Try harder" are not *specific* goals).

Self-Evaluation 2: Pet Peeve Presentation

After giving your presentation, respond to each of the following questions in a paragraph/short essay form. Your evaluation must be typed and double-spaced. Self-evaluations may be no more than two pages in length.

1. Discuss how this presentation was different from your "past, present and future" presentation. How did you gain your audience's attention in this presentation? How did you organize this presentation?

2. How were you able to support your "pet peeve"? What sources did you cite in your presentation

that gave you credibility? What types of verbal supportive material did you use to explain or illustrate your "pet peeve"?

3. Comment on your delivery for this presentation. How did your delivery change or improve for this presentation? How did you use gestures, movement, or vocal emphasis to demonstrate to the audience your emotions?

4. Discuss how your personal involvement with the topic improved your presentation. Did your delivery improve with this presentation? What areas do you need to continue to work on in your delivery (volume, vocal emphasis, gestures, and movement)?

Self-Evaluation 3: Informative Presentation

After giving your presentation, respond to each of the following questions in a paragraph/short essay form. Your evaluation must be typed and double-spaced. Self-evaluations may be no more than two pages in length.

1. Why did you choose your topic? How did your topic relate to your audience? Why was this topic fascinating to you?

2. Discuss the effectiveness of your introduction. Did you state the thesis of your presentation? How did you gain the audience's attention? How did you establish your credibility as an "expert" on this topic?

3. Discuss the body of your presentation; comment on the appropriateness/effectiveness of your verbal supportive material. What specific types of verbal supportive material did you include in your presentation (examples, explanations, testimonials, narratives, statistics, comparisons, definitions)?

4. Discuss the conclusion of your presentation. How did you tie your conclusion to the specific purpose/thesis statement of our presentation?

5. What do you feel were your strengths in preparing for this assignment? In what areas do you feel you need to improve? What specific goals will you set to improve on organization and content of your next presentation?

Self-Evaluation 4: Impromptu Presentation

After giving your presentation, respond to each of the following questions in a paragraph/short essay form. Your evaluation must be typed and double-spaced. Self-evaluations may be no more than two pages in length.

1. Discuss how comfortable that you felt speaking about a subject with only a few minutes of preparation. How has your confidence grown through the presentations and class activities this semester?

2. Discuss how you gathered your thoughts and ideas just before you spoke. How did your experience with the informative presentation help you with your impromptu presentation?

3. How did you include verbal supportive material for this presentation? What verbal supportive material did you include to support your main ideas (examples, explanations, testimonials, narratives, statistics, comparisons, definitions)? How effective were they?

4. Discuss your delivery for the impromptu presentation. What did you do that you felt was effective? What could you have done that would have improved your presentation?

5. Comment on your conclusion. Do you feel that your conclusion was adequate? Explain. How could you have improved your conclusion?

Self-Evaluation 5: Team Presentation

After giving your presentation, respond to each of the following questions in a paragraph/short essay form. Your evaluation must be typed and double-spaced. Self-evaluations may be no more than two pages in length.

1. Discuss how your team prepared for your preparation. Discuss how well your team worked together to include all of the members' ideas and research.

2. Discuss your team's plan for the presentation. Do you feel your team clearly stated your thesis for the presentation and previewed your main ideas? Explain.

3. Did your presentation flow together well? Were your ideas organized and easily followed by the audience? Why or why not? Discuss ways that you could improve the coordination of your material between the members of your team.

4. Discuss the overall delivery of your team. Was your presentation presented with good vocal quality and enthusiasm? Comment on how presenting in a team effected your own personal delivery and confidence.

5. Discuss how your team used visual aids in your presentation. Were they effective or not? Explain your answer. Discuss how you could improve the use of your visual aids in your presentation.

6. What did you learn from the team presentation? What would you do differently next time?

Self-Evaluation 6: Persuasive Presentation

After giving your presentation, respond to each of the following questions in a paragraph/short essay form. Your evaluation must be typed and double-spaced. Self-evaluations may be no more than two pages in length.

1. Why did you choose your claim? How did your claim relate to your audience? How is this issue significant to the lives of your audience members?

2. How did you justify your position with regards to this claim? What types of supportive material did you provide to support your position? Comment on the appropriateness/credibility of your documented sources.

3. What specific emotional appeals did you use to persuade your audience to accept your position? Discuss the effectiveness/appropriateness of your motivational appeals based on your analysis of the audience.

4. Comment on your overall presentation skills. How do you feel your use of visual aids, movement, attire, and vocal delivery affected your credibility/effectiveness? In what areas do you feel you need improvement?

5. What specific goals will you set to improve your overall presentation skills in terms of movement, attire, and vocal delivery?

Outside Speaker Evaluation

Throughout the semester, there are various free presentations offered at the university and in the community. For this assignment, you will attend one presentation delivered by a speaker who is neither a member of your class nor a professor (current or past). Presentations not sponsored by the university are subject to approval by your instructor. You will then submit an evaluation of the presentation based on the principles of public speaking as discussed in class and in your textbook.

Your evaluation of the speaker's presentation should not be a verbatim report of what was said nor your reaction to the speaker's message; don't focus on whether you agreed with the speaker or not. Assess the speaker's performance as a means of demonstrating your knowledge and understanding of public speaking.

All papers must be in the following format:

- 2 to 2.5, double-spaced, pages of text.

- Cover page:
  Your name
  COM 161- section #
  Time/day of class
  Date
  Instructor's Name

- Number all pages except cover sheet.

- Your discussion must be organized in essay format and address all the areas under the following headings:

SPEAKING SITUATION: Identify the speaker, his/her source of credibility, the topic, the audience, and the speaking situation.

PRESENTATION PURPOSE: Identify the speaker's general goal and specific objective. In your opinion, was the speaker successful in fulfilling that purpose? Justify your answer.

AUDIENCE ANALYSIS: Identify the three areas of analysis: audience size and appropriate demographics, situation, and attitude. How did the speaker adapt his/her message to the audience and the situation (i.e. language, delivery, supportive material)?

ORGANIZATION: Discuss the elements needed for the introduction, preview of main points, main ideas, transitions between main points, and conclusion. Was the presentation well organized and easy to follow? Justify your answers. What organizational pattern was evident in the presentation?

CONTENT: Briefly discuss the value of the presentation content. What types of supportive material were used? Did the speaker use any visual aids? Were they helpful? Explain.

DELIVERY: Discuss the speaker's appearance, eye contact, gestures, movement, volume, pitch, articulation, pronunciation vocal variety, vocalized pauses, etc.

FINAL EVALUATION: What was the speaker's greatest strength? Greatest weakness? If this presentation was delivered in class and you were the instructor, what grade would you have assigned the speaker and why?

Overall Semester Self-Evaluation

Carefully read Ch. 11—*Communicating, Leading and Listening*. Ch. 11 reviews why learning how to "sell yourself and your ideas" is the purpose of this course. The ability to present your ideas well so others buy into those ideas is vital for career success. Those communication skills are the essence of being an effective employee, coworker, and leader. Are you now more employable? Will you be a more effective coworker? Will people follow you? Based on content from Ch. 11, evaluate how you have developed by answering the following questions:

1. Look back at where you started in your "Past, Present and Future" presentation and how your communication skills and competencies have developed throughout this semester. How much progress have you made? What did you learn about yourself as a communicator? What new skills do you most value? What are the most important lessons you learned about being a competent communicator? Provide examples from each presentation and make reference to feedback you received from your instructor.

2. How will your career benefit from having developed stronger presentation skills? What knowledge, skills, and abilities have you gained that will make you a better employee and coworker? Explain why based on content from Ch. 11.

3. Will people follow you? Explain why the communication competencies you developed in this course will make you a more competent leader. Relate your evaluation to ethos, logos, and pathos, as well as processes of change. Consider the "5 P's of Great Leaders" (p 223). Assess how well you now manifest these communication traits having taken this course.

Guidelines:

- 2.5 to 3 full pages of double-spaced text.

- A cover-page including your name, COM 161 section #, time/day of class, and instructor's name.

- Organize your self-evaluation by numbering your answers to each question.

- Any "direct quotes" from the textbook must be in "quotations" and include page numbers—such as, "Speaking is formal" (p. 221).

- Plagiarism in any form, including failure to use quotations and page numbers for any direct quotes from the textbook, will result in a "zero" on this assignment.

- Evaluation will be based on mechanical and grammatical quality, as well as the quality of analysis and depth of insight.

Appendix C: Peer Evaluations Forms

Peer Evaluation Form – Pet Peeve

Your Name: _____

Speaker's Name: _____

Rate the speaker on each point

| *5-very good!!!* | *4-good!* | *3-okay.* | *2-needs some help!* | *1-missing!!!* |

Organization and Content:

Introduction:
Gained audience's attention, established credibility	5 4 3 2 1
Identified topic, stated thesis	5 4 3 2 1
Previewed main points	5 4 3 2 1

Body:
Main points clear/well-developed	5 4 3 2 1
Effective explanations, descriptions, etc.	5 4 3 2 1
Documented sources clearly cited	5 4 3 2 1
Effective organization, transitions, use of language	5 4 3 2 1

Conclusion:
Signaled the end	5 4 3 2 1
Reviewed main points	5 4 3 2 1
Effective closing statement	5 4 3 2 1

Delivery:
Extemporaneous, conversational delivery	5 4 3 2 1
Direct and inclusive eye contact	5 4 3 2 1
Demonstrated vocal variety	5 4 3 2 1
Clear articulation and pronunciation	5 4 3 2 1
Effective gestures, movement, facial expressions	5 4 3 2 1

OVERALL EVALUATION:
What did the speaker do most effectively?

What should the speaker pay special attention to next time?

Peer Evaluation Form – Pet Peeve

Your Name: _____

Speaker's Name: _____

Rate the speaker on each point

    5-very good!!!   *4-good!*   *3-okay.*   *2-needs some help!*   *1-missing!!!*

Organization and Content:

Introduction:

Gained audience's attention, established credibility	5 4 3 2 1
Identified topic, stated thesis	5 4 3 2 1
Previewed main points	5 4 3 2 1

Body:

Main points clear/well-developed	5 4 3 2 1
Effective explanations, descriptions, etc.	5 4 3 2 1
Documented sources clearly cited	5 4 3 2 1
Effective organization, transitions, use of language	5 4 3 2 1

Conclusion:

Signaled the end	5 4 3 2 1
Reviewed main points	5 4 3 2 1
Effective closing statement	5 4 3 2 1

Delivery:

Extemporaneous, conversational delivery	5 4 3 2 1
Direct and inclusive eye contact	5 4 3 2 1
Demonstrated vocal variety	5 4 3 2 1
Clear articulation and pronunciation	5 4 3 2 1
Effective gestures, movement, facial expressions	5 4 3 2 1

OVERALL EVALUATION:

What did the speaker do most effectively?

What should the speaker pay special attention to next time?

Peer Evaluation Form – Informative Presentation

Your Name: _____

Speaker's Name: _____

Rate the speaker on each point

5-very good!!!   4-good!   3-okay.   2-needs some help!   1-missing!!!

Organization and Content:

Introduction:

Gained audience's attention; established credibility	5 4 3 2 1
Stated topic and thesis; previewed main points	5 4 3 2 1

Body:

Main points clear/well-developed	5 4 3 2 1
Effective transitions and organization	5 4 3 2 1
Variety of effective supporting material	5 4 3 2 1
Used vivid, descriptive language	5 4 3 2 1
Cited at least 3 documented sources	5 4 3 2 1
Content adapted to situation/audience	5 4 3 2 1

Conclusion:

Signaled the end	5 4 3 2 1
Reviewed main points	5 4 3 2 1
Strong closing statement	5 4 3 2 1

Delivery:

Extemporaneous, conversational delivery	5 4 3 2 1
Direct and inclusive eye contact	5 4 3 2 1
Demonstrated vocal variety	5 4 3 2 1
Clear articulation and pronunciation	5 4 3 2 1
Effective gestures, movement, facial expressions	5 4 3 2 1
Creative and effective use of "visual aids"	5 4 3 2 1

OVERALL EVALUATION:

What did the speaker do most effectively?

What should the speaker pay special attention to next time?

Peer Evaluation Form – Informative Presentation

Your Name: _____

Speaker's Name: _____

Rate the speaker on each point

    5-very good!!!   *4-good!*   *3-okay.*   *2-needs some help!*   *1-missing!!!*

Organization and Content:

Introduction:
Gained audience's attention; established credibility	5 4 3 2 1
Stated topic and thesis; previewed main points	5 4 3 2 1

Body:
Main points clear/well-developed	5 4 3 2 1
Effective transitions and organization	5 4 3 2 1
Variety of effective supporting material	5 4 3 2 1
Used vivid, descriptive language	5 4 3 2 1
Cited at least 3 documented sources	5 4 3 2 1
Content adapted to situation/audience	5 4 3 2 1

Conclusion:
Signaled the end	5 4 3 2 1
Reviewed main points	5 4 3 2 1
Strong closing statement	5 4 3 2 1

Delivery:
Extemporaneous, conversational delivery	5 4 3 2 1
Direct and inclusive eye contact	5 4 3 2 1
Demonstrated vocal variety	5 4 3 2 1
Clear articulation and pronunciation	5 4 3 2 1
Effective gestures, movement, facial expressions	5 4 3 2 1
Creative and effective use of "visual aids"	5 4 3 2 1

OVERALL EVALUATION:
What did the speaker do most effectively?

What should the speaker pay special attention to next time?

Peer Evaluation Form – Impromptu Presentation

Your Name: _____

Speaker's Name: _____

Rate the speaker on each point

5-very good!!!   *4-good!*   *3-okay.*   *2-needs some help!*   *1-missing!!!*

Organization and Content:

Introduction:
Gained audience's attention; established credibility   5 4 3 2 1
Identified topic, stated thesis   5 4 3 2 1
Previewed main points   5 4 3 2 1

Body:
Main points clear/well-developed   5 4 3 2 1
Effective explanations, descriptions, etc.   5 4 3 2 1
Used vivid, descriptive language   5 4 3 2 1

Conclusion:
Reviewed main points   5 4 3 2 1
Reinforced the overall theme, strong closing statement   5 4 3 2 1

Delivery:
Extemporaneous, conversational delivery   5 4 3 2 1
Direct and inclusive eye contact   5 4 3 2 1
Demonstrated vocal variety   5 4 3 2 1
Clear articulation and pronunciation   5 4 3 2 1
Effective gestures, movement, facial expressions   5 4 3 2 1

OVERALL EVALUATION:
What did the speaker do most effectively?

What should the speaker pay special attention to next time?

Peer Evaluation Form – Impromptu Presentation

Your Name: _____

Speaker's Name: _____

Rate the speaker on each point

5-very good!!!   *4-good!*   *3-okay.*   *2-needs some help!*   *1-missing!!!*

Organization and Content:

Introduction:
Gained audience's attention; established credibility   5 4 3 2 1
Identified topic, stated thesis   5 4 3 2 1
Previewed main points   5 4 3 2 1

Body:
Main points clear/well-developed   5 4 3 2 1
Effective explanations, descriptions, etc.   5 4 3 2 1
Used vivid, descriptive language   5 4 3 2 1

Conclusion:
Reviewed main points   5 4 3 2 1
Reinforced the overall theme, strong closing statement   5 4 3 2 1

Delivery:
Extemporaneous, conversational delivery   5 4 3 2 1
Direct and inclusive eye contact   5 4 3 2 1
Demonstrated vocal variety   5 4 3 2 1
Clear articulation and pronunciation   5 4 3 2 1
Effective gestures, movement, facial expressions   5 4 3 2 1

OVERALL EVALUATION:
What did the speaker do most effectively?

What should the speaker pay special attention to next time?

Peer Evaluation Form—Team Problem-Cause-Solution Presentation

Student's Name: _____ Topic: _____

Team Members: _____

Rate the speaker on each point

5-very good!!!　　*4-good!*　　*3-okay.*　　*2-needs some help!*　　*1-missing!!!*

Introduction:　　　　　　　　　　　　　　　　　　　　　5 4 3 2 1
Gained audience's attention. Established credibility and goodwill.
Stated topic, thesis and purpose. Previewed the main ideas.

Body:
Problem　　　　　　　　　　　　　　　　　　　　　　　　5 4 3 2 1
　Vividly explained the history, prevalence, and significance of a compelling problem.
　Illustrated how the problem affects the audience and others.
　Provided ample, credible support.
Cause　　　　　　　　　　　　　　　　　　　　　　　　　5 4 3 2 1
　Reviewed and explained the problem's underlying causes.
　Linked causes to effects (direct/indirect, short/long-term, etc.).
　Provided ample, credible support.
Solution　　　　　　　　　　　　　　　　　　　　　　　　5 4 3 2 1
　Identified and explained the "best" solution (what, who, how, when, where, etc.)
　Argued why it will directly address the causes of the problem.
　Argued why it is superior to other possible solutions. Addressed any objections.
　Illustrated the solution's benefits for those affected.

Conclusion:　　　　　　　　　　　　　　　　　　　　　5 4 3 2 1
Signaled the end of the presentation.
Reviewed and reinforced the main points of the argument.
Effective closing statement.

Team Content and Delivery:　　　　　　　　　　　　　5 4 3 2 1
Used a wide variety of supporting materials.
Adapted topic to the audience.
Used vivid/descriptive language.
Effective use of visual aids.
Provided smooth transitions between members.
Extemporaneous, conversational delivery.
Direct and inclusive eye-contact.
Strong use of vocal variety, minimal vocalized pauses.
Effective gestures, movement, facial expressions.
Displayed energy, conviction, enthusiasm.
Delivered as a "team"—united in voice and content.

OVERALL EVALUATION:
What did the speaker do most effectively?

What should the speaker pay special attention to next time?

Peer Evaluation Form—Team Problem-Cause-Solution Presentation

Student's Name: _____ Topic: _____

Team Members: _____

Rate the speaker on each point

| *5-very good!!!* | *4-good!* | *3-okay.* | *2-needs some help!* | *1-missing!!!* |

Introduction: 5 4 3 2 1
Strong Gained audience's attention. Established credibility and goodwill.
Stated topic, thesis and purpose. Previewed the main ideas.

Introduction:
Problem: 5 4 3 2 1
   Vividly explained the history, prevalence, and significance of a compelling problem.
   Illustrated how the problem affects the audience and others.
   Provided ample, credible support.
Cause: 5 4 3 2 1
   Reviewed and explained the problem's underlying causes.
   Linked causes to effects (direct/indirect, short/long-term, etc.).
   Provided ample, credible support.
Solution: 5 4 3 2 1
   Identified and explained the "best" solution (what, who, how, when, where, etc.)
   Argued why it will directly address the causes of the problem.
   Argued why it is superior to other possible solutions. Addressed any objections.
   Illustrated the solution's benefits for those affected.

Conclusion: 5 4 3 2 1
Signaled the end of the presentation.
Reviewed and reinforced the main points of the argument.
Effective closing statement.

Team Content and Delivery: 5 4 3 2 1
Used a wide variety of supporting materials.
Adapted topic to the audience.
Used vivid/descriptive language.
Effective use of visual aids.
Provided smooth transitions between members.
Extemporaneous, conversational delivery.
Direct and inclusive eye-contact.
Strong use of vocal variety, minimal vocalized pauses.
Effective gestures, movement, facial expressions.
Displayed energy, conviction, enthusiasm.
Delivered as a "team"—united in voice and content.

OVERALL EVALUATION: 5 4 3 2 1
What did the team do most effectively?

What should the team pay special attention to next time?

"Team Members" Evaluation Form

Evaluate the contributions of each team member in the planning and preparation of the presentation by rating him/her from 10 (very satisfied) to 1 (very dissatisfied). Consider each member's efforts to help the team succeed, participation in meetings, and his/her contributions to the content/visuals/outline/etc. Do consider each member's unique life situation and what efforts he/she made to contribute in light of any extenuating circumstances. Be as discerning and understanding as possible. If every member of your team was GREAT, give them each a "10". However, if a team member blatantly neglected his/her responsibilities, give him/her a "1". Provide a brief explanation of each evaluation.

Team member's name_____

Very Satisfied 10 — 9 — 8 — 7 — 6 — 5 — 4 — 3 — 2 — 1 Very Dissatisfied

Explanation:

Team member's name_____

Very Satisfied 10 — 9 — 8 — 7 — 6 — 5 — 4 — 3 — 2 — 1 Very Dissatisfied

Explanation:

Team member's name_____

Very Satisfied 10 — 9 — 8 — 7 — 6 — 5 — 4 — 3 — 2 — 1 Very Dissatisfied

Explanation:

Team member's name_____

Very Satisfied 10 — 9 — 8 — 7 — 6 — 5 — 4 — 3 — 2 — 1 Very Dissatisfied

Explanation:

Your name _____ Instructor _____

Time/Day/Section# _____

275

Peer Evaluation Form – Persuasive Presentation

Your Name: _____

Speaker's Name: _____

Rate the speaker on each point

| *5-very good!!!* | *4-good!* | *3-okay.* | *2-needs some help!* | *1-missing!!!* |

Organization (Monroe's Motivated Sequence):

Attention   5 4 3 2 1
    Strong attention getter, captivated the audience
    Established credibility, previewed topic/issue

Need   5 4 3 2 1
    Clearly established a compelling problem
    Problem vividly explained and illustrated
    Tied the problem to audience, made it personal to them

Satisfaction   5 4 3 2 1
    Clearly identified a specific solution to the problem
    Solution explained/described (what, when, how, etc.)

Visualization   5 4 3 2 1
    Vividly illustrated the positive outcomes of the solution
    Visualized the solution's benefits, advantages for everyone
    Visualized the consequences if the solution is not adopted
    Overcame objections

Action   5 4 3 2 1
    Clear, specific, motivating call for action
    Reviewed main ideas
    Strong closing statement

Content:

Used effective emotional appeals and logical appeals	5 4 3 2 1
Used a wide variety of supporting materials	5 4 3 2 1
Adapted to audience's attitudes/values	5 4 3 2 1
Used vivid, descriptive language	5 4 3 2 1
Cited at least 4 sources	5 4 3 2 1
Creative and effective use of "visual aids"	5 4 3 2 1

Delivery:

Extemporaneous, conversational delivery	5 4 3 2 1
Direct and inclusive eye contact	5 4 3 2 1
Strong use of vocal variety	5 4 3 2 1
Effective gestures, movement, facial expressions	5 4 3 2 1
Displayed energy, conviction, enthusiasm	5 4 3 2 1

OVERALL EVALUATION:

What made the speaker most persuasive and effective?

What should the speaker do to be more persuasive next time?

Peer Evaluation Form – Persuasive Presentation

Your Name: _____

Speaker's Name: _____

Rate the speaker on each point

5-very good!!!　　　*4-good!*　　　*3-okay.*　　　*2-needs some help!*　　　*1-missing!!!*

Organization (Monroe's Motivated Sequence):

Attention　　　　　　　　　　　　　　　　　　　　　　　　5 4 3 2 1
　　Strong attention getter, captivated the audience
　　Established credibility, previewed topic/issue

Need　　　　　　　　　　　　　　　　　　　　　　　　　5 4 3 2 1
　　Clearly established a compelling problem
　　Problem vividly explained and illustrated
　　Tied the problem to audience, made it personal to them

Satisfaction　　　　　　　　　　　　　　　　　　　　　　5 4 3 2 1
　　Clearly identified a specific solution to the problem
　　Solution explained/described (what, when, how, etc.)

Visualization　　　　　　　　　　　　　　　　　　　　　5 4 3 2 1
　　Vividly illustrated the positive outcomes of the solution
　　Visualized the solution's benefits, advantages for everyone
　　Visualized the consequences if the solution is not adopted
　　Overcame objections

Action　　　　　　　　　　　　　　　　　　　　　　　　5 4 3 2 1
　　Clear, specific, motivating call for action
　　Reviewed main ideas
　　Strong closing statement

Content:

Used effective emotional appeals and logical appeals　　　5 4 3 2 1
Used a wide variety of supporting materials　　　　　　5 4 3 2 1
Adapted to audience's attitudes/values　　　　　　　　5 4 3 2 1
Used vivid, descriptive language　　　　　　　　　　　5 4 3 2 1
Cited at least 4 sources　　　　　　　　　　　　　　　5 4 3 2 1
Creative and effective use of "visual aids"　　　　　　　5 4 3 2 1

Delivery:

Extemporaneous, conversational delivery　　　　　　　　5 4 3 2 1
Direct and inclusive eye contact　　　　　　　　　　　　5 4 3 2 1
Strong use of vocal variety　　　　　　　　　　　　　　5 4 3 2 1
Effective gestures, movement, facial expressions　　　　5 4 3 2 1
Displayed energy, conviction, enthusiasm　　　　　　　5 4 3 2 1

OVERALL EVALUATION:

What made the speaker most persuasive and effective?

What should the speaker do to be more persuasive next time?

Peer Evaluation Form – Alternate Team "Persuasive" Presentation

Your Name: _____

Speaker's Name: _____

Rate the overall team on each point

5-very good!!!   4-good!   3-okay.   2-needs some help!   1-missing!!!

Organization (Monroe's Motivated Sequence):

<u>Attention</u>   5 4 3 2 1
   Strong attention getter, captivated the audience
   Established credibility, previewed topic/issue

<u>Need</u>   5 4 3 2 1
   Clearly established a compelling problem
   Problem vividly explained and illustrated
   Tied the problem to audience, made it personal to them

<u>Satisfaction</u>   5 4 3 2 1
   Clearly identified a specific solution to the problem
   Solution explained/described (what, when, how, etc.)

<u>Visualization</u>   5 4 3 2 1
   Vividly illustrated the positive outcomes of the solution
   Visualized the solution's benefits, advantages for everyone
   Visualized the consequences if the solution is not adopted
   Overcame objections

<u>Action</u>   5 4 3 2 1
   Clear, specific, motivating call for action
   Reviewed main ideas
   Strong closing statement

Team Content: and Delivery

Used effective emotional appeals and logical appeals	5 4 3 2 1
Used a wide variety of supporting materials	5 4 3 2 1
Adapted to audience's attitudes/values	5 4 3 2 1
Used vivid, descriptive language	5 4 3 2 1
Cited at least 2 sources per member	5 4 3 2 1
Creative and effective use of at least 2 "visual aids"	5 4 3 2 1
Smooth transitions between team members	5 4 3 2 1
Extemporaneous, conversational delivery	5 4 3 2 1
Direct and inclusive eye contact	5 4 3 2 1
Strong use of vocal variety	5 4 3 2 1
Effective gestures, movement, facial expressions	5 4 3 2 1
Displayed energy, conviction, enthusiasm	5 4 3 2 1
Delivered as a "team"—united in voice and content	5 4 3 2 1

OVERALL TEAM EVALUATION:

What did the team do most effectively?

What should the team pay special attention to next time?

Peer Evaluation Form – Alternate Team "Persuasive" Presentation

Your Name: _____

Speaker's Name: _____

Rate the overall team on each point

5-very good!!! *4-good!* *3-okay.* *2-needs some help!* *1-missing!!!*

Organization (Monroe's Motivated Sequence):

<u>Attention</u> 5 4 3 2 1
   Strong attention getter, captivated the audience
   Established credibility, previewed topic/issue

<u>Need</u> 5 4 3 2 1
   Clearly established a compelling problem
   Problem vividly explained and illustrated
   Tied the problem to audience, made it personal to them

<u>Satisfaction</u> 5 4 3 2 1
   Clearly identified a specific solution to the problem
   Solution explained/described (what, when, how, etc.)

<u>Visualization</u> 5 4 3 2 1
   Vividly illustrated the positive outcomes of the solution
   Visualized the solution's benefits, advantages for everyone
   Visualized the consequences if the solution is not adopted
   Overcame objections

<u>Action</u> 5 4 3 2 1
   Clear, specific, motivating call for action
   Reviewed main ideas
   Strong closing statement

Team Content: and Delivery

Used effective emotional appeals and logical appeals	5 4 3 2 1
Used a wide variety of supporting materials	5 4 3 2 1
Adapted to audience's attitudes/values	5 4 3 2 1
Used vivid, descriptive language	5 4 3 2 1
Cited at least 2 sources per member	5 4 3 2 1
Creative and effective use of at least 2 "visual aids"	5 4 3 2 1
Smooth transitions between team members	5 4 3 2 1
Extemporaneous, conversational delivery	5 4 3 2 1
Direct and inclusive eye contact	5 4 3 2 1
Strong use of vocal variety	5 4 3 2 1
Effective gestures, movement, facial expressions	5 4 3 2 1
Displayed energy, conviction, enthusiasm	5 4 3 2 1
Delivered as a "team"—united in voice and content	5 4 3 2 1

OVERALL TEAM EVALUATION:
What did the team do most effectively?

What should the team pay special attention to next time?

Peer Evaluation

Speaker's Name: _____ Your Name: _____

- Logos:

- Ethos:

- Pathos:

- Strengths:

- Areas to Improve:

- What I liked best about your speech (and why)

Peer Evaluation

Speaker's Name: _____ Your Name: _____

- Logos:

- Ethos:

- Pathos:

- Strengths:

- Areas to Improve:

- What I liked best about your speech (and why)

Peer Evaluation

Speaker's Name: _____ Your Name: _____

- Logos:

- Ethos:

- Pathos:

- Strengths:

- Areas to Improve:

- What I liked best about your speech (and why)

Peer Evaluation

Speaker's Name: _____ Your Name: _____

- Logos:

- Ethos:

- Pathos:

- Strengths:

- Areas to Improve:

- What I liked best about your speech (and why)

Peer Evaluation

Speaker's Name: _____ Your Name: _____

- Logos:

- Ethos:

- Pathos:

- Strengths:

- Areas to Improve:

- What I liked best about your speech (and why)

Peer Evaluation

Speaker's Name: _____ Your Name: _____

- Logos:

- Ethos:

- Pathos:

- Strengths:

- Areas to Improve:

- What I liked best about your speech (and why)

Peer Evaluation

Speaker's Name: _____ Your Name: _____

- Logos:

- Ethos:

- Pathos:

- Strengths:

- Areas to Improve:

- What I liked best about your speech (and why)

Peer Evaluation

Speaker's Name: _____ Your Name: _____

- Logos:

- Ethos:

- Pathos:

- Strengths:

- Areas to Improve:

- What I liked best about your speech (and why)

Peer Evaluation

Speaker's Name: _____ Your Name: _____

- Logos:

- Ethos:

- Pathos:

- Strengths:

- Areas to Improve:

- What I liked best about your speech (and why)

Peer Evaluation

Speaker's Name: _____ Your Name: _____

- Logos:

- Ethos:

- Pathos:

- Strengths:

- Areas to Improve:

- What I liked best about your speech (and why)

Peer Evaluation

Speaker's Name: _____ Your Name: _____

- Logos:

- Ethos:

- Pathos:

- Strengths:

- Areas to Improve:

- What I liked best about your speech (and why)

Peer Evaluation

Speaker's Name: _____ Your Name: _____

- Logos:

- Ethos:

- Pathos:

- Strengths:

- Areas to Improve:

- What I liked best about your speech (and why)

Peer Evaluation

Speaker's Name: _____ Your Name: _____

- Logos:

- Ethos:

- Pathos:

- Strengths:

- Areas to Improve:

- What I liked best about your speech (and why)

Peer Evaluation

Speaker's Name: _____ Your Name: _____

- Logos:

- Ethos:

- Pathos:

- Strengths:

- Areas to Improve:

- What I liked best about your speech (and why)

Peer Evaluation

Speaker's Name: _____ Your Name: _____

- Logos:

- Ethos:

- Pathos:

- Strengths:

- Areas to Improve:

- What I liked best about your speech (and why)

Peer Evaluation

Speaker's Name: _____ Your Name: _____

- Logos:

- Ethos:

- Pathos:

- Strengths:

- Areas to Improve:

- What I liked best about your speech (and why)

Peer Evaluation

Speaker's Name: _____ Your Name: _____

- Logos:

- Ethos:

- Pathos:

- Strengths:

- Areas to Improve:

- What I liked best about your speech (and why)

Peer Evaluation

Speaker's Name: _____ Your Name: _____

- Logos:

- Ethos:

- Pathos:

- Strengths:

- Areas to Improve:

- What I liked best about your speech (and why)

Peer Evaluation

Speaker's Name: _____ Your Name: _____

- Logos:

- Ethos:

- Pathos:

- Strengths:

- Areas to Improve:

- What I liked best about your speech (and why)

Peer Evaluation

Speaker's Name: _____ Your Name: _____

- Logos:

- Ethos:

- Pathos:

- Strengths:

- Areas to Improve:

- What I liked best about your speech (and why)

Appendix D: Presentation Critique Sheets

"Past, Present and Future" Critique Sheet   25 POINTS

Student's Name: _____

3 items: _____

Introduction: _____ /3
Gained audience's attention
Stated name
Previewed main points

Body: _____ /10
Main points clear/well-developed
Effective explanations, descriptions, etc.
Effective organization, transitions, use of language

Conclusion: _____ /2
Signaled the end
Reviewed main points
Effective closing statement

Delivery: _____ /10
Extemporaneous, conversational delivery
Direct and inclusive eye contact
Demonstrated vocal variety
Clear articulation and pronunciation
Effective gestures, movement, facial expressions
Creative and effective use of items as "visual aids"

Deductions:
Violated time limit (2–3 minutes)   (_____)

Final Score _____ /25

"Past, Present and Future" Critique Sheet

Student's Name: _____

3 items: _____

Introduction:
Gained audience's attention
Stated name
Previewed main points

Body:
Main points clear/well-developed
Effective explanations, descriptions, etc.
Effective organization, transitions, use of language

Conclusion:
Signaled the end
Reviewed main points
Effective closing statement

Delivery:
Extemporaneous, conversational delivery
Direct and inclusive eye contact
Demonstrated vocal variety
Clear articulation and pronunciation
Effective gestures, movement, facial expressions
Creative and effective use of items as "visual aids"

Deductions:
Violated time limit (2–3 minutes)

Overall Grade: _____

"Pet Peeve Presentation" Critique Sheet   40 POINTS

Student's Name: _____

Topic: _____

Introduction: _____ /5
Gained audience's attention, established credibility
Identified topic, stated thesis
Previewed main points

Body: _____ /20
Main points clear/well-developed
Effective explanations, descriptions, etc.
Documented sources clearly cited
Effective organization, transitions, use of language

Conclusion: _____ /5
Signaled the end
Reviewed main points
Effective closing statement

Delivery: _____ /10
Extemporaneous, conversational delivery
Direct and inclusive eye contact
Demonstrated vocal variety
Clear articulation and pronunciation
Effective gestures, movement, facial expressions

Deductions: (_____)
Violated time limit (3–4 minutes)
Inadequate preparation outline

                                          Final Score _____ /40

"Pet Peeve Presentation" Critique Sheet

Student's Name: _____

Topic: _____

Introduction:
Gained audience's attention, established credibility
Identified topic, stated thesis
Previewed main points

Body:
Main points clear/well-developed
Effective explanations, descriptions, etc.
Documented sources clearly cited
Effective organization, transitions, use of language

Conclusion:
Signaled the end
Reviewed main points
Effective closing statement

Delivery:
Extemporaneous, conversational delivery
Direct and inclusive eye contact
Demonstrated vocal variety
Clear articulation and pronunciation
Effective gestures, movement, facial expressions

Deductions:
Violated time limit (3–4 minutes)
Inadequate preparation outline

Overall Grade: _____

"Informative Presentation" Critique Sheet   100 POINTS

Student's Name: _____

Topic: _____

Introduction: _____/10
Gained audience's attention; established credibility
Stated topic and thesis; previewed main points

Body: _____/40
Main points clear/well-developed
Effective transitions and organization
Variety of effective supporting material
Used vivid, descriptive language
Cited at least 3 documented sources
Content adapted to situation/audience

Conclusion: _____/10
Signaled the end
Reviewed main points
Strong closing statement

Delivery: _____/20
Extemporaneous, conversational delivery
Direct and inclusive eye contact
Demonstrated vocal variety
Clear articulation and pronunciation
Effective gestures, movement, facial expressions
Creative and effective use of "visual aids"

Outline: _____/20
Quality of preparation outline in assigned format

Deductions: (_____)
Violated time limit (4–5 minutes)

                                          Final Score _____/100

"Informative Presentation" Critique Sheet

Student's Name: _____

Topic: _____

Introduction:
Gained audience's attention; established credibility
Stated topic and thesis; previewed main points

Body:
Main points clear/well-developed
Effective transitions and organization
Variety of effective supporting material
Used vivid, descriptive language
Cited at least 3 documented sources
Content adapted to situation/audience

Conclusion:
Signaled the end
Reviewed main points
Strong closing statement

Delivery:
Extemporaneous, conversational delivery
Direct and inclusive eye contact
Demonstrated vocal variety
Clear articulation and pronunciation
Effective gestures, movement, facial expressions
Creative and effective use of "visual aids"

Outline:
Quality of preparation outline in assigned format

Deductions:
Violated time limit (4–5 minutes)

Overall Grade: _____

"Impromptu Presentation" Critique Sheet   25 POINTS

Student's Name: _____

Topic: _____

Introduction: _____ /3
Gained audience's attention; established credibility
Identified topic, stated thesis
Previewed main points

Body: _____ /10
Main points clear/well-developed
Effective explanations, descriptions, etc
Used vivid, descriptive language

Conclusion: _____ /2
Reviewed main points
Reinforced the overall theme, strong closing statement

Delivery: _____ /10
Extemporaneous, conversational delivery
Direct and inclusive eye contact
Demonstrated vocal variety
Clear articulation and pronunciation
Effective gestures, movement, facial expressions

Deductions:
Violated time limit (2–4 minutes)   (_____)

                                    Final Score _____ /25

"Impromptu Presentation" Critique Sheet

Student's Name: _____

Topic: _____

Introduction:
Gained audience's attention; established credibility
Identified topic, stated thesis
Previewed main points

Body:
Main points clear/well-developed
Effective explanations, descriptions, etc
Used vivid, descriptive language

Conclusion:
Reviewed main points
Reinforced the overall theme, strong closing statement

Delivery:
Extemporaneous, conversational delivery
Direct and inclusive eye contact
Demonstrated vocal variety
Clear articulation and pronunciation
Effective gestures, movement, facial expressions

Deductions:
Violated time limit (2–4 minutes)

Overall Grade: _____

Team "Problem-Cause-Solution" Critique Sheet   150 POINTS

Student's Name: _____ Topic: _____

Team Members: _____

Introduction: _____ /10
    Gained audience's attention. Established credibility and goodwill.
    Stated topic, thesis and purpose. Previewed the main ideas.

Body: _____ /60
Problem:
    Vividly explained the history, prevalence, and significance of a compelling problem.
    Illustrated how the problem affects the audience and others.
    Provided ample, credible support.
Cause:
    Reviewed and explained the problem's underlying causes.
    Linked causes to effects (direct/indirect, short/long-term, etc.).
    Provided ample, credible support.
Solution:
    Identified and explained the "best" solution (what, who, how, when, where, etc.)
    Argued why it will directly address the causes of the problem.
    Argued why it is superior to other possible solutions. Addressed any objections.
    Illustrated the solution's benefits for those affected.

Conclusion: _____ /10
Signaled the end of the presentation.
Reviewed and reinforced the main points of the argument.
Effective closing statement.

Team Content: _____ /25
Used a wide variety of supporting material; related topic to the audience.
Used vivid/descriptive language.
Cited 2 sources per member.
Used two effective visual aids.
Provided smooth transitions between members; delivered as a team in one united voice.

Student's Individual Delivery   _____ /25
Extemporaneous, conversational delivery.
Direct and inclusive eye-contact.
Strong use of vocal variety, minimal vocalized pauses.
Effective gestures, movement, facial expressions.
Displayed energy, conviction, enthusiasm.

Team Outline: _____ /20
Quality of preparation outline in assigned format (1per team)

Deductions: (_____)
Violated time limit/max
Inadequate contribution to the team planning/preparation (up to -25 points)

                                         Final Score _____ /150

Team "Problem-Cause-Solution" Critique Sheet

Student's Name: _____ Topic: _____

Team Members: _____

Introduction:
Gained audience's attention. Established credibility and goodwill.
Stated topic, thesis and purpose. Previewed the main ideas.

Body:
Problem:
Vividly explained the history, prevalence, and significance of a compelling problem.
Illustrated how the problem affects the audience and others.
Provided ample, credible support.
Cause:
Reviewed and explained the problem's underlying causes.
Linked causes to effects (direct/indirect, short/long-term, etc.).
Provided ample, credible support.
Solution:
Identified and explained the "best" solution (what, who, how, when, where, etc.)
Argued why it will directly address the causes of the problem.
Argued why it is superior to other possible solutions. Addressed any objections.
Illustrated the solution's benefits for those affected.

Conclusion:
Signaled the end of the presentation.
Reviewed and reinforced the main points of the argument.
Effective closing statement.

Team Content:
Used a wide variety of supporting material; related topic to the audience.
Used vivid/descriptive language.
Cited 2 sources per member.
Used two effective visual aids.
Provided smooth transitions between members; delivered as a team in one united voice.

Student's Individual Delivery
Extemporaneous, conversational delivery.
Direct and inclusive eye-contact.
Strong use of vocal variety, minimal vocalized pauses.
Effective gestures, movement, facial expressions.
Displayed energy, conviction, enthusiasm.

Team Outline:
Quality of preparation outline in assigned format (1 per team)

Deductions:
Violated time limit/max
Inadequate contribution to the team planning/preparation (up to -25 points)

Overall Grade: _____

Alternate "Team Persuasive Presentation" Critique Sheet
150 POINTS

Student's Name: _____   Topic: _____

Team Members: _____   _____

_____   _____

Organization (Monroe's Motivated Sequence):   _____ /75
Attention:
    Strong attention getter, captivated the audience
    Established credibility, previewed topic/issue
Need:
    Clearly established a compelling problem
    Problem vividly explained and illustrated
    Tied the problem to audience, made it personal to them
Satisfaction:
    Clearly identified a specific solution to the problem
    Solution explained/described (what, when, how, etc.)
Visualization:
    Vividly illustrated the positive outcomes of the solution
    Visualized the solution's benefits, advantages for everyone
    Visualized the consequences if the solution is not adopted
    Overcame objections
Action:
    Clear, specific, motivating call for action
    Reviewed main ideas
    Strong closing statement

Team Content: _____ /25
Used effective emotional appeals and logical appeals
Used a wide variety of supporting materials
Adapted to audience's attitudes/values
Used vivid, descriptive language
Cited at least 2 sources per member
Creative and effective use of at least 2 "visual aids"
Smooth transitions between team members
Delivered as a "team"—united in voice and content

Student's Individual Delivery: _____ /25
Extemporaneous, conversational delivery
Direct and inclusive eye contact
Strong use of vocal variety
Effective gestures, movement, facial expressions
Displayed energy, conviction, enthusiasm

Team Outline: _____ /25
Quality of preparation outline in assigned format

Deductions: (_____)
Violated time limit (15 min. total; 3–5 per member)
Inadequate contribution to the team planning/preparation process (up to -25)

                                                   Final Score _____ /150

Alternate "Team Persuasive Presentation" Critique Sheet

Student's Name: _____ Topic: _____

Team Members: _____ _____

_____ _____

Organization (Monroe's Motivated Sequence):
Attention:
    Strong attention getter, captivated the audience
    Established credibility, previewed topic/issue
Need:
    Clearly established a compelling problem
    Problem vividly explained and illustrated
    Tied the problem to audience, made it personal to them
Satisfaction:
    Clearly identified a specific solution to the problem
    Solution explained/described (what, when, how, etc.)
Visualization:
    Vividly illustrated the positive outcomes of the solution
    Visualized the solution's benefits, advantages for everyone
    Visualized the consequences if the solution is not adopted
    Overcame objections
Action:
    Clear, specific, motivating call for action
    Reviewed main ideas
    Strong closing statement

Team Content:
Used effective emotional appeals and logical appeals
Used a wide variety of supporting materials
Adapted to audience's attitudes/values
Used vivid, descriptive language
Cited at least 2 sources per member
Creative and effective use of at least 2 "visual aids"
Smooth transitions between team members
Delivered as a "team"—united in voice and content

Student's Individual Delivery:
Extemporaneous, conversational delivery
Direct and inclusive eye contact
Strong use of vocal variety
Effective gestures, movement, facial expressions
Displayed energy, conviction, enthusiasm

Team Outline:
Quality of preparation outline in assigned format

Deductions:
Violated time limit (15 min. total; 3–5 per member)
Inadequate contribution to the team planning/preparation process

Overall Grade: _____

"Persuasive Presentation" Critique Sheet   150 POINTS

Student's Name: _____

Topic: _____

Organization (Monroe's Motivated Sequence):   _____ /75

Attention:
  Strong attention getter, captivated the audience
  Established credibility, previewed topic/issue
Need:
  Clearly established a compelling problem
  Problem vividly explained and illustrated
  Tied the problem to audience, made it personal to them
Satisfaction:
  Clearly identified a specific solution to the problem
  Solution explained/described (what, when, how, etc.)
Visualization:
  Vividly illustrated the positive outcomes of the solution
  Visualized the solution's benefits, advantages for everyone
  Visualized the consequences if the solution is not adopted
  Overcame objections
Action:
  Clear, specific, motivating call for action
  Reviewed main ideas
  Strong closing statement

Content: _____ /25

Used effective emotional appeals and logical appeals
Used a wide variety of supporting materials
Adapted to audience's attitudes/values
Used vivid, descriptive language
Cited at least 4 sources
Creative and effective use of "visual aids"

Delivery: _____ /25

Extemporaneous, conversational delivery
Direct and inclusive eye contact
Strong use of vocal variety
Effective gestures, movement, facial expressions
Displayed energy, conviction, enthusiasm

Outline and Audience Analysis Report: _____ /25

Quality of preparation outline and analysis report in assigned format

Deductions: (_____)

Violated time limit (5–7 minutes)

                    Final Score _____ /150

"Persuasive Presentation" Critique Sheet

Student's Name: _____

Topic: _____

Organization (Monroe's Motivated Sequence):
<u>Attention:</u>
    Strong attention getter, captivated the audience
    Established credibility, previewed topic/issue
<u>Need:</u>
    Clearly established a compelling problem
    Problem vividly explained and illustrated
    Tied the problem to audience, made it personal to them
<u>Satisfaction:</u>
    Clearly identified a specific solution to the problem
    Solution explained/described (what, when, how, etc.)
<u>Visualization:</u>
    Vividly illustrated the positive outcomes of the solution
    Visualized the solution's benefits, advantages for everyone
    Visualized the consequences if the solution is not adopted
    Overcame objections
<u>Action:</u>
    Clear, specific, motivating call for action
    Reviewed main ideas
    Strong closing statement

Content:
Used effective emotional appeals and logical appeals
Used a wide variety of supporting materials
Adapted to audience's attitudes/values
Used vivid, descriptive language
Cited at least 4 sources
Creative and effective use of "visual aids"

Delivery:
Extemporaneous, conversational delivery
Direct and inclusive eye contact
Strong use of vocal variety
Effective gestures, movement, facial expressions
Displayed energy, conviction, enthusiasm

Outline and Audience Analysis Report:
Quality of preparation outline and analysis report in assigned format

Deductions:
Violated time limit (5–7 minutes)

Overall Grade: _____

Appendix E: Student Data Sheet

Department of Organizational Communication

COM 161

Student Data Sheet

Name: _____ COM 161 Section Number:_____

Address:_____

Email: _____
Year: Freshman   Sophomore   Junior   Senior
Major: _____

Hometown: _____

Job(s) you hold or have held: _____

_____

_____

"Dream" job/position you would like to have:_____
Hobbies or special interests:

    1._____

    2._____

    3._____

What type of "public speaking" opportunities have you had in the past?_____

_____

Evaluate how the thought of giving a presentation makes you feel:
    Very nervous/apprehensive 5 ----- 4 ----- 3 ----- 2 ----- 1 Very excited/no apprehension
What else does your professor need to know about you to meet your needs in becoming a successful
COM 161 student? _____

_____

_____

_____

_____

_____

Contract Agreement: I have read the course syllabus. I am aware of the expectations, policies, and requirements provided by the professor, lecturer and/or lab instructor. I understand and agree to abide by those expectations, policies and requirements.

Student Signature: _____ Date:_____

Appendix F: Quizzes

COM 161 – Introduction to Public Speaking

Quiz 1

1.

2.

3.

4.

5.

6.

7.

8.

9.

10.

Name_____

Date_____

Lab Number _____

Lab Instructor _____

COM 161 – Introduction to Public Speaking

Quiz 2

1.

2.

3.

4.

5.

6.

7.

8.

9.

10.

Name_____

Date_____

Lab Number _____

Lab Instructor _____

Quiz 3

1.

2.

3.

4.

5.

6.

7.

8.

9.

10.

Name_____

Date_____

Lab Number _____

Lab Instructor _____

COM 161 – Introduction to Public Speaking

Quiz 4

1.

2.

3.

4.

5.

6.

7.

8.

9.

10.

Name _____

Date _____

Lab Number _____

Lab Instructor _____

COM 161 – Introduction to Public Speaking

Quiz 5

1.

2.

3.

4.

5.

6.

7.

8.

9.

10.

Name_____

Date_____

Lab Number _____

Lab Instructor _____

COM 161 – Introduction to Public Speaking

Quiz 6

1.

2.

3.

4.

5.

6.

7.

8.

9.

10.

Name_____

Date_____

Lab Number _____

Lab Instructor _____

Quiz 7

1.

2.

3.

4.

5.

6.

7.

8.

9.

10.

Name_____

Date_____

Lab Number _____

Lab Instructor _____

Quiz 8

1.

2.

3.

4.

5.

6.

7.

8.

9.

10.

Name_____

Date_____

Lab Number _____

Lab Instructor _____

COM 161 – Introduction to Public Speaking

Quiz 9

1.

2.

3.

4.

5.

6.

7.

8.

9.

10.

Name_____

Date_____

Lab Number _____

Lab Instructor _____